A JOURNEY WITH MARGARET THATCHER

A JOURNEY WITH

MARGARET THATCHER

FOREIGN POLICY UNDER THE IRON LADY

ROBIN RENWICK

Biteback Publishing

First published in Great Britain in 2013 by
Biteback Publishing Ltd
Westminster Tower
3 Albert Embankment
London SE1 7SP
Copyright © Robin Renwick 2013

ISBN 978-1-84954-533-4

10 9 8 7 6 5 4 3 2 1

A CIP catalogue record for this book is available from the British Library.

Set in Adobe Caslon Pro

Printed and bound in Great Britain by
CPI Group (UK) Ltd, Croydon CR0 4YY

CONTENTS

I believe that together we really did contribute to changing our world.
– Margaret Thatcher to Mikhail Gorbachev, at the time of her resignation

PROLOGUE

What follows does not purport to be a detached account of Margaret Thatcher's achievements in foreign policy. I was one of her advisers and was involved in a good many of the episodes described – the Rhodesia settlement and, in Washington, the Falklands War and nuclear missile negotiations, in 'getting our money back' from the European Community, the negotiation of the Single European Act, the Namibia settlement and the transition from apartheid to democracy in South Africa. I have sought to explain how it was that someone who, throughout her tenure, was criticised by much of the British foreign policy Establishment, succeeded in her ambition to restore Britain's standing and influence in the world, in contrast to the disrepair in which it had fallen at the time she became Prime Minister. The journey with her was never lacking in excitement or achievement. How exactly was this high-wire act performed?

On the morning of 25 June 1984, the Prime Minister's motorcade whisked her from Orly airport to the Château of Fontainebleau. She was greeted in the courtyard by President Mitterrand and a full guard of honour in their resplendent uniforms. The French, as she observed, know how to do these things properly. There was a round of applause from the bystanders. Although hardly a favourite of the French press, she always got a friendly reception from the public in France, for whom she was a highly recognisable *monstre sacré*. The other heads of government were, to them, indistinguishable one from the other, apart from the massive Chancellor Kohl.

She got on well with Mitterrand, infinitely preferring him to his aloof and chilly predecessor, Giscard d'Estaing. He had established a mildly flirtatious relationship with her ('he likes women', as she observed), which worked because he had proved to be a true ally when it counted, during the Falklands War. It was his close friend and Minister for Europe, Roland Dumas, who said that he had described her as having 'the eyes of Caligula and the mouth of Marilyn Monroe!' She always chose an even more than normally elegant suit for these encounters with the French, and there was never a blonde hair out of place.

That afternoon, the heads of government discussed the state of the world economy, causing her to fret at what she regarded as delaying tactics. At last they got to the European Community budget. She told the others that she was not going to accept any more temporary solutions for the British budgetary contribution, a cause she described as 'getting our money back'. There was going to have to be a permanent solution. Mitterrand referred the issue to the Foreign Ministers to discuss that evening and reverted to an account of his recent visit to Moscow.

She found all this frustrating, as she made very clear to those of us accompanying her en route through the forest of Fontainebleau to the Hôtellerie du Bas-Bréau near the village of Barbizon, a favourite haunt of Robert Louis Stevenson and numerous French artists and writers from the turn of the century.

Here, the heads of government and their Foreign Ministers were due to have their separate dinners. On that warm summer evening, we waited on the terrace for her to emerge. Ever meticulous, she had kept the menu, revealing that they had dined on foie gras, lobster, rack of lamb and raspberry soufflé.

To her extreme annoyance, the Foreign Ministers' meeting had proved to be a fiasco. We had not expected much better with the small and pompous French Foreign Minister, Claude Cheysson, as chairman. In an attempt to woo him, the Foreign Secretary, Geoffrey Howe, had used his favourite tactic of inviting him to spend a weekend at the Foreign Secretary's beautiful country house at Chevening. The visit had not been an unqualified success as I had to help M. Cheysson extricate himself from the maze, where he was not tall enough to see over the hedges.

The Foreign Ministers had wasted most of their time listening to Cheysson's own account of world affairs. On the budget issue they had simply 'clarified the points of difference', with Cheysson suggesting that we might get between 50 and 60 per cent of our contribution back. When this was reported to the Prime Minister, who was consulting with us on the terrace of the hotel, clutching her whisky and soda, she exploded with rage. 'How dare they treat Britain in this way?' she stormed. 'Have they forgotten that we saved all their skins in the War?'

She was upset that the Treasury's favourite scheme, whereby our contribution would be based on our relative prosperity, had been rejected by everyone. I said that I doubted if the Treasury scheme was best for us anyway. With Greece, Ireland and Italy already in the Community, Spain and Portugal about to join it, and the improvement in our own economic performance, it could work against us over time. David Williamson, her trusted adviser from the Cabinet Office, and I told her that we still believed we could work things out with the French. We were told to go and try.

As it by now was past midnight, we set off to rouse my French counterpart, Guy Legras, from his hotel. We agreed with him a text providing for the permanent automatic correction of our contribution as it was to be embodied in Community law and changeable, therefore, only by unanimity. But we left the percentage figure blank. Legras said that Mitterrand would not go above 60 per cent. We told him that there would be no settlement at less than two-thirds of our contribution back. But having learned something by this time of Margaret Thatcher's psychology, we were absolutely determined to leave it to the Prime Minister herself to set the final figure. Otherwise she would never accept that it was the best that could have been achieved.

Next morning she felt that we had shown the 'brains and determination to retrieve something from this debacle'.[1] Roland Dumas had a private life that was colourful even by French political standards. He was the epitome of 'gauche caviar' (members of the French left with expensive tastes). But he was also a born negotiator. We knew that he wanted an agreement at Fontainebleau, as did Mitterrand's key assistant, the beautiful and very capable Élisabeth Guigou, and that they would advise their President to accept a version of our proposal.

In the European Council meeting the Prime Minister was accompanied by Geoffrey Howe and by the combative and cerebral Michael Butler,[2] who, as our ambassador to the European Community, had done much to pave the way for success. The text we had agreed with Legras was circulated to the heads of government. There ensued an acrimonious debate, with the Prime Minister insisting on a 70 per cent correction and the others rejecting it. When an exasperated Mitterrand finally proposed 65 per cent, she said that he could not refuse her one percentage point more, then called a time-out. Emerging from the meeting, this was the time to settle, she felt. She did not believe that more could be achieved. With considerable relief, we agreed.

The Germans, outmanoeuvred, were going to have to foot most of the bill. Hans Tietmeyer, then in the finance ministry, was particularly cross. But, as we had hoped and anticipated, Chancellor Kohl was not prepared to block an agreement negotiated with the French. The others grudgingly acquiesced.

One Mitterrand aide, Jacques Attali, who was not even present in Fontainebleau, was later to claim that the Prime Minister was so disappointed that she burst into tears. In fact, she was quietly triumphant, and not without reason. For it was, in monetary terms, the most valuable agreement any British government has ever negotiated. It has saved this country billions of pounds in every subsequent year. This outcome could never have been achieved without the ferocious energy and intransigence with which Margaret Thatcher had pursued her goal, at whatever cost to her relations with others.

Not long afterwards, standing with her at a window at Chequers, I found her gazing at a landscape of yellow oilseed rape, planted with subsidies from the European Commission. 'This,' she hissed, 'used to be a green and pleasant land!'

☞

There followed another European episode that illustrated vividly Margaret Thatcher's modus operandi. Discussions had been continuing for years on plans for the Channel Tunnel, with little progress, until it came to a meeting with the Prime Minister before she set off to Paris for another encounter with Mitterrand in December 1984.

These large set-piece meetings with her ministers and officials around the Cabinet table at No. 10 before each important European meeting had become a ritual with her. At this stage of her prime ministership, she would wade overnight through every page of the voluminous material provided for her. Each of us then would be subjected in turn to an inquisition about its contents. Officials summoned to these meetings who had not attended them before found the experience frankly terrifying. Her ministers did not enjoy them either. She would glare around the room, suspecting most of her advisers to be afflicted with terminal dampness, verging on treason. As Michael Butler observed, these encounters were not for the faint-hearted.[3] He and I had found from experience that the prerequisite was to be better prepared than she was – and then to stand our ground. She had little time for those who did not argue back and delighted in excluding one distinguished ambassador from all future meetings when he failed to do so.

The argument about the Channel Tunnel was opened by the Secretary of State for Transport, Nicholas Ridley, who made clear that he was against it, not on any technical or financial grounds, but in principle – for, apparently, visceral reasons. This, at the time, was thought to be the attitude of the Prime Minister as well. An official from his department was subjected to a fearful inquisition. Why could there not be a bridge instead? What was the point of a tunnel if you could not drive through it? And so on.

Margaret Thatcher's main concern, however, was her very shrewd suspicion that the project would cost far more than the contractors were telling us and that, when this happened, the government would be asked to foot the bill. Michael Heseltine was in favour of public funding. After all, he pointed out, we funded tunnels under the Mersey. Whatever one thought of this argument, it was the one least likely to appeal to her.

Geoffrey Howe, for all his pro-Europeanism, also had no enthusiasm for the project because of the impact he feared the through traffic would have on his constituency in Surrey. So the lonely task of arguing for it was left to Michael Butler, supported by me. We pointed out the advantage to British manufacturers of being able to freight shipments through the tunnel to many of their main export markets overnight. Above all, we argued, whatever we thought of the financial projections, the banks had undertaken to fund the project themselves. How could it possibly be compatible with the philosophy of the Thatcher government to prevent them from doing so? This earned us a basilisk stare.

The meeting ended, as usual, with the Prime Minister not revealing her intentions as we all trooped off with her to Paris. That evening, when she returned to the embassy from her private dinner with Mitterrand, she gave us her usual meticulously careful account of what had been said, on every other subject. At the end of which she casually announced: 'And by the way, we decided to give the go-ahead for the Channel Tunnel.'

She thoroughly enjoyed this *coup de théâtre*, which produced a strangled gasp from Geoffrey Howe, whose worries about his constituency were cheerfully brushed aside.

INTRODUCTION

'I OFFENDED ON MANY COUNTS'

Visiting the United States as Leader of the Opposition in 1975, Margaret Thatcher was greeted by an article in the *Wall Street Journal* describing Britain as the sick country of Europe, brought about not by any defeat or disaster, but by the policies of its governments and their 'resigned acceptance' by its people. When she described how she proposed to change this, she was accused of running Britain down abroad. In his farewell despatch from the Paris embassy, subsequently published by *The Economist*, Sir Nicholas Henderson described the fading of our influence in Europe and the world as a result of economic weakness: 'Our economic decline has been such as to sap the foundations of our diplomacy.'[4]

She saw it as her mission to arrest and reverse that decline, not only economically but also in terms of our standing in the world. Not many believed her to be capable of doing so. Describing an early meeting with the permanent secretaries of all the major government departments, she found it a dismal experience, as they did not believe that much could or even should be changed, while she had very different ideas. When she said that together they could beat the system, they protested, 'But we are the system!' She never fully trusted the civil service – and was right not to do so, given its capacity for inertia – but was always looking for outstanding figures within it, which she found, among others, in her successive private and Cabinet secretaries. Without Robin Butler, Robert Armstrong, Andrew Turnbull and others like them, she could never have accomplished what she did.

Charles Powell, her closest foreign policy adviser, came from the Foreign Office, before being partially disowned by it because of his closeness to her. Her combative and very effective Press Secretary, Bernard Ingham, was retrieved from the Department of Energy, despite having been a *Guardian* writer and lifelong Labour supporter, because she felt she could get on with him – and she did.

I and others found it refreshing to deal with a Prime Minister whose question was not 'What shall we say?' but 'What shall we do?' Unusually among parliamentarians, she had formidable executive capacities, devoting ferocious energy to ensuring implementation of her policies, not just their formulation. This determination to act as a managing director, and not as a chairman *primus inter pares*, was both the secret of her success and the source of massive friction with her colleagues. An inveterate workaholic, she spent her weekends, evenings and early mornings devouring papers in far more detail than most of her ministers, leading at times to unpleasant surprises for them. Her whole life was politics, as was Harold Wilson's, but, unlike Wilson, wheeling and dealing were not her style.

She never sought or expected any easy popularity. A polarising figure who distrusted consensus, she was prepared to court and incur unpopularity in pursuit of her goals. She knew, as was made very clear by them to her, that a large section of the media simply could not stand her. She very firmly believed that in the end, and by the electorate, she would be judged by results.

My own experience with her never was that she could not be persuaded to change her mind, and in fact she was persuaded to do so far more often than she ever publicly admitted – provided she was convinced that the persuader shared the same fundamental objectives. She arrived at conclusions by a process of arguing from first principles, including thinking the unthinkable, to be absolutely certain that the unthinkable just might not work after all. With those members of the mandarinate she trusted (a trust which had to be earned), she did not fear that any leak of private discussions would appear in the press next day, as it quite frequently did with her ministerial colleagues.

Her two key foreign policy advisers in the Falklands War, Nicholas Henderson and Tony Parsons, were both Whigs by nature, with no sympathy for her monetarist policies. Yet both developed a real admiration for her. As Henderson observed, she was remarkably unstuffy and devoid of any trace of pomposity. She had undoubted star quality and an ability to rise to the occasion. They respected her determination to do what was best for Britain, even when they disagreed about her tactics. They also admired her concern always to look her best, even at the end of a difficult or frustrating day, leaving her male counterparts exhausted in their crumpled suits. She was no feminist, but very conscious of her femininity. In Nigel Lawson's words, 'She was convinced that her authority … would be diminished if she were not impeccably turned out at all times. She was probably right.'[5] In the male-dominated and constantly photographed world in which she had to operate, she did not believe she could ever afford to appear with a hair out of place, and she virtually never did.

She devoted exceptional care and intensity to the preparation of her speeches, which made her a very effective orator, as every speech delivered by her was so extensively reworked that it indisputably was *her* speech, whoever initially contributed to it. Anyone helping her had to expect every single page to be rewritten many times, or discarded, with papers strewn across the floor, in a process lasting typically until the small hours of the day on which the speech was to be made. A firm believer in the power of words and of ideas, on such occasions she could never be accused of going through the motions.

Accompanying her to international summit meetings was always a challenging but also an exhilarating experience, due to her determination to be the best-prepared head of government in the room. She would emerge from each dinner with her counterparts, seize a stiff whisky, kick off her shoes and give us a detailed and often hilarious account of what had transpired, while preparing her plan of action for the next day.

She was no killjoy, offering a relieved George Shultz a scotch and soda at the British embassy in New Delhi with the words: 'There is only so much orange juice one can stand.'⁶ At the end of the Reagan administration, Shultz held a dinner in her honour at the State Department at which he presented her with the 'order of the handbag', observing that at whatever was the crucial moment in international meetings she would fish out of her bag a text which, he contended, more often than not would be the basis for what was eventually agreed.

In seeking to promote British interests, which she was exceptionally determined about doing, she had an instinctive distrust of the foreign policy elite in Britain, who she suspected, for instance, of wanting to engineer a handover of the Falklands to Argentina, or of Gibraltar to Spain, regardless of the principle of self-determination. She saw herself rather as expressing the views of the mass of the British people, in whose common sense she placed more faith than in that of the intelligentsia.

She did not resent argument – it was in fact her favourite pastime – so long as it was conducted away from the press. On two occasions John Major feared he had endangered his chances of promotion by getting into quite fierce arguments with her, only to be told by her husband, 'she will have enjoyed that' and to find himself promoted in the next reshuffle.[7] Michael Butler found, as I and others did, that she positively welcomed serious argument and had a high regard for those who argued with her most effectively.

She was fearless politically – and not only politically, as she showed in the rubble of the Grand Hotel in Brighton. She also was a remarkably nerveless risk-taker. The risks were calculated, but taken nonetheless, far more than they had been by her predecessors.

Her faults – bossiness, stridency, high-handed treatment of her colleagues – were of the same dimension as her virtues. As one member of her Cabinet observed: 'She was an absolutely rotten chairman', incapable of holding back until the debate swung her way. 'However, the times required a chief executive and not a chairman.'[8]

In his book *Our Age*, Noel Annan, himself a luminary of the liberal intellectual Establishment which, he contended, dominated thinking for decades after the war, expressed his dismay at the intensity of their antagonism to 'this remarkable woman, far less hollow than her predecessors, elected and re-elected to lead her country, the victor over Argentinian militarists and trade union militants'.[9] They achieved a cheap victory at her expense by voting down the proposal that her alma mater Oxford should confer on her an honorary degree. How then, asks Annan, did she prove so much more successful than her critics combined? How did she succeed where they had failed in arresting and reversing the country's economic and international decline?

☞

Margaret Thatcher's foreign policies were the subject of great controversy at the time. She was accused of being Ronald Reagan's poodle, though no less poodle-like politician did I ever encounter in the course of my career. Her views on Europe, regarded with horror by the Foreign Office and many of her colleagues, triggered her downfall as Prime Minister. Her hard-line stance against the Soviet Union was felt to be far too confrontational. Just as controversial were her views on South Africa, indulgent attitude towards the Shah of Iran and General Pinochet, support for Israel and publicly expressed fears about German unification. The continued expression of her strong views on Europe and Bosnia after her loss of office caused difficulties for her successor, John Major, and attracted fierce disapproval. The purpose of this book is to examine her successes in foreign policy and her failures, and to what extent subsequent events have tended to prove her right or wrong.

Although she always regarded herself as true blue and instinctively in touch with the views of Conservative supporters around the country (an instinct which deserted her when it came to the poll tax), I was never able to regard her as being in any way a typical or normal member of the Conservative Party. She was far more interested in ideas than most practising politicians usually turn out to be. She also came much closer than any other political leader I have known to saying what she really thought and doing what she said. There was an element of straightforward class warfare in her attitude to the party hierarchy in the face of their attempts to patronise her. She came from a family that was neither poor nor rich and which had to save up for any small luxury. Her experience at Oxford was at the other end of the spectrum to the Bullingdon Club. She did not join the Union because, in her day, women could not become members. In any case, she did not like its brittle, showy debates. She joined the Conservative Association instead.

She regarded her victory in the leadership battle against Heath as a shattering blow to the Conservative Establishment, which had fought her unscrupulously all the way. The label 'grocer's daughter' was pinned on her by her own side, not by her opponents. Although Willie Whitelaw became her loyal deputy, his late entry into the contest, having failed to mount the challenge himself and with no alternative policies to Heath, was typical of the behaviour she expected of a Tory grandee. She was regarded by them as having become leader by accident, and probably not for long, with Heath constantly trying to stage a comeback, if necessary through a national unity government. Callaghan, too, patronised her whenever he could.

When she became Prime Minister, these problems were compounded. Her experience was that many of the men she dealt with in politics demonstrated precisely those characteristics they attributed to women – vanity and an inability to make difficult decisions. There were also plenty of them who simply could not abide working for a woman. The idea that women were the weaker sex was, to her, a joke. On more than one occasion she told the rest of her Cabinet: 'You men, you are so weak!' In the eyes of her Tory critics, she was not just a woman, but 'that woman', someone 'not just of a different sex, but of a different class', a person with an alarming conviction that the values of Middle England should be brought to bear on the mess the Establishment had created.[10]

When it came to the Falklands, John Nott could not think of any male leader who would not have looked for an honourable way out.[11] She was not interested in a way out. As for honour, that entailed defeating the aggression. Against formidable odds, she was playing to win.

As she observed, she offended on many counts. When she dropped Christopher Soames from her Cabinet, he gave her the impression that he felt that the natural order of things was being violated and that he was, in effect, being dismissed by his housemaid. This was unfair to Soames, who had served with success as ambassador in Paris, Britain's first Commissioner to the European Community and Governor of Rhodesia. Ian Gilmour, on being dismissed, described the government as steering 'full speed ahead for the rocks' and bent on creating a *Clockwork Orange* society. In private she used to describe one type of Tory she couldn't abide as the 'false squire', much heartier and tougher on the outside than when push came to shove. Not that she had much time for the real squires either, regarding many of them as belonging, in summer at least, to 'Chiantishire'.

As she took office, hardly any of her Cabinet colleagues believed that she had any better chance of facing down the unions than Heath, Wilson or Callaghan had done and she herself was very cautious on this subject through her first term. Nor was there any real buy-in from most of her colleagues for the idea of privatising huge swathes of British industry. Monetarism was regarded as an alien doctrine and the Conservative Party was supposed to be non-doctrinaire anyway. To her fury, opposition to her economic policies from the 'wets' in the Cabinet manifested itself in the form of constant leaks and briefings against her. The Conservative Party chairman, Peter Thorneycroft, publicly confessed himself to be suffering from 'rising damp'.

Urged to modify her economic policies in the name of consensus, she replied that, to her, consensus seemed to be the process of 'abandoning all beliefs, principles, values and policies in search of something in which no one believes, but to which no one objects ... What great cause would have been fought and won under the banner "I stand for consensus"?'[12]

She herself acknowledged later that the money supply was too tightly controlled, deepening the recession. The hugely controversial 1981 Budget was intensely unpopular and denounced by 364 economists. Yet it was followed by eight years of economic growth at an average rate of well over 3 per cent per annum. Britain had gone from being the slowest-growing to the fastest-growing major economy in Europe.

It also was followed by her success in selling hundreds of thousands of council homes to their tenants, in requiring the trade unions to hold ballots before calling a strike and in privatising huge swathes of British industry – all of them reforms which appear in retrospect to have been self-evidently what was required, but which none of her predecessors had the courage even to begin to undertake.

In her wake, privatisation policies were adopted by a host of other governments around the world. She had become a figure of worldwide significance, a claim that could not be made for any other British Prime Minister in the past century save for her hero, Winston Churchill.

The arguments about Europe that divided the government in her third term are highly relevant to events in the eurozone today. Throughout her time as Prime Minister, Margaret Thatcher fought running battles with other senior members of her Cabinet – Geoffrey Howe, Nigel Lawson, Michael Heseltine and others – about policy towards Europe in general and the movement towards monetary union in particular. Her attitude was that if the other eleven member countries of the European Community wanted to pursue a monetary union, the British government could not stand in the way. But she wanted no part in this project for Britain. To her, it entailed a completely unacceptable transfer of sovereignty. She also had some fundamental doubts about the project itself: 'With countries at different levels of economic development, fiscal policies and rates of inflation, the most flexible and realistic method of economic adjustment is via floating exchange rates.'[13] She very shrewdly suspected that a monetary union could not long endure without a transfer of fiscal sovereignty as well.

She herself acknowledged that the aspect of her foreign policy in which she met with unambiguous failure was her Canute-like resistance to German reunification, concerned that it could destabilise Gorbachev and the reformers in Moscow. While her attitude in this respect was self-defeating, she was more prescient than others about the *consequences* of reunification and right that it would fundamentally change the balance of power in Europe. Once coupled with monetary union, reunification would result in a eurozone dominated by Germany, one within which other member states would suffer severely from their inability any longer to remain competitive by devaluing their currencies.

'80 CLEARLY THE BEST MAN AMONG THEM'

In Paris at the time of a major crisis in French politics, culminating in his return to power, I used to listen to General de Gaulle explaining to his compatriots that he had 'a certain idea of France'. He did not see France as a country of middling importance, with a rather dismal post-war history, unable to arrest its own decline or to exert much influence in the world. He saw his country as one with unique qualities, a majestic history and the capacity under the right leadership – his own – to restore its economic fortunes and its rightful influence in the world.

Margaret Thatcher, on becoming Prime Minister and in the run-up to doing so, could be heard using rather similar language. She lacked de Gaulle's credentials to do so, but she had the same sense of mission to re-energise a country regarded at the time as the sick man of Europe and restore Britain's influence and standing in the world. The waning of that influence, largely as a consequence of our economic decline, was chronicled by Sir Nicholas Henderson, with whom I served in Paris at the time, in a famous despatch published in *The Economist*, which led the new Prime Minister to appoint him as her ambassador in Washington. I did not enjoy, any more than Sir Nicholas, being patronised by my friends and colleagues in the Quai d'Orsay at a time when France was riding high and Britain very low.

Margaret Thatcher felt that, post-Suez, the British foreign policy elite had gone from believing that Britain could do anything to an almost neurotic belief that Britain could do nothing. Her conviction that this was very far from being the case was based on her upbringing, the example of Churchill's wartime leadership and her own intensely patriotic sense of what the country should aspire to be.

The lessons learned in the early years of her life were a constant point of reference for her. Fourteen years old at its outbreak, she was very much a child of the war. Born in the family flat above her father's grocery shop in Grantham, in her memoirs she paints a near-idyllic picture of growing up in a hard-working Methodist family in a provincial town which, to her, epitomised the virtues of Middle England at the time.

Well before war was declared, she observed, 'we knew just what we thought of Hitler'. An avid cinemagoer, she watched with distaste the rallies of strutting brownshirts, so alien to the British or at any rate the Grantham way of conducting politics. Her father, Alfred Roberts, was a Rotarian and aware that Hitler had crushed Rotary in Germany. After the German annexation of Austria in 1938, for a while the Roberts family looked after a young Austrian Jewish refugee en route to join relatives in South America. She told them what it was like to live as a Jew under an anti-Semitic regime.

Yet, when the Munich Agreement was reached, the sentiment in the Roberts family, as across the country at the time, was simply relief that a war had been avoided. Following the German invasion of Poland, on the morning of Sunday 3 September 1939, instead of going to church, the family huddled around the radio to hear Neville Chamberlain's announcement that Britain was now at war.

Grantham was the recipient of twenty-two air raids during the war. Alfred Roberts was frequently out on air-raid duty. The war news was unremittingly bad. Yet the family, like millions of others, never wavered in its conviction that, somehow, the war would be won. With Churchill as its leader, they felt there was almost nothing Britain could not do. The teenage Margaret Roberts did some work for service canteens and succeeded in her efforts to win a place at Somerville College, Oxford in October 1943, taking pride in the fact that she was the first member of her family to go to Oxford or Cambridge.

There she studied chemistry under the redoubtable Professor Dorothy Hodgkin. The left-wing Principal of Somerville, Dame Janet Vaughan, regarded her as a 'beta chemist' and an 'oddity' because she was a Conservative. She did not bother to invite her to her parties because 'she had nothing to contribute, you see'.[14]

Even at this stage a true-blue undergraduate, she campaigned for the Conservatives in the 1945 general election. Listening to Churchill's assertion in a radio broadcast that socialism would require 'some sort of Gestapo' to enforce it, her reaction was: 'He's gone too far.' Yet she was horrified at the election result. She simply could not understand how the electorate could do this to the man who had led them through the war.

While the Conservative Party in the post-war period was dominated by advocates of the middle way, she made a first discovery of F. A. Hayek's book, *The Road to Serfdom*. She did not, she confesses, fully grasp its significance until she was reintroduced to it by Keith Joseph in the 1970s.

She was untroubled by any doubts as to the justification for using atomic weapons to bring an end to the war in Japan. She disagreed with Churchill, 'for whom my admiration knew no bounds', about the need to bring India to independence. A student of Koestler's *Darkness at Noon* and of Karl Popper's *The Open Society and its Enemies*, she applauded Churchill's 'iron curtain' speech at Fulton Missouri in March 1946, notwithstanding the criticism it received as 'warmongering' at the time.

Having graduated with second-class honours in chemistry, she was offered a job with a plastics company near Colchester (having lost another because 'this young woman has much too strong a personality to work here'). Adopted as the Conservative candidate for the unwinnable constituency of Dartford, it was there that she met the managing director of a paint and chemicals company, Denis Thatcher, whom she grew to admire as a no-nonsense Conservative who knew more about economics than she did. She later moved to the laboratories of J. Lyons in Hammersmith as a food research chemist.

Appalled at Aneurin Bevan's description of the Tories as 'lower than vermin', she admired Clement Attlee as a serious man and patriot, 'all substance and no show', despite abhorring his party's policies of nationalisation and the apparently indefinite extension of wartime controls. When Attlee died in 1967, she praised him for having had 'an exceptionally clear mind – and in politics that is every bit as important as a highly intellectual mind and sometimes more so'.[15] Exactly the same could have been said about her.

Dartford proved impossible to win in 1950 and 1951, but she got married to Denis Thatcher and spent her evenings studying for her law exams, from which she was not deflected by the arrival of twins. She passed her Bar finals and in the process became convinced of another of the principles she was to enunciate throughout her political career: the overriding importance of the rule of law. Her two wartime ventures – the Falklands and the first Gulf War – both had a firm foundation in international law. Respect for this principle, however, was never to prevent her from trying to induce successive Attorneys-General to give her the advice she wanted.

She chose not to stand in the 1955 election, following Churchill's handover to Anthony Eden. Disaster was not long in coming when President Nasser seized control of the Suez Canal in July 1956. Margaret Thatcher shared the prevailing view that Britain should not be pushed around by Nasser but drew some lessons from the subsequent debacle. She shared her husband's disgust at the stoppage of operations when British troops were on the verge of occupying the Canal Zone. She concluded that Britain should not get into a military operation unless determined and able to finish it. Its actions must be in accordance with international law.

Many of her colleagues blamed the United States and a wave of anti-Americanism affected many in her party. She drew the opposite conclusion, that Britain should never again find itself on the opposite side to the United States in a major international crisis affecting British interests. She saw Harold Macmillan's great and lasting achievement as rebuilding the relationship with the United States. He was unable, however, to diminish the debilitating impact of what she saw as the Suez syndrome on the British political class.

Having been turned down in three other constituencies, Margaret Thatcher got herself adopted as Conservative candidate for the safe seat of Finchley. Concerned at accusations of anti-Semitism against the local party, she made a particular effort to recruit more Jewish Conservatives, which helped her to win the seat in the 1959 election.

When she arrived in Parliament, her male colleagues were amused by her extreme seriousness. She was never a part of their club. Peter Rawlinson observed that they all smiled benignly as they looked at her blue eyes and blonde hair. 'We, and all the world, had no idea what we were in for.'[16]

The main dispute within the Conservative Party at the time was over Colonial Secretary Iain Macleod's 'scramble from Africa', with Lord Salisbury, supporter of the white settlers, denouncing him as 'too clever by half'. Considering that he was applying Tory modernisation to colonial policy, Margaret Thatcher had no hesitation in backing Macleod.

In 1961 she received from Macmillan her first very junior government appointment in the Ministry for Pensions and National Insurance, about as unglamorous a position as there was to find. Harold Macmillan seemed to operate on an entirely different plane to her. She found him brilliant but elusive, admired him as the consummate politician who had restored Conservative fortunes after Suez but worried about his attitude to public spending and chameleon-like nature. She was not alone in this. When told by a friend that he had just seen Macmillan, Rab Butler enquired: 'And which Macmillan did you meet – the great-grandson of a Scottish crofter or the son-in-law of a duke?'

Her minister, John Boyd-Carpenter, found she very quickly mastered the complexities of social security and showed a capacity for work that astonished him. The Permanent Secretary, Sir Eric Bowyer, one of the first of many mandarins to underestimate her, protested that she would 'turn up looking as if she had spent the whole morning with the coiffeur and the whole afternoon with the couturier'. One more perceptive official noted that 'her assertion that her aim is to get things done has to be taken seriously'.[17] Her passion for statistics led her solemnly to announce one day in the House of Commons that she had a red-hot figure, to gales of laughter. Tributes were regularly paid in Parliament to her charm, of which she had plenty – then and later – when she chose to use it.

Her early encounters with the British Establishment led to an impatience and intolerance for it far deeper than that of any Labour Prime Minister. They also led her to the conclusion that she must find a way to impose her will on the civil service as, otherwise, it would impose its will on her – as, in her view, it had done with her predecessors.

By 1962 Macmillan's political skills had deserted him. The sacking of one-third of his government was described in the House of Commons as 'laying down his friends for his life'. In January 1963, de Gaulle vetoed the British application to join the European Economic Community (EEC). While Margaret Thatcher was later to find his reasons for doing so perceptive (he saw Britain as insular, maritime, unlike the continental European countries and likely to put its interests in the wider world ahead of those of Europe), at the time she saw the EEC as essentially a trading bloc, did not regard the European Free Trade Association (EFTA) or the Commonwealth as much of an alternative and firmly believed that it was right for Britain to join.

Disappointed by Alec Douglas-Home's decision to resign after the loss of the 1964 general election, she was persuaded by Keith Joseph to vote for Ted Heath although her acquaintance with Heath, even at that time, 'had never risked developing into friendship'.[18] She found him, as did many of her other colleagues, lacking in human warmth. Yet he was a far more ardent pro-European than his opponent, Reggie Maudling. A relative liberal on social issues, she supported the Private Members' Bills decriminalising homosexuality and abortion. In 1967 she was appointed to the shadow Cabinet.

In the same year she had made her first visit to the United States on a six-week leadership programme. The excitement she felt at the reception she received and at her visit to the NASA space centre stood in stark contrast to the grim reality of a week-long visit to the Soviet Union made in the aftermath of the invasion of Czechoslovakia. As shadow Minister of Transport, she had been invited to visit the Soviet Union to admire the Moscow metro. She used the opportunity to rush around visiting nuclear power stations as well. The drab streets and empty shops confirmed her view that communism was an alien creed, contrary to human nature, and that in the end, therefore, it could not endure. As explained by her biographer, John Campbell, in terms of the battle of ideas, she never wavered in the conviction that the Cold War was there to be won.[19] The surprise Conservative victory in the June 1970 election brought her into the Cabinet as Secretary of State for Education.

In that capacity she devoted her formidable energies to a massive new school-building programme, but ran into a political firestorm caused by the Treasury's insistence on cutting the subsidy for free milk in schools, leading to her being denounced as 'Mrs Thatcher, milk snatcher' and 'the most unpopular woman in Britain'.

There was little evidence by this stage that many children over the age of seven wanted or needed free milk, and what was being terminated was the legal requirement to provide it. But, hurt and upset by the uproar, she blamed the Treasury for precipitating a massive political storm for an absurdly small saving (£9 million). She would have preferred to be remembered for the rebuilding of 2,000 primary schools.

She deserved to be remembered also for preventing the Open University from being strangled at birth by Iain Macleod, who had vowed to withdraw funding for it. What many of her colleagues saw as a socialist project to deliver inferior degrees via television programmes, she saw as a way of making educational opportunity available to those who otherwise could not afford it.

Immersed in her work at the Department of Education, she paid remarkably little attention to the larger strategic issues facing the Heath government. She was not part of Heath's inner circle and scarcely spoke on the broader issues in Cabinet. She was wholeheartedly in favour of the negotiations to secure British entry to the EEC, completed by Heath in 1971. There was concern about the budgetary contribution, but the White Paper on entry claimed reassuringly, but misleadingly, that: 'There is no question of any erosion of essential national sovereignty … The common law will remain the basis of our legal system and our Courts will continue to operate as they do at present.' The one foreign policy issue on which she strongly but privately dissented, expressing her disagreement in Cabinet, was the decision to impose an arms embargo on Israel as well as on the Arab states in the Arab–Israeli war.

The Heath government staggered from crisis to crisis. The attempt to curb trade union power through the Industrial Relations Act was an abject failure. The government was the loser in a confrontation with the National Union of Mineworkers (NUM) in February 1972, as picketing rendered it impossible to access coal reserves. Heath embarked on a failed attempt to implement a policy to limit wages and incomes through consultations with the union leaders and the Confederation of British Industry.

By December 1973, Britain was operating a three-day week to conserve energy. Faced with the prospect of another miners' strike, Heath called a general election in February 1974, which the Conservatives lost. Margaret Thatcher did not forget that the support of business leaders who had urged the government to stand firm simply melted away. While the interventionist policies, corporatist style and pursuit of a wages and income policy epitomised everything she fought against later, she did not contest Heath's economic policies as a member of his Cabinet and, with Keith Joseph, would have been pretty much alone in doing so had she tried.

She was regarded as one of the few successes of the Heath government. When she left the Department of Education, *The Guardian* wrote: 'Her support for primary schools, polytechnics, the raising of the school-leaving age, and the new nursery programme will all provide more help to working-class children than the Labour programme actually did.'[20]

By this time she had developed very serious doubts about Heath's policies, largely on the grounds that they simply had not worked. Heath seemed to her not to be willing to learn any lessons from what had been tried and failed and to go on instead proposing more of the same. Now her closest political friend and mentor, Keith Joseph, disappointed not to become shadow Chancellor, opted instead to concentrate on research, founding the Centre for Policy Studies, where she became his vice-chairman. Declaring that he had himself 'only recently become a Conservative', Joseph reintroduced her to Hayek's *The Road to Serfdom* and, this time, she did not fail to notice the dedication 'To the socialists of all parties'. To Heath's fury, in June, Joseph made a speech lumping together the mistakes of both Labour and Conservative governments, talking about 'thirty years of socialist fashions'. In September, with inflation at 17 per cent, he rejected the view that an incomes policy could contain it; this could only be done by controlling the money supply.

In the October 1974 election, which Labour narrowly won, she was still far enough away from full acceptance of these ideas to propose subsidising mortgage interest rates. She also proposed enabling council house tenants to buy their houses. These were about the only two popular features of the Conservative manifesto. She was infuriated by Heath's last-minute suggestion of a government of national unity, to which he knew she was strongly opposed. She decided to support Keith Joseph in a challenge to Heath for the party leadership, only for him to destroy whatever chances he might have had by lamenting the threat to the 'human stock' in Britain from the rising proportion of children being born to mothers 'least fitted to bring children into the world'.

She decided to stand instead, against the advice of her husband ('you haven't got a hope').

To general amazement, in February 1975 she defeated Heath in the first-round poll of her parliamentary colleagues, then easily saw off belated challenges from Willie Whitelaw and Geoffrey Howe. Described at the time as the peasants' revolt, she was elected by the backbench MPs. Virtually the entire party leadership had voted for Heath. In response to rumours that she was anti-Common Market, she issued a statement, as she put it, 'endorsing Europe'. On the Labour side of the House, Barbara Castle confided to her diary her private solidarity with this extraordinary opponent who 'so clearly was the best man among them'.[21]

II

'THE ODD WOMAN OUT'

The conventional wisdom at the time was that Margaret Thatcher became Prime Minister with no knowledge or experience of foreign affairs. That certainly was the view of most of the grandees in her Cabinet. She had served in government only in domestic departments and in Cabinet only as Secretary of State for Education. Compared with her senior colleagues like Peter Carrington or Christopher Soames, her practical experience was negligible. Ian Gilmour felt that he knew more about these matters than she did and that was the sentiment of several other members of her Cabinet, as well as of the majority of political commentators.

This was to underestimate very seriously the energy and determination she devoted to foreign policy and meetings with foreign leaders during her period as Leader of the Opposition. She was far more interested in ideas than many of her colleagues and was, for instance, the western leader most strongly influenced by Alexander Solzhenitsyn and his writings about the true nature of the Soviet regime. The themes she developed in this period remained a constant refrain through much of her tenure as Prime Minister.

The first challenge she faced as Leader of the Opposition

was the referendum on Britain's membership of the European Economic Community. The 'renegotiation' by the Labour government of the terms of entry had been achieved mainly with smoke and mirrors. As a diplomat in the British embassy in Paris at the time, I was asked by Harold Wilson, en route to see President Giscard, how to tell him in French that he proposed to smuggle the ball out on the blind side.

Europe was very much Heath's issue. There were suspicions that his successor was less enthusiastic but she did genuinely believe that it would be foolish for Britain to leave the EEC. She saw it as providing an economic bond with other western European countries, which was of strategic significance. But, disliking high-flown rhetoric about Britain's European destiny and not seeing Europe as central to her policies, she was more than happy to leave the leadership in the referendum campaign to Heath, despite their frigid personal relations. Nor was she at all enthusiastic about referenda in general, except in the event of some major constitutional change, which she did not believe to be the case at the time. In retrospect, she admitted, she should have realised that the subordination of UK law to European law resulting from accession to the Treaty of Rome did represent such a major constitutional change. But few were disposed to acknowledge this then. In Parliament she rejected the argument put forward by the government that the case of continued EEC membership was unique and a referendum was required. It was rather a device to help the Labour Party and government overcome their internal divisions.

She launched the Conservative pro-EEC campaign at a press conference presided over by Heath but, thereafter, *The Sun* commented on her subsequent largely invisible role in the campaign: 'Missing: one Tory leader. Answers to the name of Margaret Thatcher. Mysteriously disappeared from the Market Referendum campaign eleven days ago.' The referendum was won easily, with a two-thirds majority, encouraging Heath to believe that he could make a political comeback, possibly as head of a coalition government.

A visit by her to Paris provided a contrast between the ebullience of the Prime Minister, Jacques Chirac, and the monarchical airs of President Giscard. But she found the Prime Minister's residence, the Hôtel Matignon, and the Elysée making the same statement about the historic grandeur and national pride of France. The French, she felt, would always put their national interests first in their dealings with the Community, a sentiment she found oddly reassuring.

In July 1975 the Belgian Prime Minister, Leo Tindemans, came to see her about his report on European union. She indicated that a Conservative government would have a more positive attitude to Europe than Labour, but argued for organic growth rather than grand plans imposed from the centre. Conservative MPs had divided views about direct elections to the European Parliament, but were able to defeat the proposal to hold them in Britain on the basis of proportional representation.

The far more difficult issue was the attitude the opposition should take to the embryonic European Monetary System (EMS). In 1972 Britain had joined in the first attempt at the coordination of European currencies – the so-called 'snake' – as a way for Heath to demonstrate the country's European credentials. It is astonishing in retrospect that so important a decision came to be taken with virtually no debate. Heath's management of his Cabinet was every bit as autocratic as Thatcher's was, or became. Sterling came under such pressure that Heath had to withdraw within six weeks.

In March 1979, eight of the nine member states of the EEC signed up to a fresh attempt at currency coordination through the EMS. The Callaghan government elected not to join. Margaret Thatcher in opposition exploited to the full the fact that this was due to sterling's weakness under Labour, but neither she nor her advisers had a view on what to do themselves. Geoffrey Howe believed that a Conservative government, with the right economic policies, would have been able to join and feared that the alternative meant surrendering the direction of the EEC to the 'Franco-German high table'. Nigel Lawson saw that the EMS had a political objective, the next stage of European unity, but that the discipline which was its 'sole merit' might prove to be so unpopular as to invite political suicide. His reluctant conclusion was that Britain should join anyway, but his best hope was that the system would simply collapse because of the pressures on other currencies. Margaret Thatcher's conclusion was that they should adopt a positive general approach to the EMS while avoiding any specific commitments.

A cause close to her heart, more than to those of her successors today, was to improve cooperation between the right-wing parties in the European Parliament. Addressing the German Christian Democratic Union (CDU) party conference in Hanover in May 1976, she denounced Euro-communism.

In some European countries we now see communist parties dressed in democratic clothes and speaking with soft voices. Of course, we hope that their oft-proclaimed change of heart is genuine. But every child in Europe knows the story of Little Red Riding Hood…

She worried that Willy Brandt's détente policy had had the unintended effect of promoting neutralist attitudes and was relieved at the robustness of his successor, Helmut Schmidt, who she found to be a good deal less socialist than most members of her shadow Cabinet. But her main objective was to forge an alliance in Europe between the Conservative Party and the CDU, to be known as the European Democratic Union (EDU). Aware of the German determination to work things out with the trade union leaders, she acknowledged that this was feasible – provided they were German. At her first meeting with the Christian Democrat leader Helmut Kohl, she found him amiable and instinctively sound on the important issues, but deliberate, ponderous and far more difficult for her to engage with than the trenchant Helmut Schmidt. The relationship between them was not helped by the fact that neither spoke the other's language. In the course of her travels, she established a rapport with the future Dutch Prime Minister, Ruud Lubbers, but not with the Christian Democrats in Italy, who declined to participate in the EDU.

She was not immune to flattery. When the Spanish Foreign Minister descended on her, he asked if he might speak frankly. 'I had been told, madam, of your formidable intelligence, but no one had warned me of your beauty.' Douglas Hurd was appalled, 'thinking the impertinence would annoy. I had a lot to learn.' When Woodrow Wyatt gushed to her in similar fashion a decade later, 'not bad for sixty', was her response.[22]

In a speech in Brussels in June 1978 she described the EEC as not merely an economic entity, but as having a wider strategic purpose. As a zone of stability, democracy and prosperity adjoining Soviet-controlled eastern Europe, it could act as a magnet drawing others away from communism. Western countries should be more cautious, she argued, about technology transfer and the granting of cheap credits to the Soviet bloc.

☞

The consistent central theme of her foreign policy speeches as Leader of the Opposition was the need for the West to show greater unity and determination in standing up to the Soviet Union, which was still pursuing expansionist policies in various parts of the world. The Vietnam War had ended in communist domination of the whole of Indo-China. The post-Watergate paralysis of US foreign policy was to render it impossible for America to respond to the Soviet intervention in Angola. She and President Ford's Secretary of State, Henry Kissinger, came over time to share a similar view of world affairs. He became a special confidant of hers, on whom she relied for insights into developments in the US and elsewhere and into the characters and motivations of the array of world leaders with whom he kept in touch. She admired his intellectual brilliance and agreed with his generally hawkish sentiments. She wholeheartedly approved of Kissinger's initiative in normalising relations with China.

At this time, however, she had grave misgivings about the whole strategy of détente, which, in the absence of any real change in Soviet behaviour, she regarded as verging on appeasement. Nor had she failed to notice that the strategic arms limitation talks (SALT) had not resulted in any actual reduction in the number of Soviet nuclear missiles at all. It was only later, when she learned the full extent and very real dangers of Soviet paranoia from the KGB defector, Oleg Gordievsky, that she came to understand Kissinger's success in creating a stable framework within which the US and Russia could discuss nuclear issues with each other.

Alarmed at the preparations for the Helsinki conference with the Russians on mutual and balanced force reductions (MBFR) and human rights, she made a major speech on the subject on 26 July 1975. Much of it was written with the aid of Robert Conquest, historian of Stalin's terror and a determined critic of his successors. Deliberately, she did not consult the shadow Foreign Secretary, Reginald Maudling, or anyone else who might have wanted to tone it down. She began with the huge military imbalance in Europe and rapid expansion of the Soviet Navy. She called for 'real' détente, as against Brezhnev's contention that peaceful coexistence was compatible with intensification of the struggle to undermine pro-western regimes around the world. Respect for human rights would be the litmus test of any real change. No flood of words from the conference would mean anything unless it was accompanied by demonstrable progress in the free movement of people and ideas.

The reaction showed, in her own words, that she was the odd woman out. The Helsinki agreement was generally welcomed. Maudling was understandably furious not to have been consulted and disagreed with her anyway. In retrospect she acknowledged that enshrining human rights in a treaty gave dissidents in eastern Europe leverage which they exploited quite successfully. In her view, however, this would have been to little avail but for the subsequent western, especially American, renewal of resolve and defence build up. On a visit to Romania, against Foreign Office advice, she presented Ceaușescu with a list of political prisoners whom she urged him to release.

On a visit to America at this time, she was confronted by an article in the *Wall Street Journal* declaring that 'Great Britain is the sick country of Europe ... It has been brought to this by the calculated policies of its government and by their resigned acceptance by the people.'[23] In a speech in New York she attacked the 'progressive consensus', in particular the notion that the state should engineer the redistribution of wealth and incomes. To her irritation, a senior member of the British embassy staff gave a counter-briefing against her. She found President Ford to be large and friendly, but epitomising the limitations of a 'safe pair of hands'.

In September 1975 the Cubans, with Soviet assistance, began to pour troops into Angola. Congress debarred Kissinger and Ford from supporting the anti-communist forces there. The warnings in her speech about Helsinki began to look more prescient. This triggered a further speech by her on the threat posed by Soviet imperialism, warning of the imbalance between NATO and Warsaw Pact forces in central Europe, where western forces were outnumbered by 150,000 men, nearly 10,000 tanks and 2,600 aircraft. This got a much more favourable reception and a priceless gift from the Soviet army newspaper *Red Star*, which denounced her as the 'Iron Lady'. Visiting the British Army on the Rhine, she was thrilled to be photographed driving a tank.

The election of Jimmy Carter as President at the end of 1976 brought new challenges. She welcomed his emphasis on human rights, but not on disarmament. Nor did she believe that human rights issues could be pursued regardless of the political context. In her view, the Carter emphasis on human rights in Iran helped to undermine the Shah, leading to the far more oppressive and anti-western regime of Ayatollah Khomeini.

She met Carter in London in May 1977 and in Washington on a visit in September. He felt himself to be more comfortable with Callaghan than with her. Despite her growing doubts about his foreign policy, she liked him personally. She was not convinced, however, by his advocacy of a comprehensive nuclear test ban. Nor did she agree with the administration's approach to the Rhodesia problem and flirtation with sanctions against South Africa.

The Russians, meanwhile, were providing military support for the unsavoury regime of Colonel Mengistu in Ethiopia. The Soviet dissidents Orlov, Sharansky and Ginsburg were given long jail sentences in flagrant disregard of the Helsinki Accords.

At this point, from her perspective, a ray of hope appeared, in the form of Governor Reagan of California, who had run against Gerald Ford for the Republican nomination in 1976 and planned to run again in 1980. The Governor was not being taken seriously by the Callaghan government, who fobbed him off with a meeting with the deputy Foreign Minister, Roy Hattersley, nor by the Republican Party foreign policy Establishment, aligned behind George Bush, who was planning to run against him. She met him twice as Leader of the Opposition; Denis Thatcher had been very impressed by a speech he had made to the Institute of Directors.

She found Reagan to be a kindred spirit, advocating tax cuts as the route to wealth creation and stronger defences as the alternative to détente. Here was someone who 'thought and felt' as she did and who occupied a similar position not only in the political spectrum in America, but in his own party. Accustomed to and priding herself on making instinctive judgements about people, her reaction to Ronald Reagan was wholly positive, aided by his undoubted charm and extreme courtliness towards women, a quality she liked, admired and was to exploit very effectively in subsequent years.[24]

At the beginning of 1976 she had visited Egypt, Syria and Israel. She felt a strong affinity for Israel and the traditional Arab regimes. Most of her shadow Cabinet colleagues were traditional Tory Arabists. She was adamantly opposed to Palestinian terrorism, but accepted that there could be no lasting peace without a solution to the Palestinian problem. She was impressed by the Egyptian President, Anwar Sadat, who was setting out on an anti-Soviet course and warned her against the Ba'athists in Syria. She flatly refused to ride on a camel. With President Assad, preoccupied with his plans to intervene in Lebanon, there was no meeting of minds. Asked at a press conference why she would not recognise the Palestinian Liberation Organisation (PLO), she insisted that they must renounce terrorism, earning her the approbation of Golda Meir in Israel.

In this period before the Camp David Accords, she tried to convince Israeli ministers that Sadat at least might be thinking of making peace. She was taken to visit a kibbutz near the Golan Heights. Carol Thatcher had not been impressed by her prior stay in a kibbutz and her mother regarded the whole idea as an unnerving and unnatural collectivist social experiment. Feeling cold on the Golan Heights, she was photographed wearing the flak jacket of an Israeli general.

Margaret Thatcher was one of the last western political leaders to visit Iran while the Shah was still in power. While there was growing dissent, the very experienced and highly regarded

British ambassador, Tony Parsons, still believed that the army could contain the situation. No one foresaw how quickly the regime would crumble.

In late 1976 and early 1977, she visited eight countries in Asia. A visit to Singapore cemented the mutual admiration she had already established with the Prime Minister, Lee Kuan Yew, who had demonstrated the results his version of free market capitalism could achieve in an island state devoid of natural resources. In Delhi, she empathised with Indira Gandhi, who cleared the dishes away herself after they had lunch together – a very Thatcherlike touch – but could not approve her methods, which had culminated in the imposition of a state of emergency. She got on well with the New Zealand Prime Minister Robert Muldoon, but not with his Australian counterpart, Malcolm Fraser. A speech to his Liberal Party colleagues in Canberra fell flat as the audience appeared unused to her brand of unapologetic conservatism. In April 1977 her anti-Soviet statements ensured a warm welcome for her in Beijing. The 'Gang of Four' had been ousted and disgraced, but Deng Xiaoping was still in internal exile. She was greeted by torrents of propaganda wherever she went.

She noted in retrospect that she had established friendly relations with a number of foreign leaders with less than perfect records of respect for human rights. Her job was to promote British interests. They were the rulers of their countries, so they were the people with whom she had to deal. International relations were a matter of second-best alternatives. With some foreign leaders, she sought to sup with a long spoon. In many cases, she raised human rights issues more vigorously than most of her predecessors had done. But her style, tempered as it always was by a solid dose of realpolitik, could not have been more different from that of Jimmy Carter.

The 1978 Conservative Party conference was marked by a fierce disagreement about Rhodesia. Peter Carrington argued strongly against accepting an amendment demanding the lifting of sanctions, a line defended by the shadow Foreign Secretary, John Davies, in a speech marked by loud heckling. In Parliament there was a revolt by 114 Conservative MPs against the shadow Cabinet's decision to abstain on the order renewing sanctions. Margaret Thatcher had considerable sympathy with the rebels. The party leadership, meanwhile, was still divided as to how to respond to the government's attempts at a wages and incomes policy. When Geoffrey Howe produced a memo commending the German 'talking shop' approach in dealing with the unions, her response remained that the German talking shop worked 'because it consists of Germans'.

In their parliamentary exchanges, the Prime Minister, Jim Callaghan, continued to treat her in an extraordinarily patronising way. 'I am sure that one day the Rt Hon. Lady will understand these things a little better', he told her on one occasion. On another he said: 'The Rt Hon. Lady is too young to be living in the past.'[25] These tactics worked; he consistently was rated more highly than her in the opinion polls. She sympathised with the difficulties he faced as the successor of Harold Wilson, whom she had always liked personally, but whose politics she regarded as consisting mainly of artful dodging. She respected Callaghan's efforts to impose moderation on the labour movement. But he could scarcely complain when she responded to the collapse of the government's incomes policy and its humiliation at the hands of its allies in the trade union movement with withering scorn.

The already severe winter of 1978/9 was marked by a flood of public and private sector strikes, with demands for huge pay increases in defiance of the government's incomes policy. The industrial chaos of the 'winter of discontent' dealt a fatal blow to the rapidly diminishing authority of the Callaghan government. The Prime Minister, returning from a summit meeting in Guadeloupe plus a stay at Sandy Lane in Barbados, did not actually use the words 'Crisis? What crisis?' on descending from his plane, but that was the impression he sought to give. On 22 March the opposition tabled a 'no confidence' motion which the government lost by one vote.

The ensuing election campaign started in the worst possible way with the murder by an Irish National Liberation Army (INLA) car bomb of the shadow Northern Ireland Secretary and her close associate, Airey Neave. In the course of the election she declared that, 'Unless we change our ways and our direction, our glories as a nation will soon be a footnote in the history books.' As the campaign developed there were continuing worries by her colleagues about her commitment to new legislation on trade union reform and her leadership of the campaign. The size of the Conservative lead appeared to be steadily shrinking. As it did, she noted with disgust the party hierarchy quickly losing confidence in her. She was convinced that, as a woman leader, she would be given just one chance to win an election. If she failed to do so, they would get rid of her. Victory by an overall margin of forty-four parliamentary votes came as a considerable relief.

III

'A LONG-STANDING SOURCE OF GRIEF'

The most pressing international problem confronting Margaret Thatcher when she became Prime Minister was that of Rhodesia. It had, as she said, been a long-standing source of grief to successive British governments. Harold Wilson's credibility never fully recovered from his statement in response to Ian Smith's unilateral declaration of independence in 1965 that economic sanctions would put an end to the rebellion in 'weeks rather than months'. The agreement reached by Sir Alec Douglas-Home with Smith in 1971 fell a long way short of majority rule and was rejected by the African population. Even Henry Kissinger had tried and failed to defuse this time bomb. For the Callaghan government, David Owen had teamed with the Carter administration to present a plan which was rejected both by Smith and the Patriotic Front leaders, Joshua Nkomo and Robert Mugabe. On being appointed Head of the Rhodesia Department in the Foreign and Commonwealth Office shortly before the election, I was told that I was being given responsibility for a pretty hopeless cause, but also to come up with some new ideas.

Ian Smith, meanwhile, was pursuing the so-called 'internal settlement'. Having reached agreement with one African leader,

Bishop Muzorewa, and his colleagues, they organised elections in April 1979 in which the African population was able to vote for the first time. The Patriotic Front parties were neither invited nor willing to participate. As Leader of the Opposition, Margaret Thatcher despatched a team led by Lord Boyd, who many years before had served as Colonial Secretary, to witness the elections. Impressed by the high turnout (over 60 per cent), he reported that the elections had been fairly conducted, creating a presumption that the incoming Conservative government would lift sanctions and recognise Muzorewa.

Rhodesia was the foreign policy issue on which the Labour and Conservative parties were furthest apart. Ian Smith had quite a following in Britain. Having visited the country on the eve of the elections, I had found Bishop Muzorewa likeable and well-disposed but, manifestly, not really in charge and, even if he had been, he did not appear capable of running a government. I was able to establish a relationship with the person who *was* in charge, General Walls, a charismatic military commander accustomed to leading his men from the front, who was well aware that while his forces were winning every battle, they were losing the war, and the country badly needed to seek to normalise relations, at any rate with us. In Mozambique, where he and his guerrilla forces were based, I found Mugabe as coldly dislikeable and intransigent as ever, a would-be African Robespierre, and two days after seeing Nkomo at his headquarters in Lusaka, the Rhodesians had destroyed the house in which we met, in an attempt to kill him.

As we prepared for a change of government, it was clear that the Conservatives would not be prepared simply to continue the policy of their predecessors towards Rhodesia and nor was that desirable anyway.

Trying to look at the problem with a fresh eye, we believed that many of our difficulties arose from our continuing to accept nominal responsibility for Rhodesia without ever actually seeking to exercise that responsibility. We continually had promised more than we could perform, because we had never been prepared to intervene decisively ourselves. The idea that we should consider doing so had always been rejected by the bureaucracy and politicians alike as far too risky.

I had never met Margaret Thatcher but it seemed to me that the argument that we should not recognise the outcome of the elections in Rhodesia because that would annoy the Commonwealth and imperil our shrinking assets elsewhere in Africa had not the faintest chance of being accepted by her. But if we did recognise a Muzorewa government which attracted no other support and then went under, that would do further damage to our interests and reputation. The new Prime Minister just might, we thought, be prepared to consider a much bolder plan, which was what the by now desperate circumstances required. This would need to be based on Britain playing a far more direct and adventurous role than any previous government had been prepared to contemplate.

The Foreign Office had greeted with a sigh of relief the appointment of Peter Carrington as Foreign Secretary, after its sometimes turbulent relationship with David Owen. Carrington was a great public servant, rather than a politician, and knew the Rhodesia problem all too well. The very patrician Carrington detested the Rhodesian Front and their right-wing supporters in his own party who regarded Ian Smith (who still bore the scars of the injuries he had suffered while serving as an RAF pilot in Italy during the war) as a kindred spirit and the rebellion he had led against the Crown as a mere peccadillo.

Carrington, who had an even more distinguished war record himself, had no more time for Smith than he did for the bluster of Nkomo and intransigence of Mugabe, or for the means by which they were seeking to liberate their country. Carrington suspected, as I did, that Alec Douglas-Home might well be correct in suggesting that what they wanted was 'one man, one vote – once'. Muzorewa had emerged the victor in an election which compared quite favourably with most others held elsewhere in independent Africa. Nkomo's bombastic performances and Mugabe's public commitment to a Marxist one-party state had done nothing to endear them to British opinion. Muzorewa seemed the only herbivore in the Rhodesian jungle.

The implication of Lord Boyd's report was that the problem, in effect, was solved. We told Carrington that we did not agree. The Zimbabwe–Rhodesia constitution was designed to keep control over the armed forces, police, civil service and judiciary in the hands of the whites. Even if we did so, no other western or African country would be prepared to recognise the government. The Carter administration would not do so. The war would continue and we did not believe that Muzorewa would survive.

With a war in progress, the Foreign Office view understandably had been that it would be extremely unwise to get more directly involved. But if the situation deteriorated to the point of collapse, we faced the prospect of having to help evacuate the 140,000 British citizens or persons entitled to claim citizenship in Rhodesia in circumstances reminiscent of the last weeks of the Algerian war. There was, I was convinced, no low-risk policy in relation to Rhodesia.

There obviously was no possibility of agreement on the Anglo-American proposals. So far as the Carter administration was concerned, they were well-nigh sacrosanct. But that negotiating approach had been based on efforts to devise a plan that would be accepted by Mugabe and Nkomo. Even if they did, it never was clear, as President Kaunda of Zambia put it, who was to bell the cat and how the Rhodesians were to be brought to surrender power.

Margaret Thatcher was surprised to find the Foreign Office advocating a far more muscular approach.

The first major decision was that this was going to be a purely British initiative and not an Anglo-American enterprise. Callaghan and Owen had clung to the Americans but, on this issue, they had become part of the problem. It was Carter who had rendered the Anglo-American proposals non-negotiable by accepting the Tanzanian President Julius Nyerere's demand that, whatever the electorate decided, the future army must be based on the liberation forces. What attracted the Prime Minister most about our plan was its boldness. She liked the idea of Britain acting as the decolonising power. Carter's Secretary of State, Cyrus Vance, agreed with relief that we should take the lead. In the debate on the Queen's speech, the Prime Minister said that 'we intend to proceed with vigour to resolve the issue'. It was a promise not many believed the government capable of keeping.

We told her that the Zimbabwe–Rhodesia constitution was unlike any other on the basis of which we had granted independence, as the real power remained in the hands of the Rhodesian military commanders. She agreed that this must be remedied before the country could be brought to independence.

Finally, we sought to persuade her that bringing the country to independence would not be of much avail nor would a Muzorewa government have much chance of surviving, if we could not get the support of the neighbouring countries and seek a way to wind down the war.

For this very nasty small war was getting steadily worse. To counter the incursions by Mugabe's guerrillas in Mozambique and Nkomo's in Zambia, the Rhodesians were launching ferocious cross-border raids to disrupt infiltration and destroy the neighbouring countries' infrastructure. They also were arming groups opposed to the government in Mozambique, fuelling a full-scale civil war. As for Mugabe's tactics, one of the principal methods used to bring areas of the country under his forces' control was the torture, mutilation and execution of village headmen in front of the villagers.

The Conservative Party manifesto had included a promise to bring Rhodesia to independence 'with wide international acceptance'. David Harlech, who had served with distinction as ambassador to the US under President Kennedy, was despatched to see the heads of government of the neighbouring states. The Prime Minister was not at all keen that he should meet Nkomo and Mugabe, whose forces had carried out atrocities, but 'unpleasant realities had to be faced'.[26] Harlech's report convinced her that without changes to the Rhodesian constitution, no other African country would recognise Muzorewa. The war would continue and so would support for it by Rhodesia's neighbours.

At this point the South African Foreign Minister, Pik Botha, descended on us in London. Pik Botha was one of the most 'enlightened' (*verligte*) members of the South African government, but that was not saying much at the time. He gave Peter Carrington and his deputy, Ian Gilmour, a 45-minute lecture on the iniquity of western policy in southern Africa, alleging constant moving of the goalposts, and allowing precious little time for reply. Bent on revenge, I telephoned 10 Downing Street to ensure that when Pik Botha saw the Prime Minister he did not get a word in edgeways.

Our next visitor was Bishop Muzorewa. A decent man, he always seemed small and insignificant in meetings with him, lacking Nkomo's vast girth and bluster and Mugabe's viperish intelligence. Margaret Thatcher told him that there would have to be a new constitution, comparable to those of our other former colonies, but that if others opposed a settlement we regarded as reasonable, we would be prepared to go ahead anyway.

Our plans for the Commonwealth conference in Lusaka depended on taking the others by surprise. For the other heads of government still were convinced of her intention to recognise Muzorewa. Zambia, including its capital, had been treated as a free-fire zone by the Rhodesian army and air force for many months. I had to warn the Rhodesian commander, General Walls, against attacking the country during the conference. As the RAF VC10 neared Lusaka, Peter Carrington asked the Prime Minister why she was donning dark glasses. Mrs Thatcher feared that, on arrival, acid might be thrown in her eyes.[27] There was a sharp exchange with him when he suggested that the meeting was going to be a damage-limitation exercise, an expression she claimed never to have heard before! It was alien to her thinking, on this as on other occasions.

She also was accompanied by Sir Antony Duff, deputy head of the Foreign Office. A very unusual official, Duff belonged to a school and generation that believed that it was Britain's role not just to observe and, from time to time, deplore the state of the world, but to do something about it. A former submariner with a distinguished war record, he combined personal authority, good humour and a steeliness of spirit in measures calculated to impress both white and black Rhodesians, as they did Carrington and Margaret Thatcher. He was, in Douglas Hurd's description, 'one of those good-looking, grand-mannered officials who could exercise great influence over her once they had gained her trust'.[28] She was to appoint him subsequently as head of MI6 and then of MI5.

On arrival she was confronted by a hostile press conference and the news that the Nigerian government was nationalising BP's assets in Nigeria. This was her first encounter with Kenneth Kaunda and Julius Nyerere, who between them had destroyed the economies of Zambia and Tanzania. Both much preferred lecturing us on Rhodesia to dealing with their problems at home, though Nyerere had put an end to the appalling regime of Idi Amin in Uganda. The discussion on Rhodesia, expected to be stormy, was opened by Nyerere. What was required in Rhodesia, he argued, was a genuinely democratic constitution and elections in which all parties could participate.

The Prime Minister proceeded to upstage him by agreeing. They had, she said, lost few opportunities to remind us that it was our responsibility to bring Rhodesia to legal independence. We would be proposing a new constitution and elections to be held under British, not Commonwealth, control. The conference ended with the improbable sight of Margaret Thatcher dancing with Kenneth Kaunda. She was far too polite to mention that on returning to her accommodation one evening, the ceiling had collapsed and there was no running water.

She told the press that the problem was to find a solution which would bring an end to the war. But she added, to my dismay, that she had no plans to send British troops to Rhodesia. This was a decision we were going to have to get reversed.

The way was now open for us to put forward the plan we had been working on for months. We intended to insist that agreement must first be reached on the independence constitution. This was the opposite of what had been attempted in previous negotiations, when efforts had been made to get agreement first on a ceasefire and power-sharing arrangements, rather than dealing with the fundamental problem. If agreement could be reached on the constitution, we reasoned, then the war would be reduced to a competition for power between the parties which, instead, might be coerced into settling it in elections under impartial control.

President Nyerere sent the Prime Minister a message that Britain should not approach the independence conference at Lancaster House as a neutral power arbitrating between the contending groups. We must act as the decolonising power. He wondered how we could secure sufficient authority on the ground to organise elections. I enjoyed drafting her reply stating that we intended to do exactly that. The era of talks about talks was over.

In the run-up to the conference, it was explicitly agreed by Thatcher that she must not seek to play any part in it, otherwise the participants would constantly be appealing against Carrington to her. This included having nothing whatsoever to do with Ian Smith, despite the pleas of his supporters in her party. Having resolved to leave the negotiating entirely to Carrington, who she liked and trusted more than any other Foreign Secretary, she played a very effective role behind the scenes with the African Presidents who converged on London during the conference.

On 14 August, however, a note from No. 10 recorded that they were approaching the conference in 'rather different ways'.

The Prime Minister wished to do everything possible to enable it to succeed and bring about agreement on the constitution. Carrington regarded such agreement as 'virtually inconceivable' and tended to regard the conference as a means of enabling Britain to get off the Rhodesia hook.[29]

As the conference convened, veterans of Rhodesia negotiations looked on more in pity than in hope. Few saw much reason to believe that it would not turn into another in the apparently unending series of initiatives that had flourished briefly before leading nowhere.

At the previous conference, convened by the Labour government in Geneva, Nkomo and Mugabe had objected to the chairmanship and allowances for the delegates, simply filibustering until the meeting was called off. When they tried similar tactics on this occasion, they were told that the conference would proceed with whoever chose to attend it.

We presented a classic decolonising constitution to both sides, providing for genuine majority rule with protections for minority rights. Muzorewa was overshadowed by the brooding and sardonic presence of Ian Smith, who had driven his country full tilt into an increasingly bloody cul-de-sac. When he complained, in his grating voice, that we were dragging out the conference while people were being killed in Rhodesia, the normally imperturbable Carrington lost his temper completely. Purple with anger, he told Smith that the responsibility for the war, which they were losing, rested squarely with him.

Ian Smith's plan was to push the government up against the deadline for the renewal of sanctions in November. Urged by Carrington to find a way to outmanoeuvre him, I told the Rhodesians that not all sanctions depended on the Southern

Rhodesia Act, which they knew was unlikely to be renewed in November. A lot of measures existed under other legislation, and these required positive, not merely negative, action to terminate them. This was regarded by Smith as an example of British perfidy. But it had the intended effect. The Muzorewa delegation accepted the constitution, overruling Ian Smith.

Nkomo and Mugabe refused to accept until everything else was agreed. The conference continued for two days without them. The next step was to decide who was to govern the country in the period up to the elections. The discovery that we intended to send a British governor with full powers to do so, dissolving the Rhodesian government and parliament, brought them back to the negotiating table. Now, they told us, they realised we were serious, which they had never believed we were before. With extreme reluctance, Muzorewa agreed to stand aside as Prime Minister; a more power-hungry politician would have refused to do so. Nkomo and especially Mugabe were bent on stringing out the conference while they pushed more of their troops across the border. The Rhodesians were responding with massive cross-border raids into Zambia and Mozambique.

Carrington and I were summoned to see the Prime Minister in her room in the House of Commons. We had presented her with a Bill providing for Britain to assume direct control of Rhodesia through a Governor with full legislative and executive powers. Reminding us that she was a lawyer, she insisted on going through every line of it. Told by the Leader of the House of Commons, Norman St John-Stevas, that there was no parliamentary time, we said that, without it, we would never get the conference to a conclusion. Overruling her parliamentary managers, she told them to get it enacted forthwith.

Next we brokered an agreement between the military commanders on both sides, requiring the Patriotic Front to assemble their forces inside the country under the protection of a Commonwealth monitoring force which, she now accepted, would have to be led by the British military. We found an unexpected, invaluable ally in the principal guerrilla leader, Josiah Tongogara, who was far more interested in a peaceful outcome than his political leader, Mugabe. At my suggestion, Christopher Soames was persuaded by Carrington to serve as Governor. Following a series of secret meetings with him in a hotel under the motorway on the Edgware Road, in which he received us clad, bizarrely, in a raincoat, Nkomo by now was telling us that he wanted to agree. Mugabe, meanwhile, kept telling me that power came from the barrel of a gun and that he had a PhD in terrorism. He was not going to agree to anything until cornered into doing so.

We warned the Prime Minister that the conference could be dragged out indefinitely unless we took decisive action to bring it to a conclusion. With her approval, we now took the extremely risky step of despatching Christopher Soames to Rhodesia – despite his own misgivings, which he expressed to the Prime Minister – and lifting sanctions before a cease-fire was agreed. The conference ended with Mugabe still holding out. Charles Powell, later to become the Prime Minister's principal foreign policy adviser, had joined us in the Rhodesia department. Through the Mozambican special representative, Fernando Honwana, we were able to persuade President Samora Machel, whose country was suffering desperately from the war, to tell Mugabe that unless he signed the agreement, there would be no further support from Mozambique. Final agreement was announced in time for it to be greeted with applause at the state banquet President Carter was holding for the Prime Minister at the White House.

On 6 December the Prime Minister saw the Rhodesian commander, General Walls, who wanted reassurance that if, as he expected, the Patriotic Front forces sought to win the elections by intimidation, he and his forces would be permitted to deal with this. He also was worried about the withdrawal of South African forces from Rhodesia. He wanted written assurances on these points. Mrs Thatcher agreed that law and order must be maintained and the means of doing so would have to be agreed between him and the Governor. She was not prepared to offer written assurances: he would have to trust in her good faith.[30]

There followed two months of extreme tension in Rhodesia, with an ever-present risk of a breakdown in the ceasefire, as Mugabe kept several thousand of his forces outside the assembly areas to intimidate the villagers, and the Rhodesian special forces contributed their own atrocities, including an attempt to assassinate Mugabe. General Walls rejected appeals by Ian Smith to suspend the process and we got through to the elections by the skin of our teeth. As the results came in and it became clear that Mugabe was going to win, Duff and I had a tense confrontation with the Rhodesian commanders, and Walls in great distress ('the enemy is now our government') appealed to the Prime Minister to declare the elections flawed, which she flatly refused to do. Peter Walls was persuaded to oppose plans by some of his colleagues to stage a coup. Mugabe in turn was persuaded to form a coalition government including Nkomo and Ian Smith's deputy, David Smith, and the British military set about integrating the Patriotic Front and Rhodesian forces.

Margaret Thatcher found it sad that Zimbabwe ended up with a Mugabe government, but political and military realities were on the side of the guerrilla leaders. She wept as she watched on TV the British flag being lowered in Salisbury. I shared her sentiments about Mugabe. But she recognised that the Muzorewa government could not have brought peace to the country, which was what it needed most. Above all, she was proud of the role we had played. The settlement, in her view, brought large benefits to Britain, enabling us to play later a positive role in Namibia and South Africa. Britain had demonstrated its ability through 'forceful diplomacy' to settle a particularly intractable international dispute. While much of the credit for doing so has gone, rightly, to Peter Carrington, and Christopher Soames also distinguished himself in his near-impossible task, success would not have been possible without Margaret Thatcher's willingness to face all the risks associated with assuming direct control in Rhodesia, which none of her predecessors had been prepared to do.

IV

'THAT LITTLE ICE-COLD BUNCH OF LAND DOWN THERE'

In January 1981, Margaret Thatcher replaced her Defence Secretary Francis Pym with John Nott, to whom she looked to get the over-extended defence budget under control. The government was committed to increasing defence spending by the NATO target of 3 per cent per annum, but the rapidly escalating costs of equipment necessitated a defence review. Nott concluded that the overriding priority must be the commitment to NATO defence in central Europe. This left no room for substantial savings from the Army or RAF and Nott decided instead on swingeing cuts in the Royal Navy surface fleet, triggering the resignation of the Navy Minister, Keith Speed.

Nott proposed, with the Prime Minister's approval, to scrap one aircraft carrier, *Hermes*, and to sell a second, *Invincible*, to Australia (though both carriers were to be replaced), to cut twenty frigates and destroyers and to scrap the two assault ships, *Fearless* and *Intrepid*.

On 8 June, she and Nott saw the First Sea Lord, Sir Henry Leach, who was exercising his right to appeal to the Prime Minister about Nott's plans. He gave her a prophetic warning in writing that: 'The proposals have been devised ad hoc in two months. It has all been done in a rush. Such unbalanced devastation to our overall defence capability is unprecedented. War seldom takes the expected form and a strong maritime capability provides flexibility for the unforeseen.'[31]

His protests were ignored.

A few months later came the evening she was never likely to forget: that of 31 March 1982. As she was working in her room in the House of Commons, Nott asked for an urgent meeting. The intelligence reports showed that the Argentine fleet, which was already at sea on 'manoeuvres', intended to seize the Falkland Islands on the Friday, 2 April. Nott added that in the Ministry of Defence's view the islands could not be retaken once they were seized, getting an instant response from her: 'If they are invaded, we have to get them back.'

At this point, in what she was to describe to the Franks Committee as the worst moment of her life, salvation appeared in the form of Admiral Sir Henry Leach. An element of farce had delayed his arrival at the meeting. Although he was in naval uniform, he was held up by the police in the central lobby and had to be rescued by one of the government whips. Quietly, calmly and confidently, he told her that he could put together a task force to be led by the two aircraft carriers Nott was planning to retire, which he believed could retake the islands. It could, he said, be ready in forty-eight hours. It would be an operation involving considerable risk, but there was no better alternative. Asked if they could recapture the islands, he said that they could and, in his opinion, they should. Otherwise 'in a few months we will be living in another country whose word counts for little'. The Prime Minister wholeheartedly agreed.

He saw her again on the following evening, noting that in these late-night sessions she was at her very best. 'Such were her stamina and resolve in a crisis that I believe she rather enjoyed them.' When asked what his reaction to the despatch of the task force would be if he were the Argentine fleet commander, his reply was: 'I would return to harbour immediately.'

The admiral could hardly be blamed for planning, more or less openly, to vanquish not only the Argentinians, but also his own Secretary of State for Defence.[32]

☞

Lord Franks's report on the invasion of the Falklands by Argentina, published after their successful recovery, ended with the words: 'We would not be justified in attaching any criticism or blame to the present Government for the Argentine Junta's decision to commit its act of unprovoked aggression in the invasion of the Falkland Islands on 2 April 1982.' Margaret Thatcher herself told Lord Franks and his colleagues that she never expected Argentina 'to invade the Falklands head on. It was such a stupid thing to do… Such a stupid thing even to contemplate doing.' When the report was published, Harold Macmillan wrote tongue in cheek to congratulate the Prime Minister on the committee of inquiry having fulfilled its function of finding that, all things considered, 'no one was really to blame'.[33]

This was regarded even at the time as a pretty generous conclusion. As Margaret Thatcher observed, the Falklands were an improbable cause for a twentieth-century war and the Americans, despite their much greater involvement in Argentina, had no more foreknowledge than she did of the Argentine intention to invade, a decision taken at very short notice by the military regime. But the signals emitted by the British government over the previous years certainly had done nothing to discourage them. In 1976, the Labour government had been prepared to offer Argentina sovereignty over the uninhabited dependencies and to consider a lease-back arrangement for the Falkland Islands themselves. For the Conservatives, Nick Ridley, deputy to Peter Carrington, had been pursuing a longstanding Foreign Office plan to persuade the islanders to accept a sale to Argentina and long-term lease-back of the islands. The Prime Minister's initial reaction was described by Carrington as 'thermonuclear', but she permitted Ridley to pursue the idea. When it was turned down by the islanders and irate backbenchers, Labour as well as Tory, 'lease-back' was taken off the table. In December 1981 a new three-man military junta took over in Buenos Aires with, as it turned out, far more aggressive intentions than their predecessors.

As part of the defence review, Nott announced the decision to withdraw HMS *Endurance* which, although an ice-breaker with no heavy armament, was Britain's only naval vessel in the South Atlantic and an important signal of commitment to the Falklands. The announcement was made over the strenuous objections of Peter Carrington in three separate minutes to Nott, copied to No. 10. Carrington warned that this would be interpreted by both the islanders and the Argentinians as a reduction in Britain's commitment to the islands and its willingness to defend them. The government also ignored a warning in Parliament from James Callaghan that 'this was an error that could have serious consequences'.[34]

Following his election as President of the United States, Ronald Reagan and his Defense Secretary, Caspar 'Cap'

Weinberger, initiated a massive increase in US military spending. Weinberger decided to equip the US Trident strategic
nuclear submarines with a new and more powerful D5 warhead.
This necessitated a renegotiation of the terms on which Britain
had the right to acquire the missiles, previously agreed with the
Carter administration.

The Pentagon was alarmed by Nott's plans for the Royal Navy.
The US officials with whom we were dealing knew that President
Reagan and Weinberger were determined that our negotiation
about the new warheads should succeed and, in financial terms,
we were able to obtain a Trident II agreement more favourable
than the initial offer of Trident I had been. But our US colleagues,
Richard Perle and Frank Miller, conducting the negotiations for
the Americans, were determined – as they saw it – to use them
to save us from ourselves. As part of the price for Trident II
they insisted, successfully, on the abandonment of Nott's plans
to scrap the Royal Navy's two remaining landing ships, *Intrepid*
and *Fearless*. *Intrepid* and *Fearless* were subsequently to prove
indispensable in the Falklands. Those who had favoured scrap-
ping without replacing them appeared to believe that our forces
would never have to undertake opposed landings again.

☛

When she became Prime Minister, Margaret Thatcher claimed
that she never thought she would have to order British troops into
combat. The first sign of trouble had come with the landing on
the British-owned territory of South Georgia on 20 December
1981 of a group of Argentine 'scrap-metal merchants', who
subsequently withdrew. Next, the military regime unilaterally

repudiated a joint statement agreed by its own diplomats following the latest round of Anglo-Argentine discussions about the Falklands, amidst increasingly aggressive rhetoric in the Argentine press. On 3 March 1982 Mrs Thatcher minuted on a telegram from Buenos Aires, 'we must make contingency plans'.[35] There was no follow-up to this. On 20 March the British learned of a further unauthorised landing on South Georgia by the 'scrap-metal merchants' who had raised the Argentine flag at Leith harbour. Protests to the Argentine government had no effect. On 25 March the Cabinet noted the 'real risk' that if HMS *Endurance* removed the Argentinians from South Georgia, Argentina could carry out some counter-action against the Falkland Islands themselves and that 'Britain would face an almost impossible task in seeking to defend the islands at such long range'.[36]

On the evening of 28 March, the Prime Minister rang Carrington from Chequers to express her anxiety about the situation. When they met next morning en route to a European Council in Brussels, they agreed to send a nuclear-powered submarine to reinforce HMS *Endurance*, which had not yet been withdrawn – but it would take two weeks to get there. Following the European Council, Carrington left on a scheduled visit to Israel, having made the unfortunate decision not to postpone it, in part because of his rather fraught relationship with the Israelis, who regarded him as pro-Arab.

There followed the dramatic meeting in her room at the House of Commons on the evening of 31 March at which it was decided to mobilise the task force to recover control of the islands.

In Washington, we had not been having much success in getting the Americans to intervene with the Argentinians about the 'scrap-metal merchants'. Secretary of State Al Haig's deputy told Sir Nicholas Henderson, to the ambassador's fury, that they intended to remain neutral in the affair. On the afternoon of 31 March, Washington time, we received a flash telegram with the intelligence showing that an invasion was imminent. I accompanied Henderson to the meeting he sought forthwith with Al Haig. As we went through the intelligence material, Haig expressed astonishment that his own services had not identified the threat themselves.

The White House agreed that President Reagan would try to speak to General Galtieri, head of the Argentinian military junta. The President had to go to the Walter Reed hospital for a medical check-up that morning. Shortly before he was due to make the call, my friend on the National Security Council (NSC) staff, Lieutenant Commander Dennis Blair, a Rhodes scholar and one of the brightest stars in the US Navy, rang to ask me if the President should tell Galtieri that if he invaded the islands, we would regard this as a *casus belli*. There being no time to consult the Foreign Office, who would have been bound to agonise over the terms of a reply, I told Blair that I was convinced we would.

In the event, it took several hours for Reagan to get through, as Galtieri kept refusing to take his call. Later that evening, Blair telephoned me to say that when, eventually, he did so, Galtieri appeared to have been drinking. He kept saying that 'the die is cast'. The same message was passed to Nico Henderson, who was entertaining Vice-President Bush at the embassy. He telephoned the Prime Minister direct to tell her the news. Waking her up at two in the morning, he found her not at all in a bellicose mood, but in a very sombre one, understanding full well the dangers that lay ahead. I asked the Ministry of Defence to warn the

Governor that he was going to have Argentine marines on his doorstep the next morning. President Reagan, in his message to the Prime Minister, said that the US had a policy of neutrality on the sovereignty issue, 'but we will not be neutral on the issue involving the Argentine use of military force'.[37]

The next day was a black one for our standing in the world. The small contingent of seventy-five Royal Marines, which was all we had to defend the islands, was quickly forced to surrender and the Argentine flag flew over Port Stanley. Undeterred by these events, the US ambassador to the United Nations, Jeane Kirkpatrick, had proceeded to attend a dinner given in her honour by the Argentine ambassador as the invasion was under way.

When I visited the National Security Council that morning, Dennis Blair asked me if we really intended to fight for these small islands, of no economic value, with a mere 1,800 British citizens on them, 3,000 miles from our nearest base. It would, he pointed out, be a difficult and dangerous operation and the Pentagon was by no means convinced that we could succeed. I said that we had, as yet, no instructions but that in my opinion we would indeed fight to recover the islands. Blair's response was: 'How can I get myself seconded to one of your carriers?'

On the evening of Friday 2 April, the Cabinet met to approve the despatch of the task force to recover the islands, with one member (probably the Chief Secretary, John Biffen) warning against encouraging a belief that a military solution could easily be accomplished. The Prime Minister had been infuriated to receive advice from the Foreign Office which, she felt, 'summed up the flexibility of a principle characteristic of that department'. This warned of the dangers of a backlash against the British expatriates in Argentina, problems about getting support in the UN Security Council, the lack of reliance to be placed on the European Community or the United States, the risk of the Soviets becoming involved and the disadvantages of being looked on as a colonial power.[38]

It was a pity that this unfortunate document did not end with the conclusion, already reached by Carrington, that despite all of the above, it was indispensable to Britain's standing in the world to recover control of the islands. It confirmed Margaret Thatcher in her distrust of the Foreign Office as an institution. Yet she greatly admired and relied upon some outstanding figures in it, acknowledging that 'no country was ever better served than Britain by our two key diplomats at this time: Sir Anthony Parsons, Britain's UN ambassador and Sir Nicholas Henderson, our ambassador in Washington, both possessed precisely those qualities of intelligence, toughness, style and eloquence that the situation required'.[39]

On the Saturday morning, the Prime Minister had to deal with the most difficult debate of her parliamentary career. In an atmosphere of jingoism and recriminations, with her own back-benchers baying for blood and the Labour Party both blaming the government and insisting that the invasion must be reversed, she made the most sober speech in the debate. Her announcement that the task force was ready to sail was greeted with approval. But she was aware of the gap between those, including many of her Cabinet colleagues, who saw it as a way of getting the Argentinians back to the negotiating table and those who believed it might actually have to fight.

Enoch Powell declared in sepulchral tones that having received with pride the soubriquet 'the Iron Lady' from the Russians, 'in the next week or two this House, the nation and the Rt Hon.

Lady herself will learn of what metal she is made'. She knew that the appearance of unanimous support would fray very quickly as others came to appreciate the full extent of the practical military problems and the risks involved in staging opposed landings against numerically superior forces 3,000 miles from the nearest British base and in the absence of any RAF air cover.

Meanwhile, John Nott had received a drubbing in the Commons debate and both he and Carrington were attacked in a meeting with Tory backbenchers. On the morning of Monday 5 April, to the regret of every one of us, Carrington decided he must resign, despite the Prime Minister's efforts to dissuade him. Nott also offered to resign, but was told he must stay until the end of the conflict. Carrington told the Prime Minister that, while he did not always agree with her, his admiration for her determination and resourcefulness was unbounded. Francis Pym was chosen to succeed Carrington as Foreign Secretary, an unfortunate choice given the lack of any real rapport or trust between him and the Prime Minister, who felt that she had exchanged an amusing Whig for a gloomy one.

The Cabinet on 6 April agreed with the Prime Minister that there would be no diplomatic solution unless it was made absolutely clear that, in the last resort, Britain was prepared to fight.[40]

In setting up the Cabinet sub-committee to deal with the Falklands crisis – the so-called War Cabinet – Margaret Thatcher was influenced by Harold Macmillan, who advised her to leave the Chancellor of the Exchequer off the committee – advice that she accepted. The effort to regain control of the Falklands was not going to be constrained by financial considerations. Throughout the conflict, however, all issues relating to the Falklands were thoroughly debated by the Cabinet and she held no less than sixty-seven meetings of the sub-committee before the crisis was over. Always meticulous about using the Cabinet Office machinery, 'sofa government' was not the style of Margaret Thatcher.

The striking feature of the Cabinet and War Cabinet discussions was that, while remaining intransigent on the two key issues of Argentine withdrawal and self-determination for the islanders, and adamant that military action must be taken if negotiations failed, she displayed no bellicose ardour, but willingness to explore any potential diplomatic solution that did not infringe those principles, whatever the difficulties it would have caused her in Parliament.

In the Washington embassy, it was clear from day one of the military operations that we were going to be critically dependent on American support. My first task was to persuade the Pentagon to divert forthwith a vessel in the mid-Atlantic carrying aviation fuel to Ascension Island, to meet the needs of the RAF.

Henderson and I went to see Cap Weinberger to say that we were going to need a great deal of equipment at very short notice, all of which would be paid for immediately. Weinberger was a passionate admirer of Mrs Thatcher and a no less passionate opponent of aggression. He instructed his staff, soon to be joined by Colonel Colin Powell, that our requests were to be dealt with immediately, outside any of the normal procedures. Any case of delay was to be referred to him directly. This opened the way for massive amounts of equipment to be flown out overnight by the RAF from the Andrews Air Force base outside Washington to Ascension Island, for use in the South Atlantic.

As Weinberger wrote afterwards, 'We all knew of the enormous military odds against Britain.'[41] He was sufficiently worried about the critical gap in our armoury – the lack of a large aircraft carrier

– to appear one day at the embassy and ask if we had considered leasing a US carrier! While grateful for the thought, it clearly was an entirely impractical one and the offer had to be politely declined. The Pentagon's official assessment doubted our ability to successfully re-invade the islands against numerically superior enemy forces in the absence of any air cover except what could be provided by the twenty Sea Harrier aircraft on our two mini-carriers.

On Saturday 3 April, Tony Parsons had succeeded in rushing through the UN Security Council without attracting a Soviet veto a resolution calling for immediate and unconditional withdrawal by the Argentines from the Falklands. Mitterrand telephoned the Prime Minister to pledge his support, which he delivered throughout the conflict. Except for Italy and Ireland, the EC countries imposed an embargo on Argentine imports.

On 6 April Margaret Thatcher sent a message to Reagan urging the US to impose economic sanctions against Argentina. They had imposed an arms embargo, but were not prepared to go further than that. They wanted to retain influence in Buenos Aires. Tom Enders, head of the Latin American bureau, was attached to trying to keep Galtieri in power. The alternative, he and several other members of the administration believed, would be a left-wing anti-American regime.

From the day after the Argentine invasion, we had warned our friends in the State Department – led by the formidable Larry Eagleburger, in charge of European affairs – that the dénouement of this crisis was likely to have as profound an impact on Anglo-American relations as the Suez affair had made. The difference, we pointed out, was that this time we were the victims of aggression and the country was united behind the Prime Minister in her determination that it should be reversed.

Very different views were being urged on Haig by Enders and the opinionated right-wing US ambassador to the UN, Jeane Kirkpatrick, who considered Latin America to be 'the most important place in the world for us'. On 8 April this provoked a stand-up row in the White House when Admiral Bobby Inman, deputy head of the CIA, told her that this was rubbish: the US must support Britain. Haig told us that, while his sympathy was with the British, he believed that the most practical expression of that sympathy would be impartial US mediation in the dispute.[42]

We forewarned the Prime Minister that Haig saw himself as the Kissingerian peacemaker in this crisis and that he was flying forthwith to London to try to mediate. At this point, both Haig and his entourage believed that their task must be to find a face-saving way to extricate the British government from the very tight corner it was in. His first meeting with Margaret Thatcher on Thursday 8 April was to provide him with a rude awakening. He was told that she would be making it clear publicly that he was not being received as a mediator but as a friend and ally, to discuss how the US could help Britain recover control of the islands.

Haig was worried that the Argentinians might ask for Soviet assistance. He wanted to avoid what he described as 'a priori judgements about sovereignty' and to persuade both sides to accept some kind of neutral interim administration after Argentine withdrawal pending agreement on the long-term future of the islands.

The US team found 'La Thatcher … really quite fetching' in a velvet two-piece suit. But Haig's ideas were dismissed by her as 'woolly'. She had not, she declared, despatched the fleet to establish some nebulous 'interim authority', but to restore British

administration. Only then should there be negotiations, subject
to the overriding condition that the wishes of the islanders would
be paramount. They were not dealing with Neville Chamberlain.
She added, disarmingly, that it was only possible to be so frank
between the closest of friends.

Haig said that the Argentinians were not wholly rational. The
Soviet Union was ready to meddle. All the Latin Americans
would support decolonisation. Galtieri might be overthrown by
somebody more intransigent. None of these arguments made
any impression on the Prime Minister.

Haig reported to Reagan that 'the Prime Minister has the bit
in her teeth', with a unified nation and an angry Parliament. She
clearly was prepared to use force, though her Foreign Secretary
did not really agree with her.[43] Francis Pym, who had won a
military cross in the Second World War, felt that he knew more
about the reality of war than she did.

A key official accompanying Haig was the British educated
General Vernon Walters, who had become a legendary figure
in the CIA. Walters, an accomplished linguist who had served
as Roosevelt's interpreter towards the end of the war, was the
United States' preferred envoy in dealing with dictators one-
on-one in their own language, starting with General Franco in
Spain. He knew the Argentine military commanders, who, he
reckoned, had bitten off more than they could chew. As he said to
me on his return from their encounter with the Prime Minister
in 10 Downing Street, 'She gripped me by the elbow and showed
me the portraits of Nelson and Wellington. I think I got the
message.' Haig reported to Reagan that the Prime Minister
appeared determined to restore the status quo ante. When
Francis Pym murmured, 'Maybe we should ask the Falklanders

how they feel about a war', this interjection, as Haig put it, was 'not appreciated by Mrs Thatcher'.[44]

Haig and Walters went on to Buenos Aires, where Galtieri had invited a crowd of 300,000 chanting patriotic slogans to greet them. Haig believed he had got some concessions from the Argentinians, only for these to be abrogated as he was boarding his plane. He shuttled back to Downing Street on 12 April. He produced a complicated plan providing for Argentine withdrawal, a British military standstill and a commission with US, Britain and Argentine representation to supervise the running of the islands pending negotiations on a lasting settlement.

This time, Mrs Thatcher patiently explored the American proposals, but Haig's phone calls to Buenos Aires produced constantly changing accounts of the Argentine position. By now she saw it as potentially advantageous to involve the Americans in an interim administration, as that would deter any further Argentine military action. But the Argentinians would first have to withdraw. She reacted fiercely to Haig's suggestion that the task force might be halted. 'The fleet', she declared, 'must steam inexorably on!'[45]

The Cabinet, however, was told by her on 14 April that under Haig's plan, the withdrawal of Argentine forces would be secured without military action. Argentina would gain representation on the interim administration and a commitment to negotiations to decide a definitive status for the islands by year end, but without any commitment to a transfer of sovereignty. The Cabinet agreed with her summing up that, 'Repugnant as it was that the aggressor should gain anything from his aggression, this seemed an acceptable price to pay.' The best insurance against a possible second Argentine invasion would be to involve the US in the interim agreement and the security of the islands thereafter.[46]

On the following day, Haig reported that the Argentinians would not agree unless there was a process leading to ultimate Argentinian sovereignty. The Prime Minister told Parliament that in any negotiations she would continue to insist on Argentine withdrawal and that the wishes of the islanders must remain paramount. The War Cabinet was told that Haig had welcomed the despatch of the task force as crucial to influencing the Argentine government in favour of a negotiated settlement. From this point on, the Prime Minister kept trying to pursue the idea of persuading the United States to offer a security guarantee for the islands in the context of an agreement, to avoid any risk of a second Argentine invasion.[47] This was a commitment the US government was not prepared to make.

As Galtieri kept talking about his 'honour', Haig realised that the combination of his machismo and the 'icy scorn and iron will' of Mrs Thatcher was likely to have an unhappy outcome. General Walters was sent to tell him that the British would fight. Galtieri said: 'That woman wouldn't dare.' Walters replied: 'Mr President, that woman has let a number of hunger strikers of her own basic ethnic origin starve themselves to death, without flickering an eyelash. I would not count on that if I were you.'[48]

Neither Henderson nor I believed that US mediating efforts were going to succeed. We told our friends in the administration that they should not imagine that both governments were going to survive: either Galtieri was going to lose power or, if the Argentinians remained in control of the islands, Margaret Thatcher would regard herself as honour-bound to resign. Yet, in the Washington embassy, we were determined that we should show ourselves willing to discuss any reasonable solution which respected the wishes of the islanders and this was the *sine qua non* for retaining American support. The same message was delivered with equal vigour by Tony Parsons from his post at the United Nations. It was received at times grudgingly by Margaret Thatcher, who suspected, with good reason, that some of her ministers and officials were much less resolute than she was in support of the islanders. But in the end she always did accept the advice of the two ambassadors.

Each plan Haig came up with was examined and modified by us until it did protect our two fundamental requirements: that the Argentine forces should withdraw and the islanders decide their own future. Neither we nor the Prime Minister believed that any amount of fudging could render this acceptable to the Argentine military junta, and Haig, whose intentions were honourable but who had none of Kissinger's intellectual power, had difficulty understanding that he was trying to bridge an unbridgeable gap.

Temperamentally hyperactive, he also seemed to be operating under serious personal strain. His excitability led him to come up with ideas which we avoided sending to London until we had managed to quash them ourselves. While Al Haig's heart was in the right place and he was trying hard to do the right thing, it was disconcerting to find ourselves dealing with a US Secretary of State who, under the strain, had developed facial tics reminiscent of Dr Strangelove.

While Tom Enders continued to promote what he believed to be the interests of his Latin American clients, the political and physical heavyweight Larry Eagleburger, later to be promoted to Secretary of State under George Bush Sr., was to remain the staunchest of allies throughout the crisis.

On 14 April Haig telephoned the Prime Minister about reports in the press that the US was providing intelligence and operational assistance to the UK over the Falklands. In an attempt to appear even-handed, Haig wanted to issue a statement that the US had not acceded to requests that went beyond the customary patterns of cooperation (considerably stretching the truth) and to refer to restrictions on our use of the US base on Ascension Island. This produced an explosive reaction from Margaret Thatcher who, reminding him that the island was British territory, got the reference to it removed. ('For Pete's sake, get that use of Ascension Island out of your statement, because it's our island and we can't exactly invade our island.')

She also told him that while she had always supported President Reagan, the US was not at present seen as supporting her. She did not want to hear any more about US even-handedness between a democratic fellow ally in NATO and a military dictatorship in Argentina.[49] Haig at this point asked the US intelligence chiefs to limit what they passed to the British. Admiral Inman told me with a smile that he had been assured that they were restricting themselves to the 'customary pattern' – which meant unimpeded cooperation with us.

On 15 April Reagan sent a message to say that he had been telephoned by Galtieri, who said he wanted to avoid a conflict. Mrs Thatcher replied that, in that event, he would need to withdraw his troops from the islands. When Reagan then telephoned her, he agreed in response to a barrage of arguments that she could not be expected to move further towards the Argentine position. He was 'deeply interested in keeping this great relationship which we have'.[50]

On 19 April Haig sent her proposals following his visit to Buenos Aires which offered no prospect of a return to the status quo before the invasion. Nor did they adequately protect the

British position on sovereignty. Francis Pym, having appeared to suggest to the House of Commons that force would not be used while negotiations were continuing, had to return to the House to retract his remarks.

On 21 April, in the Washington embassy, we were informed that our forces were about to land on and recapture South Georgia. The ambassador got permission to forewarn Haig, only to return flabbergasted from a meeting in which Haig had argued that he must inform the Argentinians. Some violent remonstrances were required to prevent this happening.

On 22 April the Cabinet was informed that Galtieri was an alcoholic and 'apparently incapable of rational thought'. It was essential that any failure to secure a negotiated settlement occurred in a way that left the United States firmly in support of the British position.[51]

That evening, the Prime Minister was told by Nott and the Chief of Defence Staff that a special forces team was in difficulty in appalling weather conditions on the Fortuna glacier in South Georgia. Two helicopters from HMS *Antrim* had crashed in attempts to rescue them. For the first time she wondered if the task they had set themselves was impossible. As she left to address a dinner at Mansion House, she heard that, near miraculously, a third helicopter had managed to land and rescue them. She insisted later on meeting the helicopter pilot herself.

On the same day, Francis Pym arrived in Washington to seek to improve Haig's latest proposals, a task in which he had no success. Haig's final proposals were now presented to the British and Argentine governments. The Argentine land forces and our naval forces were both to withdraw. There would be a joint American–British–Argentine transitional administration and negotiation for a definitive settlement with 'due regard' for the rights of the inhabitants.

This was an extremely unattractive proposition from Margaret Thatcher's point of view, though Francis Pym was eager to accept Haig's plan. The Thatcher Foundation archives contain Margaret Thatcher's own heavily annotated version of Haig's proposals, which she regarded as representing conditional surrender, as they departed from the principle that the wishes of the islanders must be paramount. She told Willie Whitelaw before a meeting of the War Cabinet that there was no way she could accept them. She then took her colleagues forensically through the document clause by clause, pointing out the deficiencies in it. The War Cabinet broadly agreed with her, but rather than rejecting Haig's proposals she was prevailed upon, at John Nott's suggestion, to propose that he should put them first to the Argentinians. Henderson regarded this as a finesse worthy of Talleyrand. We remained convinced that the Argentine military junta could not afford to withdraw from the islands without winning guarantees about their future sovereignty. 'And so,' she observed, 'a great crisis passed.' If the War Cabinet had accepted Haig's proposal, she would have resigned.[52]

On the following day HMS *Antrim* disabled an Argentine submarine caught on the surface and secured the surrender of the Argentine garrison in South Georgia under Captain Astiz who, for his activities in the internal 'dirty war' in Argentina, was wanted for the murder of civilians by both France and Sweden. It was with regret that, as a prisoner of war, he had to be handed back in the end to Argentina. The British public were invited by the Prime Minister to 'rejoice' at the recapture of South Georgia.

On 28 April the Cabinet was told by the Prime Minister

that Haig's proposals were unacceptable, as there was no firm commitment to self-determination. In discussion it was agreed that they would be seen as a sell-out by the islanders. Nor was there any safeguard against a second Argentine invasion, as the Americans were declining to provide any military guarantees.[53]

As there was still no word from Buenos Aires about Haig's proposals, on 29 April the Prime Minister sent a message to Reagan saying that the Argentinians must now be regarded as having rejected them, as in fact they did later that day. Reagan replied that it was essential to have made clear to the world that every effort was made to find a peaceful solution. They would not publish the US proposals because of the difficulty this might cause her. He recognised that she had fundamental difficulties with them, but she had not rejected them. They would make clear that the British government had acted in good faith and was left with no choice but to proceed with military action. In his diary he wrote that 'I don't think that Margaret Thatcher should be asked to concede anymore.' As Jeane Kirkpatrick reflected bitterly: 'There wasn't any question about where President Reagan stood on this issue, from start to finish.'[54]

In the meeting of the National Security Council on 30 April, Haig confirmed to his colleagues the Prime Minister's worst suspicions. His proposal, he said, had amounted to 'a camouflaged transfer of sovereignty' to Argentina. Nevertheless, the Argentinians had rejected it. Reagan asked if the 'tilt' towards Britain would not put an end to negotiations. Haig said that he was not going to give up. Jeane Kirkpatrick was confident that the Argentinians would not go to war. She expected an early UN initiative, possibly that weekend, which they would then accept. Reagan commented sardonically that 'it would be nice if, after all these years, the UN could accomplish something as constructive as averting war between the UK and Argentina'.[55]

Weinberger said that the US needed to come out of this getting credit for something, namely support for the British. He was continuing to ensure that we received forthwith all the military equipment we needed. As Richard Aldous has observed, while Haig jetted to and fro, Weinberger simply got on with the business of making sure that Britain won the war.

Late that evening, I was summoned to Eagleburger's office in the State Department to be given a paper stating that, in view of the Argentine attitude, the United States would give material support to the British in the Falklands dispute. In fact the Pentagon had long since been providing this already and Cap Weinberger had not even bothered to consult the State Department about doing so. But the statement was a clear declaration of a choice of sides and a tribute to the unrelenting efforts Nico Henderson had made, through countless media appearances and calls on every Senator, to mobilise press and Congressional support, as well as that of the administration. In the end, we were able to obtain a vote of 79:1 from the Senate in our support, stating that the US 'cannot stand neutral' and must help Britain secure full withdrawal of the Argentine forces, demonstrating where America's sympathies really lay. Henderson was advised by Senator Joe Biden to forget all the 'crap' about self-determination: 'We're with you because you are British!'[56]

Having pledged his support publicly, President Reagan disconcerted the government at home by referring to the Falklands as 'that little ice-cold bunch of land down there'! But he restored the Prime Minister's faith in him by adding that 'armed aggression must not be allowed to succeed'. Two days later, Al Haig relayed to us Reagan's view that the British forces were 'doing the work of the free world'.[57]

The way was now clear for us to make an all-important request, which I took forthwith to Weinberger's office in the Pentagon. This was for the supply of 105 AIM9L Sidewinder air-to-air missiles from the US Air Force. This was the very latest version of the Sidewinder, far more accurate and effective than its predecessor and not yet in service with many of the United States' own front-line aircraft. Nevertheless, Weinberger decreed that the missiles should be supplied. To do so, he had to order that some of these very advanced missiles should be stripped from US war planes facing the Soviets in Germany and delivered to us instead. As Margaret Thatcher was to record in her memoirs, without the latest version of the Sidewinders supplied by Weinberger, 'we could not have retaken the Falklands'.[58]

V

'THIS IS DEMOCRACY AND OUR ISLANDS'

As the task force moved south, on 28 April the government had announced the establishment of a total exclusion zone around the Falkland Islands. The Argentinians were warned via the Swiss government that any approach by Argentine warships would be regarded as hostile. The chiefs of staff were especially worried about the Argentine aircraft carrier, which could not be found, and the cruiser *Belgrano*, which was being tracked by HMS *Conqueror*. The aircraft carrier could cover 500 miles in twenty-four hours, with its aircraft giving it an additional range of 500 miles. The War Cabinet already had decided that if the carrier ventured out of Argentine territorial waters, it would have to be sunk.

Following an air attack on British ships on 1 May, the Prime Minister held an ad hoc meeting of the War Cabinet, including the Attorney-General, at Chequers on the morning of Sunday 2 May. On the advice of Admirals Lewin, Fieldhouse and Woodward, this authorised British forces to attack any Argentine naval vessel that ventured outside Argentine territorial waters thus, in the view of the chiefs of staff, posing a threat to British ships in the exclusion zone. HMS *Conqueror* thereby was author-ised to torpedo the *Belgrano*, which had ventured out of port with its destroyer escorts towards the task force. The attack was carried out that evening, resulting in the deaths of 321 members of the *Belgrano*'s crew.[59] It was later alleged in Parliament, notably by Tam Dalyell, that the sinking was calculated to disrupt new Peruvian peace proposals. In fact the decision was taken on purely military grounds and had its intended effect, as the Argentine fleet, including the carrier, did not thereafter venture out of territorial waters. Haig was appalled, berating the ambassador.

On 4 May the destroyer HMS *Sheffield* was hit and sunk by an Argentine Exocet missile. Haig, meanwhile, had not given up. Instead he orchestrated proposals from President Belaúnde of Peru which bore an uncanny resemblance to his own. The NSC staff, feeling that the conflict had reached an alarmingly new and desperate stage, urged the President to intervene more decisively. On 5 May Margaret Thatcher received a message from Reagan urging further compromise. She got the proposals amended in minor ways, but for the first time was unable to ensure that the wishes of the islanders must be respected in any long-term settlement. The US formula was that 'the two governments acknowledge that the aspirations and interests of the islanders will be included in the final settlement of the status of the islands'. The dropping of the word 'wishes' had been the subject of a prolonged argument between Henderson and Haig, but the ambassador got nowhere. Haig was adamant that it was 'an absolute sticking point for the Argentinians'.

Shaken and angry, Margaret Thatcher drafted a personal letter to Reagan, which she toned down before it was sent, expressing her frustration at constantly being asked to weaken her position. She began by stating: 'I think you are the only person who will understand what I am trying to say.' She complained that the latest US proposals did not provide unambiguously for a right to self-determination and Haig had rejected any explicit reference to it. Nor would there be a return to British administration of the islands. Nevertheless, in Cabinet on 5 May the proposals were accepted, with extreme reluctance. Francis Pym told Parliament that a small group of countries would administer the islands, pending a solution without prejudice to the wishes of the islanders. But this plan too was rejected by the Argentine military junta.[60]

Mrs Thatcher's main preoccupation by now was with the military challenge facing the task force. The *Atlantic Conveyor*, carrying nineteen replacement Harriers and other vital supplies, had no effective armament at all. The main troop carrier, *Canberra*, was a civilian passenger liner. To her alarm, further reinforcements had to be sent on another passenger liner, *Queen Elizabeth II*. She questioned whether 'this great ship' should be used for such a purpose, but was persuaded that it had to be. The military commanders advised her that the planned landings could not be delayed beyond the second half of May because of rapidly deteriorating weather conditions.

The negotiating scene now shifted to the UN, where Tony Parsons defended the British position with 'great force and brilliance'. The Prime Minister told him on 8 May that she was not prepared to compromise on self-determination for the islanders. But, she added, 'It is going to be the most awful waste of young life if we really have to go and take those islands.'[61] There were discussions with the Secretary-General, Pérez de Cuéllar, about an interim UN administration and the possibility of US military involvement, about which the Americans remained extremely wary.

On the eve of serious hostilities, Pérez de Cuéllar received an unexpected telephone call from her, asking him to do all he could to keep 'my boys' from being killed by securing Argentine withdrawal.[62]

In Haig's absence in Europe, Reagan was prompted by Tom Enders to telephone her on 13 May. Enders did not lack self-confidence. In Larry Eagleburger's words, 'Even though he is six foot eight inches tall, he *still* has a Napoleon complex!' Reagan had been given the impression that the negotiating positions were now quite close. The Prime Minister disabused him of this. Reagan said that the President of Brazil was worried that British forces were planning an attack on the Argentine mainland. The US, he said, had sided with Britain at the price of its relations with Latin America. He wanted her to hold off military action. She responded that British ships had been attacked the day before. He was concerned that the struggle was being portrayed as one between David and Goliath. In response, she pointed out the 8,000-mile distance at which the task force was having to operate. Rather improbably, she sought to persuade him of the potential strategic significance of the islands if the Panama Canal were ever closed. It was a difficult conversation, but she felt she persuaded him that he had been misinformed about Argentine concessions. She did not believe the Argentine military regime could afford to give way on withdrawal or sovereignty without being overthrown. 'I can't see Ronald Reagan getting on to her on the phone again in a hurry', was Henderson's comment.[63]

Nevertheless, she agreed that before launching an invasion, final proposals should be put to the Argentinians. Tony Parsons and Nico Henderson were summoned to Chequers on 16 May for a meeting of the War Cabinet to help draft these proposals. In Henderson's words, 'The rest of us, and in particular the FCO participants, constantly found themselves under attack for being wet, ready to sell out, unsupportive of British interests.'[64] Despite this posturing, she was persuaded to put an eminently reasonable proposal to the UN Secretary-General. It included a UN administration for the islands. The Argentine government was required to respond within forty-eight hours.

Margaret Thatcher had been prepared to go surprisingly far in these negotiations, to a point at which, had the Argentines accepted the later versions of these various proposals, she would have been in real difficulty at home, as there would have been no return to a British administration and no certainty as to the outcome of future negotiations. While she continued to fight for self-determination, it was no longer safeguarded explicitly, save by references to the UN Charter, which the Argentinians would have been bound to interpret differently. Each one of these documents carried within it the certainty of a fresh deadlock by year end. She had made some extremely unpalatable concessions because of her own realisation that a major landing would be an extremely risky operation on the outcome of which the future of her government would depend. In reality, she was prepared to go way beyond what she thought was reasonable because of the imperative need to retain American support. While the Americans fully sympathised with her determination to reverse Argentine aggression, in the longer term they did not regard the principle of self-determination as sacrosanct for a population of 1,800 people and were worried at the possibility of a semi-permanent state of hostilities in the South Atlantic.

It was an act of huge folly on the part of the Argentine military to reject these various proposals, none of which offered the prospect of a return to the status quo, and under which they would have been able to gain a role in administering the islands. They did so because, having whipped up a political frenzy in Buenos Aires, they could not face having to withdraw their forces from the islands with no certainty of a transfer of sovereignty.

The other striking feature of the way in which Margaret Thatcher handled the crisis was the very great latitude she gave to the military to develop their plans and conduct operations without any political interference. In the words of the Deputy Secretary to the Cabinet, Robert Wade-Gery, she told the chiefs of staff from the outset: "'Look, you run this war because you know how to. I don't, but when you need a political decision of any kind, if necessary at three o'clock in the morning, I will give it to you." And she was as good as her word.' While Margaret Thatcher never hesitated to micromanage the efforts of most of her ministers, she had much greater faith in the armed forces. She liked men in uniform. They in turn admired her political courage, decisiveness, fortitude when the going got tough and willingness to delegate to them. The Chief of Defence Staff, Admiral Lewin, described her as, 'from the military man's point of view, an ideal Prime Minister'. The troops regarded her as a kindred spirit, displaying the same fighting qualities as they were expected to. Brigadier Julian Thompson, who commanded the British troops in the Falklands, could think of no politician except Winston Churchill who struck such a chord with servicemen 'who usually have no time for politicians'.[65]

In the course of one of the meetings about the Falklands, Tony Parsons was interrupted by the Prime Minister three times in as many minutes. He did not take this lying down, telling her that she would get the information she wanted more quickly if she stopped interrupting him. Not long afterwards, he was appointed her foreign policy adviser.[66]

At Chequers, Admiral Lewin, Chief of Defence Staff, had noted Henderson's view that what the Americans respected above all was success and that no diplomatic problems would count for much if it were achieved as quickly as possible. Henderson found Lewin very confident of military success, though there would be casualties.

Meanwhile, she penned a fierce message to President Mitterrand about French plans to supply Exocet missiles to Peru. 'If it became known, as it certainly would, that France was now releasing weapons to Peru that would certainly be passed on to Argentina for use against us, France's ally, this would have a devastating effect on the relationship between our two countries.'[67] It is not clear whether this was sent or raised by her in person when Mitterrand visited her in London on 17 May. In any event, her intervention was successful. Acknowledging that the weapons were liable to be passed on to Argentina, Mitterrand suspended the shipment. The French also helped the British with technical details about the Exocet's capabilities.

On 18 May the War Cabinet met with the chiefs of staff. The difficulties of staging the landings in the absence of adequate air cover were clear. But with the weather rapidly worsening in the South Atlantic, they could not be delayed. A long blockade was not considered viable. Michael Foot, then leader of the Labour Party, had written to the Prime Minister urging further negotiations. By now the Argentinians had rejected the British proposals. Pérez de Cuéllar put forward a much vaguer last-minute scheme. Pym favoured delay, but in Cabinet the chiefs of staff advised that repossession of the islands was militarily feasible, although air superiority had not been achieved and during the landings some Argentine aircraft were liable to get through. They added that, throughout the conflict, they had not been denied political authority for any military activities they considered necessary. The Attorney-General confirmed that the military action being planned was fully compatible with Article 51 of the UN Charter. There would be intense pressure for a ceasefire and it was important not to give the impression of rebuffing the UN Secretary-General. Nevertheless, the Cabinet agreed that, notwithstanding the risk of losses, the priority now must be rapid military success.[68] The Secretary-General, meanwhile, reported the failure of his efforts, having received no response from the Argentinians.

On the day of the invasion, 21 May, to the task force's dismay, a brilliantly clear day dawned in the South Atlantic. The main landings began at 4 a.m., with a large and highly vulnerable flotilla, including the passenger liner *Canberra*, exposed in San Carlos Sound. The landings were carried out without a single casualty, but around midday the Argentine air force launched wave after wave of attacks against the frigates and destroyers protecting *Canberra* and the landing ships in the Sound. Their defensive missile systems functioned erratically. HMS *Ardent* was sunk and *Argonaut* and *Brilliant* were badly damaged. But the Harriers equipped with the new Sidewinders were extremely effective. Of twenty-seven AIM 9L missiles fired during the conflict, twenty-four found their targets.

Visiting Northwood, the Prime Minister did her best to seem confident, but privately asked Admiral Fieldhouse: 'How long can we go on taking this kind of punishment?' He was no less worried, but conscious also that a great deal of damage was being inflicted on the Argentine air force.[69]

Meanwhile, HMS *Coventry* was attacked and sunk, then the

Atlantic Conveyor. Although its cargo of nineteen Harriers had been flown off before the attack, three heavy-lift Chinook helicopters were lost, hugely complicating the land campaign about to begin. The task force continued to worry about the Argentine carrier, which nearly was attacked when it ventured fractionally outside territorial waters only to move back quickly into them. Margaret Thatcher and the Attorney-General, Michael Havers, pored over maritime charts at Chequers themselves, but there was never any question of attacking Argentine warships within the twelve-mile limit, despite an attempt on one occasion by Admiral Lewin to get this considered.[70] On 24 May, the Prime Minister told the War Cabinet that now that military repossession of the Falklands was in progress, opinion in Britain would insist that it be completed. The time for negotiations was over.[71]

British troops forced the surrender of a much-larger Argentine force at Goose Green, at the cost of losing their commander, Colonel 'H' Jones. As they slowly advanced across East Falkland, Tony Parsons fended off demands for a ceasefire at the United Nations. Jeane Kirkpatrick appealed to President Reagan personally to prevent the British staging a 'bloodbath' in Port Stanley which, she contended, would destroy US relations with Latin America.

On the eve of his departure with the President for the Versailles Economic Summit, at which Reagan was due to meet Margaret Thatcher, Haig summoned the ambassador. I accompanied him to this meeting. We had been forewarned by friends in the State Department that Haig would quote Churchill to us: 'In Victory, Magnanimity'. Henderson replied that Churchill had been talking about magnanimity once victory had been achieved.

As Haig continued to insist on the need for a ceasefire to save Argentine honour, we replied that, with his distinguished military record, he surely must understand that the British government could not ask servicemen to risk and in some cases lose their lives landing on the Falklands and fighting their way across the islands – only then to tell them at the moment of their victory that they must stop – with still no guarantee of an Argentine withdrawal.

Prompted by Haig, President Reagan telephoned the Prime Minister late on 31 May, having talked again to the President of Brazil. Reagan began by congratulating her on 'what you and your young men are doing down there ... you've demonstrated to the whole world that aggression does not pay', but then sought to urge on her that, as the UK had the upper hand militarily, it should now strike a deal to avoid 'complete Argentine humiliation'. The President was unable to get much beyond the word 'Margaret...' in the rest of the call. He was told that having lost valuable British ships and invaluable British servicemen's lives to return to the Falklands, she could not now let the invader gain from his aggression. There was no longer any question of an interim administration. She was sure he would have reacted in the same way if, say, Alaska had been threatened. He nervously said that Alaska was different, but she did not agree. She referred to a TV interview he had given in which he had said that if the aggressor were to win, some fifty other territories would be at risk. There would be no ceasefire without an Argentine withdrawal. 'There is no alternative', she concluded. The conversation was 'a little painful' but, she felt, had a good effect. Reagan ended by apologising for having 'intruded'.

Faced with this diatribe from the Prime Minister, the NSC staff felt that the President had sounded like more of a wimp than Jimmy Carter. In his autobiography Reagan recorded: 'She told me too many lives had already been lost for Britain to withdraw without total victory, and she convinced me.'[72]

The Prime Minister at this point had drafted, but in the end did not despatch, a direct appeal to Galtieri:

In a few days the British flag will be flying over Port Stanley. In a few days also your eyes and mine will be reading the casualty lists. On my side, grief will be tempered by the knowledge that these men died for freedom, justice and the rule of law. And on your side? Only you can answer that question.[73]

On 4 June Reagan and Margaret Thatcher were together at a G7 summit in Paris. She walked along the Rue du Faubourg St-Honoré to see him in the US embassy, 'looking great' according to the NSC staff. Henderson saw her before her meeting with Reagan: 'Glaring at me she said that she would be very reasonable in her conversation with the President, *provided I get my way.*' She was no longer prepared to compromise, telling Henderson that 'we have lost a lot of blood and it's the best blood'.[74] Wisely, Reagan saw her without Haig. He was concerned at the risk of a permanent state of war between Britain and Argentina. Her response was that the defeat of aggression would send a positive signal around the world.

Tony Parsons, meanwhile, had accomplished near-miracles in avoiding Britain having to use the veto in the UN Security Council long before this. Spain now sponsored a resolution calling for an immediate ceasefire. Britain and the US vetoed the resolution, only for Jeane Kirkpatrick, who had challenged her instructions from Washington and got them changed by Haig, to announce immediately afterwards that if the vote could be taken again, she would now abstain. Margaret Thatcher was still with Reagan at the G7 summit. An American journalist asked him about the US confusion at the United Nations. To Mrs Thatcher's amazement, he knew nothing about it. When she was asked, to avoid embarrassing him, she said she did not give interviews over lunch.[75]

In his speech to the Houses of Parliament shortly after the Versailles conference, Reagan aligned himself with the Prime Minister. British soldiers in the Falklands, he said, were not fighting for mere real estate. 'They fight for a cause, for a belief that armed aggression must not be allowed to succeed.'[76]

There followed further disasters when the landing ship *Sir Galahad*, which had not yet discharged its troops, was attacked by Argentine aircraft at Bluff Cove, and HMS *Glamorgan* was struck by an Exocet missile. But by 13 June British troops were engaged in the final assault on Mount Tumbledown, overlooking Port Stanley, and Argentine resistance collapsed. When the news of the recapture of the islands reached Washington, it was greeted with cheering in the Situation Room in the White House. In a speech a few days later Margaret Thatcher declared: 'We have now ceased to be a nation in retreat.'

On 23 June she was back in Washington. When Reagan raised the Falklands, Mrs Thatcher described the desertion of the under-supplied and demoralised Argentine conscript army by their own officers. 'We were spared nothing,' commented Henderson.[77]

There remained one final skirmish. On 12 July she told the War Cabinet that the contention by some church leaders that army personnel should be debarred from reading any of the lessons at the Thanksgiving Service in St Paul's was simply not acceptable.

In the event, an army chaplain was allowed to read one of the lessons. A suggestion by the Dean of St Paul's that the Lord's Prayer should be read in Spanish was set aside.[78]

At the end of October a new Argentine military government put forward a resolution at the UN calling for a resumption of talks on the Falklands. To pre-empt her reaction, Reagan sent her a letter saying that he did not expect her actually to enter into negotiations, but did not want to exclude them in the future. The US therefore, would support the resolution. The new British ambassador, Sir Oliver Wright, was instructed to protest to George Shultz, who had succeeded Haig as Secretary of State. In the words of George Shultz, himself a former marine, he 'read me off like a sergeant would a recruit in the Marine Corps boot camp'. Shultz's response was that, having supported Britain during the conflict, the US now had to pay attention to its interests in Latin America. He worried that Reagan would be alarmed at the Prime Minister's reaction, but found that on this subject he too 'was getting a little fed up with her imperious attitude'.

In terms of excitability, the tough, calm and unflappable Shultz was at the opposite end of the spectrum to Al Haig. Despite this tiff over the UN resolution, he was a great admirer of Margaret Thatcher. The British decision to go to war for these desolate, scarcely populated rocky islets 8,000 miles from London, he wrote, was the first marker laid down by a democratic power in the post-Vietnam era to state unambiguously that a free-world nation was willing to fight for a principle. The world paid attention to this; it was noted by the Soviets too.[79] The Argentine military was discredited and the pressure for democracy strengthened. Christopher Meyer, in Moscow at the time, observed the impact her victory had in Russia, where their nominal support for Argentina was offset by interest in this new tsarina.[80]

In Al Haig's view, the fatal miscalculation of the Argentinians was about the character of the British Prime Minister. She had been by far the strongest and shrewdest player in the game. The British had demonstrated that a free people had not only kept a sinewy grip on the values they seemed to take for granted, but were willing to fight for them, and to fight supremely well against considerable odds.[81]

As for Ronald Reagan, despite Shultz's remarks, our friends in the White House told us that one of the telephone calls from her urging him to be more stalwart – almost certainly that on 31 May – came through with several members of the NSC staff gathered with him in the Oval Office. Ronald Reagan listened intently to her arguments, unable to get a word in, then held up the phone to his staff: 'Isn't she wonderful?' he said.

There is no doubt that, in international affairs and to a significant degree also in domestic politics, the Falklands 'made' Margaret Thatcher. The Labour opposition was told that she did not believe they would have ended up firing a shot. She had well and truly answered Enoch Powell's question as to the metal she was made of. The doubts about her re-election were swept away.

Henceforth, she had to be taken seriously, including by those who disapproved most strongly of her. Having despatched the task force to recover the islands, despite the immense military difficulties and shoestring nature of the operation, she never wavered in her determination that it should do just that, unless the Argentinians withdrew meanwhile. Nor was she ever tempted by the solution a less resolute Prime Minister and Cabinet members would have settled for, namely a slow-motion transfer of control over the islands to Argentina. The cost was high: one British soldier or sailor killed for every seventh islander. But aggression had indeed been defeated. The fears of Tom Enders and Jeane Kirkpatrick that the successor regime would be virulently anti-western turned out to be entirely misplaced. In fact Margaret Thatcher could claim a fair amount of the credit for the restoration of democracy in Argentina.

One immediate casualty was Al Haig. Famous for his periodic attacks on the English language ('let me caveat that'), differences over Israel had caused him to describe Peter Carrington in one State Department meeting as a 'duplicitous bastard'. When this was reported in the *Washington Post*, he telephoned the ambassador to deny that he had said it. Two of his staff telephoned me to say that he had indeed said it, but of course he hadn't meant it!

Ronald Reagan distrusted his excitable temperament. The final straw came when, in a meeting attended also by Mike Deaver, Haig told the President that if he gave the order, he would turn Cuba into a 'parking lot' (by bombing it).[82] He was replaced by the solid, calm and reassuring figure of George Shultz.

A few months later, Margaret Thatcher made the twenty-four hour, intensely uncomfortable flight to the Falklands, most of it on a freezing cold RAF Hercules aircraft. On the soggy ground, she flatly refused to wear wellingtons to visit the graves of war heroes like Colonel Jones. Denis Thatcher reflected, on returning home, that the islands consisted of 'miles and miles of bugger all'. That, in her opinion, was not the point. The point was that the islands, and the people living there were British and, thanks to her efforts and those of the military, they had remained so.[83]

VI

'ONE COUNTRY, TWO SYSTEMS'

In 1979 the Chinese Premier and party chairman, Hua Guofeng, visited Britain. He was accompanied by Sir Percy Cradock, the British ambassador to Beijing. Sir Percy, on first acquaintance, could give the impression of being an archetypical mandarin, whose idea of excitement was a glass of dry sherry. This disguised formidable expertise about China, determined negotiating skills and a very sharp mind indeed. It was his first encounter with Margaret Thatcher and his first experience of the 'bruising but searching' meetings she always held before important visits. The ministers and officials gathered to brief her were put through the mill in a way that was to become very familiar. What was the visit for? What would we get out of it? She wanted precise answers.[84]

When the Governor of Hong Kong, Sir Murray MacLehose, saw Deng Xiaoping in March 1979, Deng said that he understood that people in Hong Kong were worried what would happen when the British lease over the New Territories, comprising most of the land area of Hong Kong, expired in 1997. Sovereignty over Hong Kong belonged to China, but Hong Kong could have a special status. Investors should 'put their hearts at ease'.

In April 1982, when Ted Heath saw him in Beijing, Deng wondered whether a solution for Hong Kong could not be found on the basis of sovereignty passing to China but Hong Kong remaining a free port and investment centre, as a special administrative region of China.

Margaret Thatcher visited China and Hong Kong in September that year, in the immediate aftermath of the Falklands War. In addressing the problem of Hong Kong she was determined to start, as she always did, from first principles, not from where the Foreign Office had got to in their thinking about it. While the lease for the New Territories indisputably did expire in 1997, sovereignty over the island of Hong Kong and a small enclave in Kowloon did not. Was Hong Kong really not viable or defensible without the New Territories? Could Hong Kong not enjoy self-determination and be brought eventually to independence like Singapore? This remained her preferred solution and she was bitterly frustrated at finding it to be beyond her grasp.

Despite what he describes as the suffering involved in this approach, Cradock regarded it as a healthy intellectual exercise: alternative theories were tested to destruction. Through a form of guerrilla warfare, she was engaged in a necessary process of convincing herself that there really were no viable alternative courses of action, that no concessions were being contemplated that did not really have to be made and that she was doing everything possible to uphold the interests of the people of Hong Kong. She hated the idea of having to hand them over to the communist regime in China. This was a mere six years after the downfall of the Gang of Four. She did not know how long the new-found moderation of the Chinese leadership would last. A passionate admirer of the territory and of its enterprise culture, she would very much have preferred not to have found herself in the position of having to negotiate away control over Hong

Kong. She accepted, however, that Hong Kong was militarily indefensible and critically dependent on supplies of food and water from the mainland.[85]

On her way to Beijing, Cradock went to see her in Tokyo. He found the embassy in a state of upheaval as, with the usual intensity she displayed in preparing for set piece occasions, she insisted that they must find a suitable Japanese proverb for her speech that evening. Various offerings were peremptorily rejected until she found one that satisfied her.

Cradock found, however, that in Beijing she presented her case very skilfully in a first meeting with the Chinese Prime Minister, Zhao Ziyang, concentrating on the need to maintain confidence in Hong Kong. Her standing and that of Britain in the world had just been enhanced by victory in the Falklands. But she found the Chinese leaders determined to bring home to her that the Falklands was no sort of precedent for dealing with Hong Kong. She needed no convincing of this both from the military and the legal viewpoints. The Chinese government had never recognised the Treaty of Nanking, which they had been forced to sign in 1842, ratifying the annexation of Hong Kong. Her negotiating aim was to exchange sovereignty over Hong Kong Island and Kowloon for the continuance of British administration over the whole territory.

She made no progress on this with Zhao Ziyang and still less in a more abrasive meeting with Deng Xiaoping on the following day. She knew that he was a realist and an economic reformer, who had been setting up special enterprise zones on the mainland. According to those present at the meeting on the British side, she put up an impressive performance. Her proposal that British administration should continue was couched as the way in which the prosperity of Hong Kong could best be assured, rather than as an objective. She wanted agreement that after 1997, Hong Kong would continue with the same system of law and the same independent currency. She made a heavily guarded but explicit offer to consider recommending a transfer of sovereignty to Parliament if the right arrangements for administration could be agreed.

Deng, however, was adamant that China was going to recover sovereignty over the whole territory in 1997. China was prepared to have talks with Britain and to listen to views from Hong Kong but, in a year or two's time, the Chinese would formally announce their intention to recover it. In her memoirs, Margaret Thatcher recalled that at one point Deng said that the Chinese could walk in and take over Hong Kong later that day if they wanted to. She said that they could indeed do so. She could not stop them. But this would cause the collapse of Hong Kong. The world would see what Chinese rule would have achieved. Percy Cradock reported this slightly differently, with Deng saying that if there were disturbances in Hong Kong, China might have to consider an earlier takeover and the Prime Minister replying as described. Anthony Galsworthy, who was sitting behind the Prime Minister taking the official record, confirms that Cradock's version is the more accurate one.[86]

After this sharp exchange, Deng became more accommodating. He told her that the British must stop money leaving Hong Kong. She said that this would cause a loss of all confidence and prevent any new money coming in. She felt that the Chinese needed to be further educated about the economic realities. Also, they did not seem to understand that the British felt a responsibility towards the people of Hong Kong. Deng, however, had offered a statement announcing the beginning of talks to resolve differences over Hong Kong. She got it modified to include 'with the common aim of maintaining the stability and prosperity of Hong Kong'.

She had been impressed by the squat, barrel-like figure, exuding immense authority, slumped casually in his chair, chain-smoking and spitting, but saw him as representing a totally alien and still brutal political system. She felt him to be 'cruel'. Cradock was surprised at her reaction. He did not see how anyone who had been at the top of the Chinese Communist Party, had survived being purged, not just once but twice, then fought his way back to the top again, could be anything other than as tough as nails, with a streak of ruthlessness as well.

Although the announcement about talks did much to help confidence in the short term, a subsequent comment by her to the press that treaties could not simply be abrogated and that a country that did so in one case could not be relied on in others brought a fierce public reaction from the Chinese, though she had been explicit in the talks with them that treaties could not be abrogated unilaterally. To her concern, for the next six months no serious talks were engaged as the Chinese insisted the British must first accept that these could only be about the transfer of sovereignty to them. In February 1983, she held a meeting with the Governor of Hong Kong, ministers and senior officials to review the position. The Chinese were indicating that they intended to make a unilateral statement about Hong Kong in June. They agreed they must try to prevent this. She had been rethinking her objectives. She wanted to build up a more Chinese administration in Hong Kong, with Britain playing a more subordinate role. She also proposed increased democracy via the Legislative Council, but the China experts cautioned against this.

She sent a private letter to the Prime Minister, Zhao Ziyang, which did have the effect of getting talks under way. In it she said that if talks led to an agreement that would safeguard the future prosperity and stability of Hong Kong, she would be prepared to recommend to Parliament that sovereignty over Hong Kong should revert to China.[87] For Cradock, who had played the leading role in persuading her, this was the 'first finesse'. The objective still was to try to convince the Chinese that British administration should continue. She did not want to give way on this at this stage in the process. She was conscious that the British negotiators had precious few cards in their hands and of the need to manage Hong Kong opinion, as expressed to her by the Governor, Sir Edward Youde, and by the business leaders on the Governor's Executive Council.

After three rounds of talks with the Chinese, she held a further review meeting on 5 September 1983. It was clear that unless they conceded the end of British administration as well as of sovereignty, the Chinese would break off the talks, inflicting great damage on Hong Kong, but the Chief Secretary, Sir Philip Haddon-Cave, and the non-official members of the Executive Council led by Sir S. Y. Chung still were resisting this.

When talks did take place on 22 September, the absence of any reassuring statements in the communiqué caused a massive capital outflow from Hong Kong. Her economic adviser, Professor Alan Walters, telephoned her from Washington to support the proposal by a senior Hong Kong official, John Greenwood, that the only effective way to restore confidence was to establish a currency board system linking the Hong Kong currency to the US dollar. Hong Kong had sufficiently large currency reserves to render this feasible. Nigel Lawson was at first reluctant and the

Governor of the Bank of England had some reservations, but they agreed on the necessity of supporting Hong Kong. The Hong Kong currency was fixed at 7.80 to the US dollar. Confidence returned to the Hong Kong financial markets. The financial press regarded this intervention as an unqualified success.

Some members of the Governor's Council still were resisting what they regarded as unnecessary concessions to the Chinese and urging the British negotiators to call their bluff. Cradock regarded this as extremely dangerous: he did not believe the Chinese were bluffing. He had to urge them to 'look into the pit' and consider carefully the consequences for Hong Kong of a collapse of the negotiations. He won little support, except from the Financial Secretary and the Commander of British forces in Hong Kong, both, understandably, more realistic than the others.

To break the logjam, Cradock proposed his 'second finesse'. On 14 October Margaret Thatcher was persuaded by him to send a further message to Zhao Ziyang expressing willingness to discuss Chinese ideas on the future of Hong Kong. She had to intervene firmly herself with the members of the Hong Kong Executive Council to get them to accept this. Talks were resumed, but it was clear by now that her hopes of establishing democratic self-government before the handover were not going to be realised. The Chinese were now threatening not to sign a treaty but simply to declare 'policy objectives' for themselves. She authorised her negotiators to spell out that Britain was prepared to explore Chinese proposals based on the absence of any link of authority or accountability between Britain and Hong Kong after 1997.[88]

Some of the China experts in the Foreign Office felt that she should have conceded more rapidly an end to British sovereignty and administration. But it was not in her nature to do so, without first assuring herself that nothing better could be achieved, and she was subject to opposite pressures from the Governor and other senior figures in Hong Kong, who had a direct line to 10 Downing St. Cradock and his negotiating team in Beijing strongly agreed that she could not afford to give way on these critical issues without having first secured the acceptance, however grudging, of the leaders of Hong Kong opinion as represented on the Governor's Executive Council and that she was going to have to play the crucial role in persuading them. When one Foreign Office mandarin told her, in exasperation, that he knew more about China than she did, she reacted calmly to this explosion, staring at her papers, before smiling and suggesting that they move on to another subject!

Feeling depressed by the Chinese attitude and her own lack of any real leverage, she telephoned the Prime Minister of Singapore, Lee Kuan Yew, for his advice. This was to send a senior emissary to explain very calmly to the Chinese that if they wished to compromise the future of Hong Kong, no one could prevent them doing so. But that would reflect very badly on their international reputation. Knowing Hong Kong well, Lee Kuan Yew was convinced that the colony could just as well be run by highly competent Hong Kong officials as by the expatriates then still in charge. She should concentrate on securing maximum autonomy for them to go on doing so. He was to be proved absolutely right in this, with the emergence at the head of the Hong Kong administration of figures like the formidably competent Anson Chan, Donald Tsang and Joseph Yam.

Meeting the 'unofficial' representatives on the Hong Kong Executive Council again in January 1984, she was struck this time by their much greater realism about what she regarded as the highly unpalatable options they had to consider. Following the meeting, she instructed officials to work out how they could give undertakings of a right of entry to the UK to Hong Kong officials who stayed in their posts until 1997.

Geoffrey Howe visited Beijing in April and again in July, accompanied by Percy Cradock, who had been appointed as the Prime Minister's foreign policy adviser, succeeding Tony Parsons. In these and other discussions it was agreed that, following the transfer of sovereignty to China, Hong Kong would enjoy a high degree of autonomy, that it would be vested with executive, legislative and judicial power, that the laws currently in force would remain basically unchanged, and that its government would be composed of local inhabitants. Foreign nationals would remain in employment in public services except at the most senior levels. It would retain the status of an international financial centre and a freely convertible currency. By now the terms on offer constituted what could be a binding international agreement. They were sufficiently clear and detailed about what would happen to Hong Kong after 1997 to reassure people there and the agreement would have force under Chinese law.

Difficulty arose over the Chinese proposal to set up a joint commission in Hong Kong to oversee the transition. The Governor feared that this could turn into a parallel government. In the event, the Chinese agreed that it should be a joint liaison group, with purely consultative powers.

In her memoirs, she paid a well-deserved tribute to Geoffrey Howe's role in what had been achieved. 'Geoffrey was always good at the actual process of negotiation … his meeting with Mr Deng was highly effective in reassuring the Chinese that we were to be trusted.' No less important a contribution was made throughout the entire negotiation by Percy Cradock, who had succeeded in winning her confidence when it had mattered most.[89]

As a result of their efforts, Margaret Thatcher's visit to China to sign the Joint Agreement in December 1984 was a preordained success. She found Zhao Ziyang as concerned about the transitional period as she was. She urged that the Basic Law to be passed by the Chinese Parliament must be compatible with the free market system and consistent with the Hong Kong legal system. She touched very lightly on the idea of expanding democracy in the period up to the handover.

With Deng Xiaoping, she told him that the stroke of genius in the negotiations had been his concept of 'one country, two systems'. He attributed this to a Marxist process of 'seeking truth from the facts'. It had in fact originally been formulated as a Chinese proposal for Taiwan.

Asked why the Chinese had set a fifty-year time frame for the agreement, Deng said that China hoped to approach the economic development of advanced countries by that time. To achieve this, China had to be open to the outside world. Maintaining Hong Kong's stability and prosperity would help China to modernise its economy. This did not mean that China would become a capitalist country, even if capitalism continued to prevail in Hong Kong and Taiwan.

In that regard, as she observed, he turned out to be completely wrong. His slogan in Shanghai that 'to get rich is beautiful' was taken so fully to heart by his compatriots as to amount to a thoroughgoing embrace of capitalism. She came away reassured that the Chinese in their own interests would seek to keep Hong Kong prosperous. Deng by this stage had decided to invite the Queen to visit China, which she proceeded to do in 1986.

But Margaret Thatcher's forebodings about the political system were borne out by the massacre in Tiananmen Square in June 1989 and the repression that followed. Zhao Ziyang was ousted from the leadership and placed under house arrest for counselling moderation. Conscious that the events in Tiananmen Square had traumatised Hong Kong, she saw the need to reassure those the British were counting on to remain in place in the territory. She also was determined to honour the debt to those who had served Britain loyally and believed, anyway, that an influx of Hong Kong entrepreneurial talent would benefit the country. So her response was to legislate to give British citizenship to 50,000 key people in the colony and their dependents.[90]

In 1992, to Cradock's alarm, relations with China took a sharp turn for the worse in response to proposals by Chris Patten, newly appointed by John Major as Governor of Hong Kong, to broaden democracy in the territory in the run-up to the handover of power. While Patten regarded these as fully compatible with the Basic Law enacted by China, which envisaged some extension of elected representation, there was no real consultation with the Chinese about them, despite promises that there would be, and they reacted very badly to them. Hong Kong business leaders initially were enthusiastic, but soon began to get cold feet as the Chinese reaction proved fiercer than they had expected. Despite her frequent differences with Patten, Margaret Thatcher proved a strong supporter of his pro-democracy reforms, despite the misgivings of most China experts, Percy Cradock among them. Senior figures like Ted Heath, Geoffrey Howe and an array of other dignitaries, Patten observed, initially were supportive. 'Only Margaret Thatcher was to remain so in public and in private ... insisting that the joint declaration signed in her name should mean what it said.' When the foreign policy Establishment seemed to turn against him, 'she was a better and stouter friend to me than she will ever know'.[91]

The Hong Kong administration, meanwhile, was run with exemplary efficiency by the Chief Secretary, Anson Chan, who described herself as Margaret Thatcher with a smile.

In response to the Patten reforms, my Chinese colleague in Washington, ambassador Ma, observed sardonically: 'Very interesting. You have discovered democracy in Hong Kong after a hundred and fifty years!' He was appointed as the first Chinese commissioner to Hong Kong after the handover. His mission, he explained to me, was to ensure that the mainland authorities did not interfere, for which he had the authority of the Prime Minister at the time, Zhu Rongji.

Margaret Thatcher's conclusion, several years after the handover, was that the Chinese to date had honoured their commitments to Hong Kong. She continued, on every subsequent visit she made to China, to enquire about Zhao Ziyang in an effort to help him by showing the Chinese leadership that the world had not forgotten about him.

As for Percy Cradock, as her foreign policy adviser, his abiding memories were of her coming down the steps from her flat to the study in Downing Street, 'beautifully turned out, with every sign of positive anticipation of a good discussion on some particularly ugly international situation'.[92]

VII

'GETTING OUR MONEY BACK'

Six days after becoming Prime Minister, Margaret Thatcher sought to disabuse her first foreign visitor, Chancellor Helmut Schmidt, of any notion that she might be a soft touch in matters to do with the European Community (EC). She had to tackle straight away the unfair budgetary burden imposed by the terms Heath had been obliged to accept in the accession negotiations, stemming from the fact that two-thirds of the EC budget was spent on agriculture, from which Britain's receipts were minimal. The 'financial mechanism' agreed during Wilson's renegotiation, which was supposed to correct an excessive British budgetary contribution, had proved to be worthless, yielding no results at all and leaving the problem to be dealt with by her. Britain, which at the time was the seventh most prosperous state in a Community of ten, was in danger of overtaking Germany as the largest and only other net contributor.

In a speech during the first direct elections to the European Parliament, she said that she believed in a 'free Europe, not a standardised Europe... We insist that the institutions of the European Community are managed so that they increase the liberty of the individual' and that they should not dwindle into bureaucracy. Nothing could have been further from the intentions of the European Commission. She was well aware that the Community continued to be shaped by the Franco-German axis, limiting Britain's ability to influence events.

At her first European Council in Strasbourg in June 1979, she tried to show willing by saying that although Britain was not in a position to join the Exchange Rate Mechanism (ERM), as Schmidt wanted her to do, the Bank of England would swap some of its reserves for ecus (the European Currency Unit). She did not rule out in her own mind the possibility of Britain joining the ERM at some point at this time. Throughout the day she tried and failed to get the British budgetary issue discussed. When the French President, Valéry Giscard d'Estaing, proposed moving to dinner, she objected until she had secured an instruction to the Commission to make proposals to deal with the matter.

Among her European colleagues, she liked and admired Helmut Schmidt despite some fierce exchanges with him. She regarded him as staunch in standing up to the Russians and, despite being head of the Social Democratic Party, far less of a socialist than most of her Cabinet colleagues. But in the course of an argument about fishing quotas in the North Sea, the Prime Minister, who had studied her brief in exhaustive detail, exclaimed: 'The trouble, Helmut, is that you don't know anything about fish.' One of my German colleagues reported that, on returning to his delegation office, Schmidt had responded by kicking the furniture.

Valéry Giscard d'Estaing was not someone to whom she ever warmed – she was far from alone in that – and she knew the feeling was mutual. She disliked his supercilious airs and his technocratic mindset. When she proceeded to say so to her advisers at some length, after a meeting with him, she was interrupted by Denis Thatcher. 'That's enough', he said, bringing her to an abrupt halt. Giscard in turn took to calling her '*la fille de l'épicier*'. She was to get on much better with his socialist successor, François Mitterrand.

She also had developed a distaste for the Italian Prime Minister Andreotti, who seemed to her to have a positive aversion to principle and a love of intrigue and of deals concluded behind closed doors. This feeling too was mutual. When, in my presence, she reminded Andreotti one day that she was a chemist, he muttered in Italian that he would never go to her for treatment, as he would be afraid she might poison him. His aversion to principle was eventually to cost him dear, as he was later indicted for relationships with the mafia.

Her demands on the budget generated much spurious indignation, with others claiming that the financial levies paid over to it belonged as of right to the Community, not to the contributing states. Even to talk in Brussels about our net contribution was regarded as like spitting in church.

She became sufficiently frustrated to start examining the possibility of withholding British payments to the EC, but baulked at threatening to do so when told by the Law Officers that she would lose the subsequent case in the European Court. To avoid having to fight these battles annually, she tried to insist that the solution must last as long as the problem. But 'they were determined to keep as much of our money as possible'. In the end she was offered a refund of £350 million, one-third of the net contribution, which she rejected. She found infuriating the way in which the others all ganged up on her and were reluctant to hear what she regarded as a fair case. 'I am only talking about our money, no one else's,' she declared. Most of the other heads of government were as upset with her as she was with them. She was, however, pleased by an article in *Le Monde* comparing her tactics to those of Charles de Gaulle.

In April 1980 the argument was resumed at a further European Council in Luxembourg. She was offered a refund of one-third of the net contribution for 1980 and less than half for 1981, which she rejected. Schmidt and Roy Jenkins, as President of the Commission, urged her to settle, but were told that the terms were unacceptable and that she was not prepared to have a settlement that only lasted for two years.

At the end of May, the Foreign Secretary, Peter Carrington, and his deputy, Ian Gilmour, went to a Council of Ministers meeting in Brussels at which they felt they had secured a reasonable settlement, winning a three-year refund of two-thirds of the net contribution. Summoned to Chequers to explain what they had agreed, far from being congratulated, they were greeted, in the words of Ian Gilmour, about as cordially as if they had brought bailiffs to repossess the place. Without even offering them the drink they were dying for, the Prime Minister bombarded them with objections. It was only after a long and difficult discussion that she was persuaded that this offer was worth accepting.[93] Her frustration stemmed largely from the realisation that this still left the whole battle to be fought again, as no permanent solution had been achieved.

Having won a greatly increased majority of 144 seats in the June 1983 election, she moved Geoffrey Howe to the Foreign Office. He was succeeded as Chancellor by Nigel Lawson. Until their differences over the Exchange Rate Mechanism and the overheating of the British economy in 1988–9, Lawson was her particular favourite. Admiring his intellectual self-confidence, she deferred to him in Cabinet more than to any other minister.

The same could not be said of her relationship with Geoffrey Howe. She wrote, a decade later, that she found him very good at negotiating texts, as befitted a distinguished lawyer, and she acknowledged the value of this in the European negotiations. But, embittered by his role in her downfall, she claimed that he 'fell under the spell of the Foreign Office where compromise and negotiations were ends in themselves'. In her view, he also showed a longing for Britain to become part of some grandiose European consensus. What she regarded as his 'misty Europeanism' was bound to put him at loggerheads with her.[94]

At this time, they were still a very effective partnership. Increasingly, however, she was unable to prevent herself regarding Geoffrey Howe as a potential rival. In her words 'quietly ambitious', he had stood against her for the leadership after her first-round victory against Heath and would, she knew, have been a far more acceptable candidate to the party hierarchy than her. In his dealings with the press, she felt that he was trying to create the image of a more emollient and 'reasonable' alternative to her. He could hardly be blamed for doing so, but it did not help relations between them.

By now, the European Commission was pressing to raise the 1 per cent VAT ceiling for the Community budget, giving her leverage in the negotiations because increasing the Community's overall budget ceiling required unanimity. She was still finding it difficult to establish much of a rapport with the new Chancellor, Helmut Kohl. She tried unsuccessfully to persuade him to nominate a German candidate to succeed Roy Jenkins as President of the Commission, instead having to settle for the French Finance Minister, Jacques Delors.

On the British budgetary contribution, Nigel Lawson and the Treasury came up with the proposal that a country with a GDP per head of 90 per cent or less of the Community average should make no net contribution at all, with the richer member states contributing more according to their prosperity. She declared that she would not agree to any increase in the Community's 'own resources' unless agricultural spending was curbed and member states' contributions matched their ability to pay. At the March 1984 European Council in Brussels, Kohl proposed a flat-rate refund of 1 billion ecus, which was rejected as representing only half the British contribution.

At this time I had been appointed as the Foreign Office Under-Secretary responsible for the negotiations with the European Community. Visits to Brussels and other European capitals convinced me that the Treasury 'safety net' scheme had no chance whatever of acceptance. Apart from altering our own contribution, it also proposed to alter those of every other member state. While most of the other governments had scarcely even bothered to study it, they were unanimous in their determination to have nothing to do with it.

As the French held the Presidency of the Community, one of my first tasks was to accompany Margaret Thatcher to Paris for a meeting with President Mitterrand in April 1984. In opposition, Mitterrand had been the leading opponent of the Fifth Republic, which he had denounced as a 'permanent *coup d'état*'. It was fascinating to observe the transformation of this consummate politician, whom I had seen in the days when he still was free to enjoy a bohemian lifestyle on the Left Bank. Now there he was, installed in the General's office, enjoying all the trappings of the de Gaulle presidency. Even his speech and posture had changed. What remained reassuringly familiar was the team of efficient and attractive young ladies on his staff.

Her tête-à-tête meeting with Mitterrand over, on the plane back to London Margaret Thatcher was gloomy about the chances of any progress on the budgetary problem. My colleague David Williamson, head of the European Secretariat in the Cabinet Office, and I were more optimistic. Because of the history of French obstructiveness and a very adversarial relationship between our delegations in Brussels, where they were described as carrying on the Hundred Years War by other means, the tendency on our part always had been to try to enlist the support of the other member states against the French. This had never met with much success and we believed that the key to a solution lay, on the contrary, in doing a deal with them. The others, we believed, could then be bounced into accepting it.

For at the time, the most difficult of the allies we had to deal with were the Germans. While the French knew their minds, my colleagues in Bonn never seemed able to make up theirs. With straight faces they would tell us that, on the one hand, they were totally opposed to any reform of the Common Agricultural Policy (CAP) (most German 'peasants' by this time were circulating in BMWs), but that, on the other, there must be no increase in the EC budget, and certainly not in the German contribution to it. For their security, the Germans looked to the United States, and, for their legitimacy, to 'Europe' and to France. In their calculations, the British finished a bad third.

So we spent many hours with our French counterparts, Guy Legras and Élisabeth Guigou (later Minister of Justice in the French government), seeking to work out with them a way forward. For Williamson and I had concluded that we must adopt a radically simplified solution, based on an automatic two-thirds abatement of the difference between what we contributed and what we received, provided this was made a permanent mechanism, enshrined in Community law and changeable only by unanimity. When we tried this on Geoffrey Howe, the response was that we could try to negotiate something on these lines – but on our heads be it if the Prime Minister didn't like it. Geoffrey Howe did not enjoy arguing with the Prime Minister, for which he could hardly be blamed, as she was often rude to him. 'I know what you are going to say, Geoffrey', is how she was said to have begun one meeting with him, 'and the answer is no'. It was made very clear to us that this was an argument we were going to have to conduct with her ourselves.

So the stage was set for the negotiation in Fontainebleau, described in the Prologue. She had achieved a major success for British diplomacy, but at a cost in terms of her personal relations with the other European leaders. She had fought with ferocious energy for this result and they were the more annoyed because, in the end, she had prevailed. The need to do so was not her fault. Given the fact that the solution we wanted had to be at the cost of all eleven other member states, a less implacably determined Prime Minister could never have achieved as satisfactory an outcome for the UK.

But in the process, she had left a lot of bruises. There was plenty of grudging admiration but, apart from her style, the others felt that, almost wilfully, she did not understand what the EC meant to them. Their countries had all been occupied and devastated in the war. The excesses of the CAP were nothing to them compared to the horrors Europe had inflicted upon itself before it was invented. The French and Danes apart, the others all positively favoured a further pooling of sovereignty, while the French had good reason to believe that the system could be used to promote their interests, having very successfully colonised the Commission and the other institutions. The Commission and others knew that they simply could not proceed without France and Germany. Without them, 'Europe' did not exist. But we had ourselves shown them that it could exist, and develop, without us.

After the bruising encounters over the British budget, the Commission under Jacques Delors was determined to try to give some new impetus to European integration. We ourselves wished to see faster progress with the directives needed to achieve a genuine single market. Such a market existed so far as material goods were concerned, but not in services, in areas like air and road transport, insurance and banking, where our competitive advantage lay.

The Commission argued that, to enable faster progress to be made and to prepare for the further enlargement of the Community, the treaties should be amended to provide for more majority voting. The Prime Minister was strongly opposed to amending the treaties, which she saw as opening Pandora's box, and to any extension of majority voting.

We circulated a paper to the other member states arguing for the creation of a genuine common market, extending also to the service industries and the professions. We also had been playing a leading part in efforts to improve foreign policy coordination. We were determined to maintain our own ultimate freedom of action and so, needless to say, were the French. But the idea that

Europe should so far as possible speak with one voice in world affairs was one we did support, so we proposed a document codifying political cooperation. Copies were given privately, in advance, to the foreign policy advisers of Kohl and Mitterrand.

As we walked across Downing Street to attend the usual meeting with the Prime Minister in London on the eve of the Milan European Council in June 1985, we were told that the French and Germans had circulated to the other member states a brand new 'Treaty of European Union'. This consisted, verbatim, of the text we had given them, plus a caption stating that this, together with the existing treaties, constituted European Union. As Margaret Thatcher observed, it was the kind of behaviour that would have got you thrown out of any London club.

The Prime Minister went to Milan determined to veto any changes to the treaties. This was a period in which the Italian government changed every few months. But this never seemed to make much difference, as we always found ourselves dealing with the wily Andreotti. Whatever else changed in the new government, he always reappeared as Prime Minister or, as in this case, as Foreign Minister. Andreotti regarded the Prime Minister as extraordinarily effective in the pursuit of her objectives, but predisposed to pay scant regard to those of others.

The same problem existed, in greater measure, with Helmut Kohl. He regarded himself as representing a more important country, with a stronger economy. He found it irksome to be told that German objectives often were contradictory – as indeed they were. Mrs Thatcher could not understand why, when faced with a choice between the United States – where her sympathies so obviously lay – and France, the Germans, resolutely, would refuse to choose. For Kohl, whose brother had been killed on

'Heavens, not another wet?' Margaret Thatcher with Alexander Haig on 8 April 1982.
© *The Economist*

Surrender of the infamous Captain Astiz on South Georgia, 26 April 1982. © Getty Images

ABOVE After the victory: Margaret Thatcher with British troops in the Falklands, January 1983. © Sgt. Bill Bain/ Defence Image Database, Imperial War Museum

LEFT 'Not a hair out of place.' Margaret Thatcher addressing the Conservative Party Conference in Brighton immediately following the IRA's attempt to assassinate her, 12 October 1984. © Bettmann/Corbis

'Someone who thought and felt as I did.' Margaret Thatcher and Ronald Reagan, June 1988.
© Gary Hershorn/Reuters/Corbis

Entente cordiale. Margaret Thatcher and Francois Mitterrand at the Elysée: ratification
of the Channel Tunnel Treaty, 29 July 1987. © Jacques Langevin/Sygma/Corbis

'Someone I can do business with': the Thatchers and Gorbachevs at Chequers, December 1984. © Getty Images

Margaret Thatcher at the 1985 NATO Summit with Ronald Reagan and Geoffrey Howe. © Getty Images

A special relationship: Margaret Thatcher and Mikhail Gorbachev in Moscow, 30 March 1987. © Getty Images

'An influence on US policy not seen since Churchill's day.' Margaret Thatcher, President Reagan and George Shultz at the White House, 18 July 1987. © Press Association

'Anchor to windward.' Margaret Thatcher and George Bush at Camp David, 24 November 1989. © George Bush Presidential Library and Museum

No meeting of minds: Margaret Thatcher and Chancellor Kohl, 18 January 1982.
© Getty Images

Margaret Thatcher, Francois Mitterrand and éminence grise (Charles Powell), 4 May 1990. © Getty Images

'Free Nelson Mandela:' Margaret Thatcher and Mandela, 4 July 1990. © Getty Images

ABOVE Facing aggression: Margaret Thatcher and George Bush in Aspen, Colorado, 2 August 1990.
© Getty Images

LEFT Leaving 10 Downing Street, 28 November 1990.
© Getty Images

the Russian front in the Second World War, Europe and the Franco-German rapprochement represented legitimacy, acceptance and a new future for his country, which were his overriding objectives. Encounters with the Prime Minister were not his favourite pastime. On one famous occasion, he ended a meeting with her, pleading pressure of business, only to be discovered devouring a large cake in a coffee house nearby.

Andreotti, meanwhile, was busy engineering an ambush in Milan. On the first day, Mrs Thatcher ruled out changes to the treaties. On the second day he called a vote on whether there should be an intergovernmental conference, which we lost by nine votes to one.

While treaty change required unanimity, the procedural decision did not. Mrs Thatcher returned to the delegation room to report what had happened. As she got up to go to her press conference, we urged her not to tell the journalists that we would not agree to any treaty change. It was, we suggested, just possible that we could negotiate changes that would be acceptable to us.

The Prime Minister swept off with no reply. But in her press conference, under intense pressure from the journalists, she did not say that we would never agree to treaty change – only that she was not convinced of the need for it. One correspondent asked if she had read an article in his newspaper criticising her style of government. 'If you think I have time to read editorials in the newspapers,' she exclaimed, 'you are sadly mistaken.'

On our return to London, Michael Butler, David Williamson and I sought and were granted a licence to explore with the other member states whether we could agree treaty changes acceptable to us. 'Yes,' we were told, 'and please bear in mind that when you come back, I may disavow you.'

While Michael Butler and his successor, David Hannay, negotiated with exceptional skill in Brussels, David Williamson and I sought, once again, to reach an understanding with the French, who had no more desire than we did to see a large extension of the powers of the Commission or the European Parliament.

My French counterpart, Pierre de Boissieu, great-nephew of General de Gaulle, was particularly adamant on this point. When Mrs Thatcher told President Mitterrand that she could accept the Boissieu plan for the Parliament, Mitterrand was delighted. 'But what is the Boissieu plan?' he enquired.

By the time of the Luxembourg European Council in December 1985, we had reached agreement on the text of a new treaty which incorporated our text on political cooperation and treaty changes to speed up decision-making on the single market. But the other member states also wanted commitments to an eventual monetary union and to the abolition of frontier controls. Neither issue was negotiable for us and, on her arrival in Luxembourg, I gave Mrs Thatcher a list of twelve points she needed to win if we were to agree to what was proposed.

This had the advantage of channelling her formidable energies in a positive direction and, after two days, and at the cost of driving the others to distraction, she had won eleven of them.

The remaining issue was the determination of the Ministry of Agriculture at all costs to maintain our ability to prevent the import of animals and plants from the other member states, come what may. By the time they had spent three hours debating this, the other heads of government had heard more than enough about our anti-rabies regime. As the discussion had reached complete deadlock, I fed into the meeting a new formula, devised by my deputy, Stephen Wall, which did allow us to maintain our controls.

A relieved Geoffrey Howe read this out to the conference. As the Luxembourg Prime Minister went around the table, Kohl, Mitterrand and the others all accepted – until he got to Mrs Thatcher, who rejected it! The others by now did not know whether to laugh or cry. A short break in the proceedings enabled us to persuade a reluctant Prime Minister to go along with our own proposal.

Margaret Thatcher subsequently sometimes gave the impression of regretting it. But, at the time, she was very pleased with the outcome in Luxembourg – the negotiation of the Single European Act. We had succeeded in obliging the others to negotiate to a large extent on terrain of our choosing – the completion of the single market.

No one who witnessed Helmut Kohl and, in due course, Jacques Chirac bellowing and thumping the table in support of German and French farmers could reasonably accuse her of having been overzealous in defence of British interests. We had at the time forged quite an effective alliance with the French. Like their President, the senior French officials had developed an admiration for Mrs Thatcher, not only as a formidable adversary when we disagreed, but as the current embodiment of the Gaullist doctrine of '*l'Europe des patries*'. They were no keener than she was to see any great extension of the powers of the Parliament or of the Commission at that time. In foreign policy, preserving French freedom of action remained an all-important objective for them.

She still felt, at this stage, that with enlargement and the drive to complete the single market, the Community was developing in a direction compatible with our interests. Later, much energy would be devoted to trying, unsuccessfully, to limit the ambitions of others, above all in relation to monetary union. Institutionally, the Foreign Office had a near-pathological fear of being left out of European construction. Yet there were obvious advantages to being 'left out' of the Schengen Agreement abolishing frontier controls. There were, or should have been, attractions in facilitating variable geometry for the enlarged Community – which is what in fact came to pass.

VIII

'WHAT BRITISH POLITICIAN WILL EVER REALLY UNDERSTAND NORTHERN IRELAND?'

No Prime Minister could have had a closer or more personal experience of Irish terrorism than Margaret Thatcher. Airey Neave, hero of the attempts to escape from the Colditz prison camp during the war, had played a crucial role in her campaign for the party leadership against Ted Heath. Appointed by her as shadow Northern Ireland Secretary, he was killed by a car bomb planted by an extremist Irish terrorist group, the Irish National Liberation Army (INLA) within the precincts of Parliament on the eve of the election in 1979.

This was followed by the murder of Lord Mountbatten and members of his family in Ireland in August 1979 and the ambush and killing by the Irish Republican Army (IRA) of eighteen British soldiers near the border with the Irish Republic. Mrs Thatcher went post-haste to Northern Ireland, receiving an enthusiastic reception in Belfast's main shopping centre before spending time with the army and police. Her attempts shortly afterwards to agree on increased security cooperation with the Irish authorities met with no response whatever from the Irish Prime Minister, Jack Lynch.

Her own instincts were, as she said herself, 'profoundly unionist', despite her sometimes troubled relationship with them.
She was firmly committed to the defence of the union. She
considered that the North was British territory, a clear majority
of whose population had through many generations regarded
themselves as British and demonstrably wished to remain so. She
had the highest admiration for the people of Northern Ireland,
who greeted her warmly on the visits she made there after nearly
every major terrorist attack, and she felt her responsibility to
them acutely.

'But what British politician,' she added, 'will ever really understand Northern Ireland?'[95] It was her realisation that this was
indeed the case that led her to move from a very conservative
position to a more adventurous one. Her starting point was
that the nationalist minority had legitimate grievances and had
suffered serious discrimination. This could not justify armed
insurrection, let alone a campaign of systematic murder, but the
political realities prevented a return to self-government based
on majority rule. Enoch Powell had been campaigning for full
integration and an end to any special status for Northern Ireland,
an idea she rejected. There was going to have to be some form of
power-sharing.

As the declared aim of all parties in the South, as reflected
in Articles 2 and 3 of the Irish Constitution, was the same as
that of the IRA, namely the incorporation of the North into the
'national territory' of a united Ireland, she believed that successive Irish governments were less than wholehearted in combating
IRA terrorism, lax in preventing terrorists from using Southern
territory as a safe haven and prone to placing obstacles in the
way of effective cross-border security cooperation.

In December 1979, Charles Haughey became the Irish Prime Minister. In 1970 he had been accused but acquitted in a case of gun-running for the IRA. Despite this unpromising background, and the allegations of corruption which followed him throughout his career, he made great efforts to charm her with skilful blarney, plus the well-chosen present of a Georgian Irish silver teapot. In December 1980 they held a meeting which the communiqué described as extremely constructive, promising to devote their next meeting to discussing the 'totality of relationships between these islands'. Haughey portrayed this as a triumph from the Irish point of view, and Irish ministers started talking about 'new institutional structures', annoying Mrs Thatcher and infuriating the unionists.

Meanwhile, she was having to cope with a serious crisis triggered by the IRA prisoners in the Maze prison in Belfast. A 'special category' status for convicted terrorist prisoners in Northern Ireland had been conceded in 1972. This was, in her view, a bad mistake and it had been ended in 1976. But earlier prisoners continued to have a special category status. Within the Maze prison in Belfast, protests had been constant, including fouling cells and breaking up furniture. In October 1980, they announced plans for a hunger strike, demanding the right to wear their own clothes, avoid any prison work and to consort with other 'political prisoners'. Her response was that there was no such thing as a political murder. Her hatred of terrorism and conviction that terrorists were murderers who should never be rewarded for their terrorism lay behind her resistance to making any concessions to the hunger strikers and in particular her refusal to grant them political prisoner status.

Haughey urged her to make some face-saving concessions.

The Catholic Church was persuaded to come out against the hunger strike. When one of the prisoners began to lose consciousness, the strike was abruptly called off. It was then started again in March 1981 by the IRA leader in the Maze, Bobby Sands. Michael Foot, Leader of the Opposition, urged the Prime Minister to make concessions to the strikers. Bobby Sands died on 5 May. In Parliament she said that he was a convicted criminal, who had chosen to take his own life. 'It was a choice that his organisation did not allow to many of its victims.' In all, ten prisoners died before the strike was called off in October.

In July 1981, Garret FitzGerald had taken over from Haughey as the Irish Prime Minister. He had first met Margaret Thatcher when she was still Leader of the Opposition. He had been told that she was a convinced unionist and was worried that, under the influence of Airey Neave, she might revert to the idea of a devolved government in Northern Ireland on the basis of majority i.e. Protestant control. He was told flatly by her that there would be no devolution without power-sharing.

In these first contacts with her, FitzGerald came to a very shrewd judgement about her. Most British politicians approached Northern Ireland as gingerly as if it were an explosive device, and were exceptionally fearful of unionist eruptions. He felt that she would be hard to persuade, but that if she were persuaded, 'she had the qualities to do something serious about the North and to stand by what was agreed'.[96] He therefore decided to make an all-out effort with her.

She was impressed by his obvious sincerity and agreed in November 1981 to set up an 'Anglo-Irish Intergovernmental Council' of ministers on both sides to discuss issues of common concern, provoking another furious reaction from the unionists.

The return of Haughey to power in Dublin in 1982 brought Anglo-Irish relations back to freezing point. Mrs Thatcher regarded him as fundamentally untrustworthy, a sentiment further reinforced when he sided with Argentina in the Falklands conflict. Chairing a Cabinet committee in July 1982, she heard the sound of a bomb exploding not far away. Bombs had exploded in Hyde Park and Regent's Park, killing eight and injuring fifty-three people.

Midway through the Falklands crisis, David Goodall became Deputy Secretary in the Cabinet Office responsible for foreign and defence affairs. He found that the loss of life by British servicemen in the Falklands campaign had caused Margaret Thatcher personal anguish. At the end of 1982, he found himself talking to her about Ireland after a dinner at 10 Downing Street. He observed that it was a scandalous fact that, at the time, the only place in the world where the lives of British soldiers' were being lost in anger was in the United Kingdom itself, in Northern Ireland. He was struck by the seriousness of her interest in Northern Ireland and the extent of her background reading on the subject. The conversation ended with her saying that, 'If we get back next time' (in the 1983 general election), she wanted to 'do something about Ireland'. Robert Armstrong, as Cabinet Secretary, also was told of her determination, once re-elected, to try to do something to change the course of events in Northern Ireland.[97]

The return of Garret FitzGerald as Taoiseach in December 1982 offered hope of an improvement. Following her victory in the 1983 election, talks were engaged between Robert Armstrong and his Irish counterpart, Dermot Nally. In September 1983, David Goodall's counterpart, Michael Lillis, told him that FitzGerald tentatively was thinking of amending Articles 2 and

3 of the Irish Constitution laying claim to Northern Ireland, in return for an Irish political presence in the North, with the involvement of Irish police and security forces there and of Irish judges in terrorist trials. This suggestion was received with scepticism in Whitehall, but attracted Mrs Thatcher's interest. The idea of Irish troops or police operating in Northern Ireland was a non-starter, just as a British proposal that the security forces on both sides should have the right to hot pursuit of terrorists within five miles of the border was flatly rejected by the Irish. But she had fully grasped the significance of FitzGerald's readiness to accept publicly, and not just privately, that Irish unification was not a feasible proposition for the foreseeable future.[98]

When they met at Chequers on 7 November 1983, FitzGerald made his case for an 'equation' whereby the Irish government would endorse the Union of Britain and Northern Ireland and increase security cooperation in return for an Irish role in the government and administration of justice in the North. He argued for 'joint authority', which she rejected. But he had persuaded her that there was a possibility of progress.

Immediately after the Irish delegation left, she held a meeting with the British participants around the fire at Chequers. She authorised Robert Armstrong and David Goodall, for both of whom FitzGerald had formed a high regard, to engage in secret discussions with their Irish counterparts and to prepare counterproposals for new forms of cooperation. Robert Armstrong was asked to lead the negotiations because she wanted to keep them firmly under her personal control.[99]

In December, she visited Harrods in the immediate aftermath of an IRA bomb attack there, finding the charred body of a teenage girl lying where she had been killed. The next day, Denis

Thatcher was spotted by the press returning to No. 10 with a clutch of shopping bags from Harrods. He was not, he declared, going to allow himself to be put off doing his habitual Christmas shopping there by some 'murdering Irishman'.[100]

The Irish put forward proposals for joint policing and mixed courts in Northern Ireland, based on ideas of 'joint sovereignty', which she could not accept. But there followed a series of exploratory meetings between officials. In return for endorsing the Union, the Irish government wanted as much involvement and influence as possible in the North. Mrs Thatcher was not prepared to bargain about an Irish security or judicial presence in Northern Ireland, but recognised the need to address nationalist concerns about the conduct of the security forces and the impartiality of the courts. She had initially been very attracted by the idea of the Irish amending the offending articles of their constitution, but the price they wanted from the British for this – 'joint authority' – was unacceptable to her and would have triggered a full-scale unionist revolt. She was prepared to agree a consultative role for the Irish government in Northern Ireland which, however, would lapse once there was an administration in which nationalists and unionists were genuinely sharing power.

On 12 October 1984 she was working until 2.40 a.m. in her rooms at the Grand Hotel in Brighton on her speech to the Conservative Party conference when the IRA very nearly succeeded in their objective of eliminating her and much of her government. A massive explosion destroyed a whole perpendicular section of the hotel. Her Private Secretary, Robin Butler, was still working with her in her suite when the explosion took place, and helped her out of the rubble of the hotel. She was evacuated to the Brighton police station, then to the Lewes Police College, but refused to return to 10 Downing Street. In the morning she saw television pictures of Norman Tebbit being pulled from the wreckage; his wife was paralysed in the attack. Anthony Berry MP and Roberta Wakeham had been killed; John Wakeham, a member of her Cabinet, was badly injured.

She told Robin Butler: 'We must make sure the conference restarts on time.' He was appalled. How could she go on with the conference when her friends and colleagues were being dug out of the rubble, he asked. 'We can't allow terrorism to defeat democracy,' was her reply.

At 9.30 a.m. precisely, she opened the conference. Having rewritten her speech once more, she knew that what she said was less important than the fact that she was still there to tell her audience that 'all attempts to destroy democracy by terrorism will fail'. Simon Jenkins observed that the foreign journalists present in Brighton were incredulous at her composure and immaculate appearance. She visited her wounded friends and colleagues in the Sussex county hospital. Her daughter, Carol, found her next day at Chequers grimly reflecting that, 'This was the day I was not meant to see.'[101] The IRA declared that she had been lucky, but they 'only had to be lucky once' in their continuing attempts to kill her.

David Goodall felt that Margaret Thatcher would have been only human if she had responded by suspending the negotiations, and half-expected her to do so. But he found that he had underestimated her courage and determination.

Her reaction was to respond not with a barrage of emergency measures – she had considered but in the end had always rejected internment without trial of terrorist suspects – but with a display of studied normality. 'Outwardly unruffled', she decreed that the negotiations must continue.[102]

By now, Douglas Hurd had become Northern Ireland Secretary. He found that meetings with her on the subject tended to start from square one. She had a great admiration for the people of Northern Ireland, but a poor opinion of unionist politicians. She would begin by saying that the answer might be to redraw the border so as to get rid of the predominantly republican areas. Hurd would reply that the orange and green ethnic map in his office showed that the communities were irretrievably intermingled. She would then denounce Irish ministers and the police for their feebleness in dealing with the IRA. But he too found that the Brighton bombing did not deflect her from her determination to try to reach an agreement with the Irish government.[103] To have any chance of success, the negotiations had to be conducted in secret, though at a very late stage the unionist leader Jim Molyneaux and Enoch Powell were offered briefings as privy councillors which, at Enoch Powell's insistence, they rejected.

The unionists had been excluded from the discussions because of the implacable opposition of both unionist parties to any Irish government involvement in the North. She liked and trusted Garret FitzGerald, despite complaining about his verbosity, and respected him as someone who was genuinely trying to change the course of events. He spoke both very rapidly and very softly, as a result of which, on one jet-lagged occasion, she fell asleep during a peroration from him, causing Charles Powell to assure him that he had written it all down and would make sure she read it! He complained that she kept calling him Gareth. 'Does she think I am Welsh?' he enquired. But she hijacked him to travel with her on her plane back from Mrs Gandhi's funeral in Delhi in order to continue their very sensitive private discussions.

In a meeting at Chequers on 18 November 1984, she sought to disabuse him of the notion that a 'joint authority' could be established for Northern Ireland. But they had a detailed discussion on ways to involve the Irish in a security commission. She regarded this as the most serious discussion she had ever had with an Irish leader. She discomfited FitzGerald by declaring at her press conference that the options of unification, confederation and joint authority were all 'out', and was genuinely upset that this caused difficulties for him in the Irish Parliament. In the light of hindsight, however, Goodall felt that it probably saved them, by forcing each side to realise the limits of what was potentially feasible for the other.[104] She then had a further positive meeting with FitzGerald at the Dublin European Council in December. She semi-apologised by saying that when people asked her direct questions, she had a weakness of giving direct answers. Geoffrey Howe felt that an extraordinary personal chemistry had developed between them.

FitzGerald kept trying to persuade her that something radical must be done to overcome the 'alienation' of the Catholic community in Northern Ireland. 'I do wish you would stop using that dreadful word, Garret,' she would reply! But on the substance, she was persuaded.[105]

Secret discussions between the two governments, led by Armstrong and Goodall, continued on the basis of a British draft formalising consultation with the Irish government about Northern Ireland. The British negotiators pressed the Irish to state publicly that there could be no change in the status of Northern Ireland without the consent of the majority of the people there. FitzGerald was impressed by their obvious sincerity in striving to reach an agreement and by the fact that, despite the reservations of others on the British side, Armstrong and Goodall had her full confidence and backing.

By now the two sides had agreed that instead of amending the Irish constitution, there would be a formal acceptance by the Irish government of Northern Ireland's status as part of the United Kingdom, unless and until its people should freely choose otherwise, in return for which the Irish government could have an institutionalised influence on British decision-making in Northern Ireland without diminishing British sovereignty – a proposition that required some skilful drafting by Robert Armstrong and his counterparts.

Garret FitzGerald made the all-important commitment that the Irish government would declare publicly its acceptance of the Union and of the fact that it could not be changed without the consent of the majority of the people of Northern Ireland in a meeting with Mrs Thatcher at the Milan European Council in June 1985, showing in her view the same political courage she was going to have to demonstrate in dealing with the unionist leaders. While this position had been hinted at by earlier Irish governments and the Irish had said at the time of the 1973 Sunningdale Agreement that they wanted to see unity 'established by consent', FitzGerald had agreed to express this in a far clearer and more high-profile manner in the form of a treaty. They had a forthright exchange about the composition of the courts in Northern Ireland and ways in which policing could be rendered more acceptable to the minority community.

At the crucial Cabinet meeting on 25 July 1985, she received vital support from Norman Tebbit, whose wife had been crippled in the Brighton bombing. FitzGerald was continuing to press for joint courts and changes to the police and the Ulster Defence Regiment. Nevertheless, dismissing the reservations of the new Northern Ireland Secretary, Tom King, she felt that they were now close to an agreement.

On 15 November 1985 she and FitzGerald signed the Anglo-Irish Agreement at Hillsborough Castle in Northern Ireland. Article I affirmed that no change in status could come about without the consent of the majority of the people of Northern Ireland and recognised that the present wish of the majority was for no change. On this basis, it was clear that the Irish government no longer contested the legitimacy of British authority over the North. The agreement allowed the Irish government to put forward its views and proposals in various areas, including security. But decisions rested with the British.

Mrs Thatcher was right in regarding this as a huge prize. Any idea that an Irish government might seek to coerce the North into a united Ireland against the wishes of the unionist community was laid to rest. The 'consultative' structures established under the agreement established a degree of joint responsibility between the two governments without which it is doubtful whether the subsequent Good Friday Agreement (following which the Irish constitution later was amended) could ever have come about.

The Prime Minister had thought that Article I and her own well-known attitude to Irish terrorism should have been sufficient to reassure the unionists about her intentions. Instead, to her fury, the unionists launched a general strike and threats of civil disobedience. She was denounced for treachery by Enoch Powell, who compared her to Jezebel. Having previously always taken him extremely seriously, this convinced her that he was more than slightly mad after all. To her disappointment, Ian Gow, who had been a close political friend, insisted on resigning from his position as a junior Treasury minister. At a dinner for her at this time, Charles Moore, editor of *The Spectator*, attacked the agreement. 'What about the Protestants?' he asked. Leaning across the table, with her usual intensity she said, 'Yes, Charles, and what about the Catholics?' She told FitzGerald that he had the glory and she had the problems, but she was not going to be deflected by the unionist protests from implementing the agreement.[106] The agreement got a positive reception internationally, especially in the United States, as showing that the two governments were working together. The Irish government's acceptance that unity could only come about with the consent of the Protestant community undercut republican propaganda to the contrary.

But to Margaret Thatcher's bitter disappointment, it did not result in any improvement in the security situation. The French intercepted a ship carrying Libyan arms for the IRA. A bomb attack killed eleven people at a Remembrance Day service at Enniskillen. She insisted on attending the rescheduled service regardless of the risk to her own security. When three Irish terrorists were killed by British security forces in Gibraltar, the funeral in Belfast turned into a mass IRA demonstration. She was appalled when two British soldiers who stumbled into a further IRA funeral were filmed being lynched by a frenzied mob.

Haughey, who had defeated FitzGerald in the 1987 Irish elections, infuriated her by making a violently anti-British speech at the UN General Assembly in March 1988, earning a stinging rebuke from her. Nor was she any better pleased when Geoffrey Howe said that he 'did not underestimate the hurt felt by the

Irish in recent months'. Security measures were reinforced, but the government rejected bringing back internment and she was persuaded not to seek to proscribe Sinn Féin. A further blow followed when the IRA killed Ian Gow with a car bomb in July 1989.

She had found the results of the Anglo-Irish Agreement disappointing. It had alienated the unionists without resulting in improved security cooperation with the Republic. This was never likely to be feasible with Charles Haughey in control. The unionists were yet to produce, in David Trimble, a leader, in Douglas Hurd's words, with a sense of the future as well as of the past.[107]

Margaret Thatcher, for all her formidable qualities, was never going to be the leader best qualified to help bring peace to Northern Ireland. The IRA were right to see her as their most implacable opponent. They would never have agreed to negotiate an end to hostilities with her. Nor would she temperamentally have been able to muster the infinite patience and care which John Major and, later, Tony Blair devoted to managing Irish sensitivities and helping to overcome the innumerable obstacles to an agreement.

Nevertheless, the Anglo-Irish Agreement was one of the indispensable building blocks on the road to a more peaceful future for Northern Ireland. Charles Haughey, who had attacked the agreement as Leader of the Opposition, declared his intention to abide by it when he returned to power. The fact that it was concluded solely by the two governments, without the political parties, turned out to be its strength. The earlier Sunningdale Agreement had collapsed when the unionists withdrew their support. But both the British and the Irish governments stuck by their commitments under the Anglo-Irish Agreement. It marked a turning point in the relationship between them and provided a foundation on which John Major and then Tony Blair were able to build towards the 1998 Good Friday Agreement and all that followed.

Garret FitzGerald had abandoned the position that a unitary state could somehow be achieved regardless of the wishes of the majority in the North. All future negotiations with the Irish government, resulting eventually in amendment to the Irish Constitution and, later, the discussions with Sinn Féin, started from this point.

She also would claim to have made clear to the IRA that they could never achieve their objectives by the route they had chosen. This was a conclusion that some of the IRA leadership were starting to come to themselves. Opaque messages started to be received to this effect. Two years after Margaret Thatcher's downfall, the Northern Ireland Catholic leader John Hume told me in Washington that there had been a revolution in IRA thinking. They were now interested in discussing a political solution. I hardly dared believe him at the time, but he turned out to be right.

IX

'TIME FOR SOME STRAIGHT TALKING WITH OUR AMERICAN FRIENDS'

As Prime Minister, Margaret Thatcher's first visit to Washington was in December 1979 to meet President Carter. Peter Carrington, her Foreign Secretary, doubted if they would get on very well. She regarded Carter as woolly-minded and ineffective in standing up to the Soviet Union. Nico Henderson, her newly appointed ambassador in Washington, viewed her visit with some trepidation. In the event, she got on better with Jimmy Carter than they had expected, because she was determined to. Her visit came six weeks after the seizure of American hostages in Iran. On arrival on the White House lawn, she declared: 'At times like these you are entitled to look to your friends for support. We are your friends, we do support you.'

The effect, in Henderson's view, was like a 'trumpet blast of cheer' to a beleaguered administration. She delivered to Congressmen a ten-minute harangue on the virtues of free markets and the evils of communism, followed by questions which she handled with her usual verve. In New York, she addressed an audience of over 2,000 at the Foreign Policy Association, telling them that 'I like questions' and that she was indeed an Iron Lady because 'I have to be'. The audience lapped this up.

As Henderson observed, American audiences liked the way she painted things in black and white, and not in shades of grey. One senior Senator told him that he could not recall any over-seas visitor who had made such an impact in so short a time as she had. He was impressed by her relationship with his friend, Peter Carrington. Carrington's stance in politics was that of a patrician; hers was pretty much the opposite. Yet they got on well together as, despite their periodic differences, she clearly liked and admired him.[108]

Her visit was followed within days by the Soviet invasion of Afghanistan. This came as less of a shock to her than it did to President Carter. She joined the Americans in impos-ing various sanctions, but was distressed to find she had no powers to prevent British athletes participating in the Moscow Olympic games.

There followed the invasion of the Iranian embassy in London by five Iraqi-trained gunmen. With the hostages' lives in danger, she had no hesitation in approving the order to the SAS to storm the embassy, which they did successfully, killing four of the hostage-takers – an incident which brought her into contact with their commander, Peter de la Billière. She headed forthwith to the Regent's Park barracks to congratulate the rescuers, one of whom told her: 'We never thought you'd let us do it.'

Two days later she attended the dinner at which the permanent secretaries told her that 'we are the system'. This was an evening, she said later, that 'etched into her soul' the contrast between the can-do spirit of the military and what she regarded as the 'better-not' attitude of some of the heads of the civil service.[109]

Margaret Thatcher greeted the election of Ronald Reagan as President of the US in November 1980 with an enthusiasm not shared by Peter Carrington and the Foreign Office, who were alarmed by his anti-Soviet rhetoric. She was impressed by his warmth, charm and complete lack of affectation. 'Above all, I knew that I was talking to someone who instinctively felt and thought as I did.'[110] She was well aware of the utter contrast between her obsession with the minutiae of every issue and his infinitely more relaxed style. But she understood instinctively his extraordinary ability to communicate with the American people, thanks to an unfettered optimism which stemmed from his own progression from an impoverished childhood to the White House.

Her positive view of Reagan was very much at odds with that of most European governments and the bulk of the world's media at the time, who thoroughly underestimated him. Depicted as a B-movie actor, he was in fact a successful two-term Governor of California – not an easy state to govern. His closest associate there and in Washington was Cap Weinberger, a Harvard *summa cum laude* who was to prove an outstandingly effective Defense Secretary. The Weinberger Doctrine, as it came to be known, consisted of ensuring that the United States had by far the world's most formidable military capability and, critically, decisive leadership in defence technology, with all this military power to be used very sparingly and, if possible, not at all. As his chief of staff, Reagan chose not his own associate, Ed Meese, but the organiser of George Bush's campaign against him for the Republican nomination, James Baker, simply because he felt that Baker was more competent. When they were joined by George Shultz, replacing Al Haig as Secretary of State, this was a truly formidable team. His principal Democratic opponent at the time, the legendary Speaker Tip O'Neill, told me and many others that he had never been as comprehensively outmanoeuvred by any President as he was by Ronald Reagan.

Margaret Thatcher was the first head of government to be invited to meet the new President in Washington on 25 February. She was accompanied by Peter Carrington, who was concerned about Reagan's policies and, in her view, inclined to pursue arguments which she was convinced would be fruitless, given Reagan's unshakeable commitment to a limited number of positions. The European allies were worried about Reagan's policies on arms control, military support for the government in El Salvador and the US budget deficit. She too feared that his plans for tax cuts would widen the deficit. But she did not agree with Carrington's desire to challenge the link the new administration was making between a Namibia settlement and the withdrawal of the 30,000 Cuban troops in Angola. She knew that Reagan would not press the South Africans on Namibia without Cuban withdrawal and thought that he was fully justified in this. She considered that quarrelling with the Americans about Central America was a counterproductive waste of time. 'There is one principle of diplomacy which diplomats ought to recognise more often: there is no point in engaging in conflict with a friend when you are not going to win and the cost of losing may be the end of the friendship.' She was, unwittingly, precisely echoing Winston Churchill, who had told Anthony Eden how foolish it was to quarrel with the Americans about 'petty issues' such as Guatemala.[III]

Larry Eagleburger, Assistant Secretary of State, had visited London and other European capitals with a dossier of evidence about Cuban support for the rebels in El Salvador. Mrs Thatcher regarded the government there as unsavoury, but accepted Reagan's determination to deal with Cuban subversion following the victory of the Sandinistas in Nicaragua and attempts to overthrow the other pro-American regimes in Central America.

The Northern Ireland Office, ever sensitive to tribal undertones, was worried that a President of Reagan lineage might be tempted to see the Northern Ireland problem in shades of green. When I confided this to his closest aide, Mike Deaver, he roared with laughter. Ronald Reagan had been brought up by his mother in what was effectively a single-parent family in Dixon, Illinois. Above and beyond his admiration for Margaret Thatcher, he was an Anglophile. He was in due course to visit the land of his ancestor, where he received an ecstatic welcome, but it made much less of an impression on him than a stay with the Queen at Windsor, which he was to describe as a 'fairy-tale experience'.[112]

As Margaret Thatcher arrived in Washington, *Time* had published an article about her entitled 'Embattled but Unbowed', reporting that her government was beset with difficulties, due to high and rising unemployment. There were doubts in the US press and among many of the Reaganites about her political prospects, and the Treasury Secretary, Donald Regan, told a Congressional committee while she was in Washington that she had been insufficiently radical in cutting taxes, just before joining a lunch in her honour. He thereby earned her lasting dislike. In reality, her economic recipes and those of Reagan were very different: she did not believe in deficit financing.

On the White House lawn, she declared that: 'We in Britain

stand with you… Your problems will be our problems, and when you look for friends we will be there.'

Having entertained her at the White House, Reagan attended a return dinner at the British embassy, at which she made a speech about the need for political leaders to display what her mentor Airey Neave had called 'two in the morning courage', making quite an impression on Reagan, who was no mean orator himself. Henderson observed: 'She is very good at rising to the occasion.'

After dinner Henderson was disappointed that the American guests were too much in awe of the Prime Minister to invite her to dance, so he did so himself. 'She loved dancing, something, so I found out, that she did extremely well … one of the few frivolous things she did as an undergraduate at Oxford was to learn ballroom dancing … It was with some difficulty that Denis eventually managed to extract her.'[113]

Despite her personal liking for Ronald Reagan and the fact that she regarded him as an ideological soulmate, Margaret Thatcher never ceased to be baffled by his apparent detachment from the normal process of running his government. Asked on one occasion by her to explain how on earth he managed this, I said that his core convictions were pride in America, standing up to the Russians and against big government. The rest he left to others. His easy charm was a huge political asset. He had an endless store of anecdotes used to illustrate the follies of mankind in general and the Democrats in particular. When asked about contradictory statements by his Secretary of State, Defense Secretary and National Security Adviser, he had replied with a smile: 'The trouble with this administration is the right hand doesn't know what the extreme right hand is doing.' She was less amused by his response to a question about his education policy, 'Do you know, I really can't remember!', a reply she found horrifying. (He regarded education as a matter for the states anyway.) While manifestly he did not have anything resembling her razor-sharp intelligence, on all important issues she regarded him as having precisely the right instincts.

At the end of March, to Margaret Thatcher's alarm, Reagan was very nearly killed by shots fired at him outside the Washington Hilton hotel by John Hinckley. Shot in the chest, with his lungs collapsing, 'I hope none of you are Democrats', he said to the surgeons about to operate on him.

On 18 April, having barely survived Hinckley's assassination attempt, Reagan insisted on drafting his own reply to a typically uncompromising message from Brezhnev. 'Is it possible', he wrote, 'that we have let ideological, political and economic philosophy and government policies keep us from considering the very real, everyday problems of the people we represent?' This met with no response from Brezhnev.[114]

Meeting Margaret Thatcher in London in July 1981, in the aftermath of the deeply unpopular Budget and at a very low point in the government's fortunes, Henderson was impressed by her vitality and will. 'She is more beleaguered now than ever before. But she remains indomitable – and immaculate. There was nothing flustered about her.' Peter Carrington told him that he would be prepared to go tiger-shooting with her, a category in which he did not place many of his colleagues. The Republicans in Washington, Henderson wrote, 'no longer see us as a beacon of the true faith. We are now a spectre that haunts them.' Yet he was not sure that it was her fault or that it would not come right in the end.[115]

Reagan recovered in time to attend the G7 summit in Ottowa, at which his economic policies came under attack from François Mitterrand and Pierre Trudeau, with Margaret Thatcher standing staunchly by him despite her own doubts about the US deficit. She urged him to discourage talk by members of his administration about a 'rising tide of neutralism' in Europe, which she feared could become self-fulfilling, and thanked him for toughening the US stand against Irish terrorism and fundraising for the IRA.

In June 1982 she addressed a special session of the UN General Assembly on disarmament in response to the Europe-wide anti-nuclear campaign. The fundamental threat to peace, she argued, was not the existence of weapons of particular types, but the disposition of some states to want to dominate others. 'Aggressors do not start wars because an adversary has built up his own strength.'

☞

She regarded the ability of the US and its allies to see through the deployment of cruise and Pershing missiles in western Europe as liable to prove a turning point in the Cold War. A combination of exaggerated American rhetoric and perennial European nervousness rendered the deployment problematic. The Labour government had supported the deployment, but she 'somehow doubted' if they would have seen it through.

Her concern was that a large swathe of European opinion did not believe that the US would put its own cities at risk by using its strategic nuclear forces to stop a Soviet attack in central Europe. Yet the overwhelming preponderance of Warsaw Pact conventional forces meant that an attack by them could only be held up for a limited period by NATO conventional forces. The NATO strategy of deterrence required there to be credible Europe-based nuclear weapons as well. The Russian deployment of SS20s was intended to ensure their dominance in that category of weapons, as well as in conventional forces.

Helmut Schmidt had been adamant about the need for a western response, despite fierce domestic resistance to the deployment of new nuclear weapons on German soil. The Dutch, Belgians and Italians, as well as the British, had committed to receiving them at a NATO meeting in December 1979.

In June 1980 the British government announced that the new missiles would be stationed at Greenham Common and Molesworth. The stage was set for an epic battle over the next several years with protesters and peace movements, generally supported by the churches, in all the recipient countries. To Margaret Thatcher's annoyance, none of these demonstrations was directed at the Soviet Union, which had caused the problem in the first place. In an interview in the Netherlands, she pointed out that the Russians had SS20s targeted on every country in Europe. 'Do you really expect us to sit back and do nothing?'

At the summit meeting in Guadeloupe in January 1979, President Carter had indicated to Callaghan that the US administration probably would be prepared to supply Britain with the new US Trident sea-based missile system as a replacement for the ageing Polaris fleet. In September 1979 the Thatcher government decided against cruise missiles, an option which had been canvassed in the Labour government by David Owen as the replacement for Polaris. On 6 December 1979 the relevant ministers decided to seek to purchase Trident missiles, a decision confirmed by the Cabinet.

Although Carter had assured her that he would supply Trident, he was worried that announcing this could trigger a Soviet response that would render it harder to get the SALT II Treaty on strategic arms limitation ratified by the Senate.

The Soviet invasion of Afghanistan at the end of the year put paid to any hope of ratification of SALT II, though both sides continued to observe it anyway. In return for supplying Trident, the Americans now wanted a commitment that Britain would increase its defence efforts and contribute to the research and development costs of the missile. They also wanted to be able to develop an air base on the British colony of Diego Garcia in the Indian Ocean. The Prime Minister considered that this made sense on strategic grounds anyway. On 2 June 1980 she finalised the terms for the acquisition of Trident with the US Defense Secretary, Harold Brown. The decision was announced in Parliament on 15 July.

When the Reagan administration came in, she was told by Weinberger in August 1981 that the US intended to proceed instead with the upgraded Trident II D5 missile system and was ready to make this available to Britain. In November, a group of ministers met to consider this offer. It was a difficult discussion in which, in her view, a number of feeble and unrealistic arguments were advanced. One minister was concerned at the impact on public opinion of acquiring a still more powerful missile; another thought it would be hard to keep Trident II out of arms control negotiations; a third felt that this raised the more fundamental question of whether Britain could afford to continue to maintain an independent strategic nuclear deterrent. Her own concerns were that the cost of the new missile might escalate and that Soviet anti-missile capabilities might increase.[116]

In January 1982 there was a further discussion. It was by then clearer that if Britain was to maintain an effective deterrent, which she was determined to do, they must acquire Trident II, while seeking to limit the cost.

She knew that Reagan and Weinberger would be anxious to help. As described elsewhere, the Americans insisted on a reprieve for the landing ships *Fearless* and *Intrepid*. They also wanted an extension of the British defence commitment in Belize. In return, thanks to Weinberger, she got a more favourable deal than for Trident I, with the British contribution to the research and development costs capped at $110 million. The total cost of Trident II was estimated at £7.5 billion, just over 3 per cent of the defence budget over the relevant period. When she heard the terms, she was delighted. She had driven this decision through some very lukewarm colleagues. The Defence Secretary, John Nott, had claimed to Carrington that two-thirds of the Cabinet and of the parliamentary party were opposed to Trident. This was highly exaggerated. The opposition was querulous and questioning, rather than serious. As news of the agreement was about to leak in the *New York Times*, the Cabinet Secretary informed ministers that it had to be announced forthwith, without further reference to Cabinet, which had earlier approved the Trident programme anyway.

☞

On 13 December 1981, with Soviet encouragement, General Jaruzelski's government sought to suppress the Solidarity movement led by Lech Wałęsa by imposing martial law in Poland.

Several European countries, including Germany, were hostile to Reagan's economic policies and attitude to arms control. Margaret Thatcher did not share these attitudes, but what she did find irritating was the way in which the Americans set about reacting to events like those in Poland in ways that inflicted more pain on their allies than on themselves or, arguably, on the Polish and Soviet regimes.

Ronald Reagan was outraged, convinced the Russians were responsible, and immediately announced sanctions against the Soviet Union including a halt to the export of equipment for the planned natural gas pipeline from Russia to western Europe. Sections of the US administration strongly disliked this project, which they thought would make Europe more dependent on the Soviet Union. But several companies in Europe, including Britain, had legally binding contracts to supply equipment which included US components for the Siberian gas pipeline. If the ban were applied to existing contracts, this would deprive British firms of over £200 million of business, affecting jobs in the engineering company John Brown especially badly.

She accepted that there was some force in the argument that if the pipeline went ahead, France and Germany would become more dependent on Soviet gas supplies. But she felt that these fears were exaggerated. In any event, neither France nor Germany were going to yield to US pressure on this. There also was American talk, unnerving to the Bank of England, about forcing Poland to default on its international debts, with severe effects on the European banks.

Reagan was determined to inflict real damage on the Soviet Union in response to the repression in Poland, with Weinberger expressing confidence that the allies might not like it but could be 'dragged along'. She was not prepared to be dragged along. She worried that there was a clear danger of US policies damaging western interests more than the interests of the communists and of provoking a major transatlantic quarrel. This, she concluded, was 'a time for some straight talking to our American friends'.

She saw Haig when he was still Secretary of State in London on 28 January 1982, raising her concerns with what she described as 'unusual vehemence'. She warned against any attempt to force a Polish default, which would hurt Poland but also cause serious problems for the western banking system. Whatever the Americans felt, the French and Germans were not going to abandon their contracts for the Siberian gas pipeline. Haig gave the impression of agreeing with her, and suggested she should send a message to Reagan, which she did. But Haig seemed increasingly isolated in Washington and was soon to be replaced.

Reagan sent her a message on 8 March stressing the need to halt or restrict export credits to the Soviet Union. Upset at European resistance to tougher sanctions in response to the repression in Poland, Reagan told his colleagues that the Europeans could have their pipeline, but not with US equipment or technology. On 18 June the Americans announced that the ban on the supply of oil and gas technology to the Soviet Union would apply not only to US companies, but also to their foreign subsidiaries and to foreign companies manufacturing American components under licence.

Mrs Thatcher was appalled by the decision and condemned it publicly. The government set about taking legislative action to frustrate the US attempt to assert extra-territorial authority. She was further annoyed when the US proposed to resume grain sales to the Soviet Union on the pretext that this would drain it of hard currency when, all too obviously, the real reason was to placate the US farm lobby.

The dispute came to a head in a meeting between her and Reagan in Washington on 21 June. Having discussed the Falklands in the immediate aftermath of the British victory, Reagan said that the pipeline sanctions too were a matter of principle. He had warned the Russians that unless Lech Wałęsa was released, there would be more sanctions. US technology could not be made available to John Brown for the pipeline. 'Mrs T.'s eyes blazed and she launched into a fierce attack on the President's decision,' wrote Nicholas Henderson.[117] She said that Britain honoured its contracts. The US was about to deliver wheat to the Soviet Union, very obviously in response to pressure from US farmers. She regarded the US position as hypocritical. After the meeting she said publicly that she was a staunch friend, but felt deeply wounded by the US decision: 'We must be pretty frank with our American friends.' Later in the year, Margaret Thatcher won this battle, with George Shultz brokering a compromise that allowed the existing pipeline contracts to be honoured.

In the midst of these arguments, in June 1982, during the last days of the Falklands conflict, Ronald Reagan made a largely ceremonial visit to Britain. He especially enjoyed riding with the Queen in the grounds of Windsor Castle. Reagan remained seriously underestimated in Europe, and nowhere more so than in Britain. In the Royal Gallery of Parliament he made a speech marked strongly by his own personal input and beliefs. Not many commentators understood its significance at the time.

Reagan started by saying that he believed the world was at a turning point. Ironically, Marx was right that they were witnessing a great revolutionary crisis, where economic demands were conflicting with those of the political order. But the crisis was happening not in the free market West, but in the home of Marxism-Leninism, the Soviet Union. It was the Soviet Union that was running against the tide of history. It was in deep economic difficulty. What he was describing was a plan and hope for the long term: the march of freedom and democracy would leave Marxism-Leninism on the ash heap of history. The ultimate determinant in this struggle would not be bombs and rockets, but a test of wills and ideas.[118]

The 'ash heap of history' phrase was borrowed from Trotsky. The majority of British and American commentators were far too sophisticated to fall for what they regarded as this crude anti-Soviet rhetoric, as were most Cabinet ministers. One commentator described his speech as 'wishful thinking, bordering on the delusional'. 'Very little can be built on the President's words,' commented *The Guardian*, adding that they reflected his 'benign blank hopelessness'. Tom Brokaw of NBC thought it 'naïve'. There was far more interest in the President's admittedly expert use of the autocue.

☞

In October 1982, Margaret Thatcher visited the Berlin Wall with Chancellor Kohl. In her speech she said that, despite all efforts to frustrate it, 'One day liberty will dawn on the other side of the wall.'

She was anxious that the unilateral disarmers were still making the running on nuclear issues. Although public opinion supported the government on the nuclear deterrent and against unilateralism, there were concerns about Trident, mainly on the grounds of cost and – above all – continuing resistance to the stationing of cruise missiles, along with an underlying streak of straightforward anti-Americanism. Unilateralism was now official Labour Party policy, with Michael Foot firmly committed to it. It received, in her view, a good deal of covert support from many in the media, including the BBC. A major campaign was being mobilised to stop the planned deployment of cruise missiles in 1983, with a permanent peace camp established at Greenham Common.

In the Washington embassy, I was responsible for liaison with the Americans on the nuclear arms negotiations. In the State Department, first Haig and then Shultz, along with their key officials, were conscious of the need to manage European sensitivities. But Weinberger and his principal deputy in the Pentagon, Richard Perle, were not really believers in arms control at all. The strategic arms limitation (SALT) agreements initiated by Henry Kissinger, they pointed out, had limited but not actually reduced the numbers of nuclear missiles, while the Russians were violating the anti-ballistic missile treaty and the prohibition of the manufacture of biological weapons. Richard Perle's hawkish statements on the subject had earned him the title of 'the Prince of Darkness'.

At this stage Reagan made the inspired appointment of ambassador Paul Nitze to conduct the intermediate-range nuclear force (INF) negotiations. The immensely distinguished, patrician and also extremely rich Paul Nitze was a formidable expert on nuclear deterrence, had served as Navy Secretary under President Kennedy, and was independent minded and very much his own man. In a private lunch on his appointment, I sought to reach an understanding with him that the only way to win the battle for European opinion was to demonstrate that we had made every possible negotiating effort before deploying the missiles – and then to go on negotiating thereafter. Paul Nitze certainly kept to his side of this bargain. He was determined, however, as was Reagan, that this time there must be real reductions in nuclear weaponry.

The Foreign Office and Ministry of Defence were proceeding on the assumption that the negotiating position would be based on the usual formula of equal limits on both sides. To their horror, Richard Perle came up with the revolutionary proposition that there should indeed be equal limits for intermediate-range nuclear missiles for both sides – and that these should be zero! This caused consternation in London and Bonn, as it was held to be non-negotiable. Margaret Thatcher did not like the 'zero option' as she feared it might contribute to decoupling US and European nuclear deterrence. This fear was exaggerated, given the array of other nuclear weapons available to NATO in Europe, and the British government was persuaded, with reluctance, to go along with the zero option.

In the run-up to the 1983 elections, in February the Prime Minister urged on Vice-President Bush, and then on Reagan, the need to take a new initiative in the INF negotiations. Paul Nitze already had assured us privately that if the Russians were prepared to accept equal numbers of missiles at some level above zero, but below what they currently had deployed, of course he would negotiate on that basis. In March this was formally incorporated into the US position as an interim proposal, the ultimate goal remaining zero. The Russians rejected the offer, preferring to rely instead on influencing European opinion to prevent deployment of the missiles.

The other highly sensitive nuclear issue in the run-up to
the election was that of control over the cruise missiles to be
deployed in Britain. There was a campaign in Parliament for a
physical 'dual key' arrangement, which had been offered by the
Americans but only if the UK purchased the missiles. In the
election campaign, it became vital for Mrs Thatcher to be able to
say publicly that no US nuclear missiles could be released from
British territory without the agreement of the British government. Although this always had been the basis for our nuclear
cooperation, the State Department was opposed to stating this
openly, as the same conditions did not apply to US nuclear weapons stationed in Germany. I appealed to the National Security
Adviser, Bud McFarlane who, having consulted his master, told
me that Ronald Reagan had responded that he would mortgage
the Washington Monument, if necessary, to help get Margaret
Thatcher re-elected. A formal exchange followed on 1 May in
which the Prime Minister agreed with Reagan the statement
that any use of the missiles would be the subject of a joint decision by the US and British governments.

In the run-up to the election she joined Reagan and the other
G7 leaders at a summit meeting in Williamsburg, Virginia, at
which she supported Reagan against attempts by Trudeau and
Mitterrand to water down support in the communiqué for the
deployment of cruise and Pershing missiles, while at the same
time attempting to negotiate to eventually eliminate such
weapons on both sides. Presented with what she regarded as
a 'weasel-worded' text, she impressed the Americans by flatly
refusing to sign it until an acceptable version was produced.

She repeated this kind of performance at the next G7 summit
in London in June 1984, where she ignored Trudeau's protests at

her 'heavy-handed and undemocratic' conduct in the chair, telling
Reagan airily that 'women know when men are being childish'.[119]

On 8 March 1983 Reagan had made a speech describing the
Soviet Union, to the horror of most European commentators, as
an 'evil empire'. Two weeks later, he caused further consternation by announcing his Strategic Defense Initiative (SDI), in
the course of which he called on the scientific community which
had given the world nuclear weapons 'to give us the means of
rendering these weapons impotent and obsolete'.

Margaret Thatcher regarded this as an unattainable dream.
But she did not agree with the absolute scepticism of many of
her officials about SDI and, in particular, the possibilities
of enhanced missile defence. As a scientist herself, she wanted to
know more about the science involved and welcomed briefings
from the Americans about it. 'Laid-back generalists from the
Foreign Office – let alone the ministerial muddlers in charge
of them – could not be relied upon,' she wrote. Science 'will
not stop for being ignored'.[120] She believed that Reagan had
grasped this essential point, but she never believed that this
could deliver the results he hoped for from it. What partially
converted her to SDI was a realisation of the impact on the
Russians, their constant attempts to drive a wedge between
her and Reagan on the subject and their concern to stop it at
almost any cost, increasing the West's negotiating leverage
with them.

The election triumphantly over, she visited Reagan again
in Washington in September. Both felt that the Soviet Union
was now more on the defensive. The Russians were going to
have to decide how to react to the deployment of INF missiles
in western Europe. They had just shot down a civil Korean

airliner, killing 269 passengers. She insisted that the British and French nuclear deterrents must not be included in the talks on strategic nuclear arms reductions (START) that Reagan was planning to launch with the Russians. He believed that once the Russians failed to prevent the INF deployment, they might start negotiating seriously; she was concerned about Soviet paranoia about their own security. But Reagan held that the Russians were now close to the limit of what they could spend on defence: their internal economic difficulties were close to reaching a point of no return. She reflected afterwards that they were 'very different people. He had an accurate grasp of the strategic picture but left the tactical detail to others. I was conscious that we must arrange our relations with the communists on a day-to-day basis in such a way that events never got out of control.'[121]

While in Washington, she made a speech to the Churchill Foundation: 'We have to deal with the Soviet Union ... not as we would like it to be, but as it is. We live on the same planet and we have to go on sharing it.'

In November 1983, NATO conducted one of its annual war games. The British intelligence services learned subsequently from Oleg Gordievsky that the Russians had genuinely believed that this might be the preparation for a first strike on the Soviet Union, causing them to place some of their nuclear-capable aircraft on alert. When Robert Gates, deputy director of the CIA, saw the report, he found it horrifying. The report confirmed Margaret Thatcher in her view that they must move beyond the rhetoric of the evil empire and engage more effectively with whatever new leadership emerged in Moscow.

The next cloud came out of a blue sky, this time in the Caribbean. For years the Reagan administration had detested the left-wing regime of Maurice Bishop in Grenada. Their suspicions were intensified when several hundred Cubans installed themselves on the island to build a new airport.

But on 19 October 1983 events took a totally unexpected turn as Bishop, returning from a visit to Cuba, was arrested by his colleagues on the Revolutionary Council. In a coup led by 'General' Hudson Austin, Bishop and five of his associates were murdered, while Austin's soldiers fired on an unarmed crowd. While Bishop did have popular support, there was no evidence that the appalling bunch of thugs who had now taken over had any at all.

The State Department issued a statement of concern about the safety of several hundred American students at a college on the island. A carrier group was diverted to the area, ostensibly for the purpose of evacuating US citizens if necessary.

Two days later, the Prime Ministers of the East Caribbean islands met in Barbados. Led by Tom Adams of Barbados and Eugenia Charles of Dominica, they decided to ask for US and British military intervention, with Jamaica also supporting the request.

The State Department, meanwhile, had been asking the Foreign Office in London what action it would take. They were told that, although Grenada was a member of the Commonwealth, its internal affairs were strictly a matter for the Grenadians. What had happened was regrettable, but we did not intend to do anything about it. We had not received any request from the Governor-General, Sir Paul Scoon (who in fact was in fear of his life). The Caribbean leaders' request for assistance was set aside.

The effect of this uncompromising response was to ensure that we were excluded from US planning.

Margaret Thatcher also was very cautious about any intervention. There were 200 British civilians whose lives could be put at risk. A British official from Barbados visited Grenada and reported that they were under no immediate threat. In addition, she could not see any legal basis to intervene.

As we were concerned about American intentions, on a Saturday morning, 22 October, I called on Admiral Jonathan Howe, Director of the Bureau for Politico-Military Affairs in the State Department. He assured me that, as yet, no decision had been taken to intervene and that the Americans were 'proceeding cautiously'. In reality, the President and Shultz had been awakened that morning in Augusta, Georgia, to be told of the East Caribbean leaders' request for intervention, and contingency planning was already underway.

Sunday began with the appalling news of the Hezbollah attack on the US Marine Corps compound in Beirut in which over 200 Marines were killed. The National Security Council went into continuous session, rendering it impossible to get to our usual contacts. They spent hours discussing the disaster in the Lebanon and the difficulty of any effective retaliation. At the end of the meeting there was a brief discussion of Grenada, following which Reagan gave the go-ahead for military intervention. Otherwise, he commented, 'the American people might as well have re-elected Jimmy Carter'.

After the meeting I was able to speak to a State Department contact, who told me that Grenada was now a subject on which there was 'no cable traffic'. By the morning, we were convinced that the Americans were close to intervening. The ambassador, Sir Oliver Wright, saw Eagleburger to press for consultation.

Although the Foreign Office was informed by lunchtime London time of our suspicion that the Americans were close to taking military action, this did not reach the Foreign Secretary, Geoffrey Howe, before he stood up in Parliament to answer questions from the opposition about US intentions. He said that he knew of no US intention to intervene. The US naval forces in the area were there to ensure the safety of US citizens.

The Americans knew that the Foreign Office was opposed to any intervention in Grenada, but the White House had been counting on a different reaction from the Prime Minister. Reagan sent the Prime Minister a message informing her that he was seriously considering the request from the East Caribbean leaders for the US to take military action. By the time this reached London, the Prime Minister was on her way to a dinner with Princess Alexandra and the US ambassador, who knew nothing about Grenada at all. By the time she returned to Downing Street there was a second message from Reagan telling her that he had decided to intervene.

Margaret Thatcher replied forthwith with a message objecting to intervention in a small independent nation, despite its unattractive regime. She telephoned the President who, by this stage, was briefing the Congressional leaders about his plans. Though disconcerted by her reaction, he made it clear that the operation would proceed. Within a few hours, US troops were landing in Grenada. The first to land were US Navy SEALs (special forces), who arrived at night at Government House, where a mightily relieved Sir Paul Scoon was delighted to sign a request for military intervention. This was regarded as sharp practice by the Foreign Office lawyers, but he had been far too terrified to do so before the US Navy SEAL team arrived to protect him.

Margaret Thatcher was furious at the embarrassment caused in Parliament and, she felt, in her relations with the Queen as head of the Commonwealth. She felt dismayed and let down by what had happened. She pointed out to Reagan the effect this unilateral US action was liable to have on British opinion at a time when her government was proceeding with the deployment of cruise missiles. The US action was indeed accompanied by a torrent of indignation in the British press at this intervention in the affairs of an independent Commonwealth country.

In an attempt to make up, Reagan telephoned her on 26 October, in the midst of an emergency debate in the House of Commons on Grenada. 'I was not in the sunniest of moods,' she wrote later. He did not have the usual difficulty of getting a word in edgeways. As he took her through the reasons for his decision, apologising for the embarrassment he had caused, he got only monosyllabic replies, in the frostiest by far of all their exchanges.

Meanwhile in Grenada, the US troops were greeted as liberators and democracy was in fact restored. There had been no real consultation because the Americans knew that we would seek to dissuade them from doing anything. George Shultz concluded that, on this subject, Mrs Thatcher was just plain wrong.[122] Years later, without much success, I attempted to persuade her, in this case, to admit that possibility herself.

As for the disaster that had overtaken the US-led multi-national force in Lebanon, she had questioned the wisdom of the venture from the outset (as had Weinberger) and limited the British contribution to a hundred men. She strongly disapproved of the Israeli intervention in southern Lebanon, engineered by the Likud government and Ariel Sharon. The suicide bomber attack on the US and French troops confirmed her view that they were a sitting target and she urged Reagan to withdraw them, which he had little option but to do. She regarded this as a classic lesson in the folly of military action without a clear objective.

☞

As the Russians remained obdurate in the INF negotiations, the moment was fast approaching when the missiles would actually have to be deployed. Greenham Common was surrounded by demonstrators and getting the missiles there by road would trigger scenes of mayhem, with serious risk of injury to both the police and demonstrators.

On instructions from the Ministry of Defence, I asked for an extremely private meeting with Richard Perle. Perle replied immediately that if the matter was as sensitive as that, the meeting could not possibly be held in the Pentagon. We met instead in a sushi bar nearby! I explained our concerns and that we would want the missiles airlifted into Greenham Common overnight on the US Air Force's giant C5 Galaxy aircraft. This plan was greeted enthusiastically by Perle, who proceeded to devote his formidable energies to implementing it.

When the missiles were deployed in Britain and elsewhere, the Russians walked out of the negotiations, as we had expected they would. In due course they were back, also as expected. By this time, Gorbachev had taken over the leadership in Moscow. The Russians suddenly accepted what had been so confidently predicted to be non-negotiable – that is, a real measure of nuclear disarmament. The INF Treaty, signed in 1987, resulted in the elimination of this entire category of nuclear weapons on both the western and Soviet side, and the removal of the missiles from Greenham Common. Mrs Thatcher and Reagan had reason to feel that this was a turning point in the Cold War – or rather the beginning of its end.

X

'I FELT AS IF THERE HAD BEEN AN EARTHQUAKE UNDER MY FEET'

In the lead-up to Reagan's re-election, the US budget deficit which, in the words of Bernard Ingham, was a 'constant source of worry to her prudent soul',[123] was starting to reduce. The British government's plans to privatise British Airways were being complicated by an antitrust case brought by the US Justice Department investigating whether price-fixing had contributed to the failure of Laker Airways. Margaret Thatcher had lobbied for more than a year for the administration to drop the case. Ten days after his re-election as President in November 1984, Reagan decided to do so, overruling the Justice Department. This was just in time for a further visit by the Prime Minister to Reagan at Camp David, where he enjoyed driving her around in a golf buggy.

She sought to convince him that Gorbachev was a new kind of Russian leader, modern-minded and more open to argument. To her alarm, he said of the Strategic Defence Initiative (SDI) that the aim was to reduce and eventually eliminate nuclear weapons. Nuclear weapons, she replied, had safeguarded the peace of Europe for the past forty years. Reflecting Oleg Gordievsky's reports, she warned against giving the impression that the US was seeking military superiority. She then produced from her handbag points she intended to make to the press, which she had already agreed with George Shultz, and put Reagan on the spot to endorse them. The US and western aim was to maintain balance, not achieve superiority. SDI testing and deployment, in view of treaty obligations, would be a matter for negotiation (a statement that infuriated the SDI hawks in the administration). The aim was to strengthen, not undercut, deterrence. East–West negotiations should aim to achieve security at reduced levels of offensive systems.

Shultz was delighted that she had bound the administration into differentiating between research and deployment of SDI in terms of US treaty obligations. On this and several other occasions, she was in fact conspiring with Shultz to ensure that the administration adopted more reasonable positions than would otherwise have been the case. Knowing the strength of her influence on Reagan, Shultz confessed afterwards that he used her 'shamelessly' for this purpose.[124] As Richard Perle observed, she never approached discussions with the Americans from a position of inferiority: 'Quite the contrary!' Kissinger felt that in this period she had achieved a degree of influence on US policy, in particular in relation to NATO and arms control, equalled only by Churchill.

In his inaugural speech for his second term as President, Reagan again talked of seeking the elimination of all nuclear weapons. This was followed almost immediately by a further visit by Margaret Thatcher to Washington in February 1985 to address a joint session of both houses of Congress. She devoted all her usual ferocious energy to preparing for this, once again writing and rewriting her speech until 4 a.m. on the day she delivered it. Reagan provided his personal autocue for her, plus tips on how to use it. In her speech she delivered an impassioned defence of the 'shield' of nuclear deterrence which had helped to keep the peace in Europe for forty years. She quoted Winston Churchill in his last speech to Congress, saying: 'Be careful above all things not to let go of the atomic weapon until you are sure and more than sure that other means of preserving peace are in your hands.' This was greeted with a standing ovation.

Geoffrey Howe, dismayed by the hawkish tone of her speech, set out to correct this in a speech of his own to the Royal United Services Institute. Questioning whether the technology would really work, he observed that there would be 'no advantage in creating a new Maginot Line of the twenty-first century in space'. This went down extremely badly with the Reagan administration. Margaret Thatcher apologised, but asked Bud McFarlane, the National Security Adviser: 'Are you keeping SDI under appropriate restraint, adhering to the ABM [anti-ballistic missile] treaty and so forth?'[125]

In July 1985 she joined an arms control seminar in Washington with Reagan, Shultz, Cap Weinberger and others. She delivered another lengthy defence of nuclear deterrence, causing Reagan to observe that 'she's not a great listener'. As she knew very well, however, all the senior members of his team agreed with her.

In November 1985 Reagan had a first meeting with Gorbachev in Geneva. Reagan 'had to admit – as Margaret Thatcher … predicted I would – that there was something likeable about Gorbachev'.[126] Gorbachev argued that SDI would trigger a new arms race. Both affirmed that 'a nuclear war cannot be won and must never be fought'. When Reagan reported on the talks to a NATO summit in Brussels, Margaret Thatcher warned that beyond the change of style, there had not yet been a change of substance on the Soviet side. They would continue to try to divide the alliance over SDI. She was 'pleased to hear' that the US would continue to abide by the ABM Treaty.

In mid-December 1985, a youthful Colin Powell was exposed to his first encounter with Margaret Thatcher, accompanying Weinberger to a meeting with her in Downing Street. The US military had held a competition to choose between a British cellular phone system called Ptarmigan and a French system with the unlikely name of Rita. Both were well ahead of US developments. It fell to Weinberger to explain to the Prime Minister why the British had lost the contract to the French. Notwithstanding her admiration for Weinberger, he was told how distressed she was at 'this shabby business. Nothing you can say will convince me that there wasn't dirty work at the crossroads. We've been cheated!'

Weinberger remained stoic under this onslaught. When he tried to explain why the US had chosen Rita, she cried, 'The French!', as if the word were an epithet. 'I am sure they did not play fair. Don't write that down, young man,' she told Colin Powell, who was both bemused and amused by her performance.[127]

On 27 December 1985, Palestinian terrorists opened fire on passengers at Rome and Vienna airports. British intelligence had evidence shared with the Americans of Libya's support for this and other acts of terrorism. The Libyan People's Bureau in London had been closed following the murder of WPC

Yvonne Fletcher in St James's Square in 1984. On 7 January the United States imposed sanctions on Libya with little consultation. Margaret Thatcher was not prepared to go along with this. Seventy-five per cent of Libyan oil was exported to Europe. She did not believe that sanctions against Libya would work and there were 5,000 British subjects there. She also warned at the time against retaliatory strikes, which she felt would be against international law. This point was rejected publicly by George Shultz: the US had the right to act against terrorist nations in self-defence and intended to exercise that right. In March the Libyans fired missiles at US aircraft patrolling off the Libyan coast; the Americans retaliated. On 5 April a bomb exploded in a discothèque frequented by US servicemen in Berlin, killing one and injuring sixty Americans. The intelligence confirmed Libyan involvement.

At 11 p.m. on 8 April, Reagan sent a message requesting support for the use of US F-111 aircraft stationed in Britain for an airstrike against Libya. Hurriedly consulting Geoffrey Howe and Michael Heseltine, Margaret Thatcher replied expressing concern at what was proposed. She wanted to know precisely what targets would be attacked and what the public justification would be. She was also worried about what would happen to British hostages in the Lebanon. She felt that there was an inclination to precipitate action in the US, while they felt the Europeans were capable only of inaction. She knew that the political cost to her of agreeing to the US request would be high.

Reagan replied that the action would not trigger a new cycle of violence. That cycle was already under way through increasingly violent Libyan acts of terrorism. Colonel Gaddafi had been encouraged, in his view, by the lack of a western response. The

US action would be aimed at Gaddafi's main headquarters and special security forces. The purpose was to show that terrorism could not be sponsored by a government without cost to the regime responsible.

The Prime Minister read and re-read Reagan's message, becoming more and more convinced that he was right. Whatever the cost to her, she felt that this was an issue on which she must back the United States. Geoffrey Howe, as Foreign Secretary, seemed against the US action. The Defence Secretary, George Younger, supported it. That afternoon she replied to Reagan pledging 'unqualified support' for action against Libyan targets that demonstrably were involved in supporting terrorist activities, and agreeing to the use of US aircraft from their bases in the UK.

At one point it seemed that the US was not intending to use F-111s from the UK, which would have eased her predicament, but it then was confirmed that they would need to do so. One of her favourite senior US officials, the very experienced General Vernon Walters, was despatched across the Atlantic as the President's envoy to see her. She told him how appalled she was that the gist of her exchanges with Reagan was being reported in the US press. They discussed the terms in which Reagan would justify the action and how much intelligence could be released to support it (causing some of the sources subsequently to dry up). The French would not permit their territory to be overflown and nor would Spain agree to do so overtly, so the US aircraft had to fly through the straits of Gibraltar.[128]

On 14 April she told the Cabinet Defence Committee that the US was justified in acting in self-defence under Article 51 (her favourite article) of the UN Treaty. The Americans had stood by us in the Falklands and the UK must support them now. Attending a reception at *The Economist* that evening, she was told by the editor, Andrew Knight, that she was looking very pale. As her complexion was never very ruddy at the best of times, she must, she felt, have looked like Banquo's ghost.[129]

Militarily, the raid was a success, but there were civilian casualties and the world television coverage concentrated on these. The reactions were even worse than she had feared. Not only the opposition but also Conservative backbenchers and newspapers criticised her permission for the use of British bases. Some members of the Cabinet very understandably felt that they should have been consulted beforehand. Even normally hawkish ministers like Norman Tebbit did not support the US action.

In the words of her foreign policy adviser, Charles Powell:

Nobody in the government supported the Americans over [Libya], absolutely nobody. She put it to the Cabinet and the only person who was vaguely in favour was Lord Hailsham, who was vaguely in favour on the somewhat eccentric grounds that his mother was American. The Foreign Office were wholeheartedly against it, believing it would lead to all our embassies in the Middle East being burned, all our interests there ruined. But she knew it was the right thing to do and she just said, 'This is what allies are for. If you're an ally, you're an ally. If one wants help, they get help.'[130]

Faced with a largely sceptical or hostile House of Commons, in a debate that, in her view, was rank with anti-American prejudice, she put up a bravura performance, as usual not giving an inch. The United States was Britain's greatest ally. They had suffered terrorist attacks and had decided to retaliate. The decision was justified and, as good allies, Britain had decided to support it.

She knew that there was still a lot of incomprehension among her own supporters. 'I felt that people were looking at me strangely, as if I had done something terrible.'[131]

The immediate consequence was the killing of two British hostages in Lebanon. The raid did appear for a while to be more effective than she had expected in producing a decline in Libyan-sponsored terrorism, but just before Christmas 1988 a bomb exploded on a Pan Am flight over Lockerbie in Scotland, killing 259 people. Three years later a Libyan intelligence official, Abdelbaset al-Megrahi, was given a life sentence by a Dutch court for this crime. At the time her support for the action earned her great credit in the US which, characteristically, she sought to parlay for specific actions by the Americans on issues of concern to her. Reagan was persuaded to make an appeal to the US Senate to pass legislation intended to make it easier to extradite IRA terrorist suspects to Britain, which they did by eighty-seven votes to ten.

One subject on which she made no progress whatever with Reagan or Shultz was the Arab–Israeli dispute. Despite her well-advertised support for Israel, she was fiercely critical of Israel's invasion of southern Lebanon. An admirer of Golda Meir and Shimon Peres, she was a determined critic of Begin, Shamir and the other Likud leaders, and she became exasperated at the US failure to put more pressure on them. She asked Shultz whether he thought that Shamir ever intended to negotiate over the West Bank or Jerusalem. His position denied basic rights to the Arabs and removed Israel's credibility. She got nowhere, but not for any lack of trying, as she consistently relayed to Reagan the concerns of the moderate Arab leaders – the Saudis, Gulf rulers, Mubarak and King Hussein – with all of whom she was on close terms. She regretted that the Israeli emphasis on the human rights of would-be Jewish emigrants from the Soviet Union was not matched by proper appreciation of the rights of landless and stateless Palestinians.[132]

☞

Following the raid on Libya, Neil Kinnock had denounced her in Parliament as Reagan's poodle. When he asked to see Reagan in the run-up to the 1987 election, the President allowed him just twenty minutes. He was told that Labour's commitment to unilateral disarmament was completely counter-productive in the nuclear arms control negotiations then underway with the Russians. Weinberger had stated publicly of Labour's defence policy: 'If you want us to go, we will go.' Anti-Americanism and unilateral disarmament, which had been in vogue the year before, became an insurmountable handicap for Labour in the 1987 election.

In October 1986 Reagan and Gorbachev held their second summit meeting in Iceland. Gorbachev offered 50 per cent cuts in the nuclear arsenals and an INF treaty, plus a comprehensive test ban treaty. The Soviet delegation, which included the new Foreign Minister Shevardnadze, had concluded that Russia had long since reached the limit of what it could afford to spend on defence. They had to try to stop the arms race. At this point Reagan stunned both sides by proposing that all nuclear weapons should be eliminated over time. The meeting foundered on Gorbachev's insistence that research on SDI must be confined to the laboratory, to which Reagan refused to agree. The US officials accompanying Reagan noted that there had been no commitment by Gorbachev to abolish all ballistic missiles, as Reagan had proposed. As Colin Powell and Richard Perle both observed, Reagan had scared his own side rather more than the Russians.[133] Gorbachev won a propaganda victory; it looked as if Reagan had rejected agreement in pursuit of an unrealisable dream. Yet the meeting did convince Gorbachev that Reagan was serious about an end to the Cold War.

Margaret Thatcher's reaction, when she heard what had happened at Reykjavik, was that it felt 'as if there had been an earthquake under my feet'. Apart from imperilling the UK Trident system, Reagan's dream of a nuclear-free world entailed abandoning the entire existing system of deterrence. She rushed across the Atlantic, meeting Shultz at the British embassy before helicoptering to Camp David. On this occasion the two principals met on their own. Declaring that it had been a wonderful meeting, as usual she produced a document from her handbag for use at the press conference which had in fact been pre-agreed with Shultz. This stated that priority should be given to an intermediate-range nuclear forces (INF) agreement, supported SDI research, noted that nuclear weapons could not be dealt with in isolation (given the need for a stable overall balance) and affirmed the President's strong support for the UK Trident programme.[134]

In the meeting at Camp David, Reagan had been briefed to forewarn her that the US was close to resuming arms sales to Argentina. When he failed to raise it, she did instead, simply saying: 'Oh, arms to Argentina. You won't, will you?' 'No,' said Reagan, to Shultz's dismay.

In turn she offered Reagan unconditional support in the scandal over covert US arms sales to Iran to finance supplies to the 'contras' opposing the Sandinistas in Nicaragua. She declared that she believed implicitly in the President's integrity. It was never proven that Reagan had approved or ever fully understood what Colonel Oliver North of the NSC staff had got up to with the 'contras'. He had, however, seen arms for Iran as an attempt to secure the release of US hostages in Lebanon, a trade that would have horrified the Prime Minister.

Visiting Washington again shortly after her 1987 election victory, her main theme was that, given that agreement had been reached on the elimination of all intermediate-range nuclear forces, there must be modernisation of short-range nuclear forces (SNF) to help ensure credible nuclear deterrence in Europe. Reagan and Shultz agreed with this.

The high point of her visit, however, was a television interview with Lesley Stahl on *Face the Nation*. Asked if she was not saddened by Iran-gate, she told Stahl repeatedly to stop being so downbeat. America was a great country, with a great President, full of enterprising, self-reliant people. She was advised to have as much faith in America as she, Thatcher, did. The US audience enjoyed her combative style rather more than the shell-shocked interviewer did. Reagan described her performance as 'magnificent'.[135] Similar treatment had been meted out earlier in the day to the ultra-right-wing Senator Jesse Helms, who, she had not forgotten, had been the sole voice in the Senate against Britain during the Falklands War.

Reagan attended his final NATO summit in Brussels in March 1988, making a moving tribute to all that the alliance had achieved. Margaret Thatcher was concerned at the success

Gorbachev was having with European opinion: NATO must not let down its guard.

Following a further Shultz–Gorbachev meeting in Moscow, General Colin Powell was sent to London to brief the Prime Minister. He reported Gorbachev as saying: 'I am going to do as much as I can. I will make it irreversible. And then someone else will come and replace me.' She advised him not to take this too seriously: 'Even I say things like that from time to time!'[136]

In June, Reagan returned to London on his way back from his own first visit to Moscow. He reassured her that he would not be rushed into finalising a new strategic arms reduction treaty. There had been no repeat of Reykjavik. He invited her to Washington to say goodbye and meet his successor after the US presidential election in November. In a speech at the Guildhall, he paid tribute to the role she had played in convincing him that he could indeed do business with Gorbachev.

In November, Margaret Thatcher made her final visit to the White House under Reagan. She was received with full military honours. Each paid a fulsome tribute to the role the other had played in bringing within sight an end to the Cold War. Reagan supported her views on SNF modernisation and Shultz congratulated her on her call for a more open and less protectionist Europe in her Bruges speech.

At the State Department, Shultz gave a dinner in her honour at which he presented her with a new handbag – in recognition, he said, of the role her bag had played in international diplomacy. At crucial times in all international meetings, he claimed, a text would be fished out of her handbag which became the statement they would adopt. 'The "special relationship" is as strong as ever,' he told Reagan, 'and remains of fundamental importance to the foreign policy of both nations.'[137]

On his last evening as President, Reagan wrote to her that their partnership had 'strengthened the ability and resolve of the western alliance to defend itself and the cause of freedom everywhere'. In her own valedictory tribute, Mrs Thatcher declared that he had achieved 'the most difficult of all political tasks: changing attitudes and perceptions about what is possible'.[138]

XI

'A SPECIAL RELATIONSHIP'

A few months after becoming Prime Minister, Margaret Thatcher attended a briefing meeting with the leading Foreign Office Sovietologists. They were told by Peter Carrington that if she said things they disagreed with, they must interrupt her. Expecting a straightforward Cold War warrior, they found they had underestimated her intellectual curiosity. In a subsequent full-day seminar at Chequers including the academics Michael Howard, Elie Kedourie and Hugh Thomas, she developed her views on nuclear weapons as a force for peace. Rodric Braithwaite, future ambassador in Moscow, was told by her afterwards that she was not at all sure that, in the event, she could press the button: 'I want grandchildren too,' she said, which he found an endearing flash of humanity.[139]

In September 1983 she convened a further seminar at Chequers, mostly of outside experts, about the Soviet Union. By this time cruise and Pershing missiles were close to being deployed in western Europe. Reagan had launched his strategic defence initiative. The Russians were embroiled in Afghanistan and the Soviet government was on the defensive in a way they had not been before. The experts in the seminar, she felt, were divided into two main camps: the political analysts tended to commit the error, in her view, of playing down the differences between the Soviet and western systems, while the historians, led by Robert Conquest, were convinced that the behaviour of totalitarian regimes was fundamentally different and they would react in very different ways to those in the West. One of her conclusions was that they must seek out whoever among the next generation of Soviet leaders could prove to be worth talking to. She was keen to expose them to the West, of which they mostly still knew very little.

It was Pierre Trudeau who first talked to her about Mikhail Gorbachev, who had visited Canada in 1983. Gorbachev had stuck to the party line on the INF negotiations, but without the 'blinkered hostility' of other Soviet leaders. The two main contenders to succeed Yuri Andropov as General Secretary of the party were thought to be Gorbachev and Grigory Romanov, who combined hard-line Marxism with an extravagant lifestyle including, to Margaret Thatcher's horror, smashing priceless crystal glasses from the Hermitage collection at his daughter's wedding.

In February 1984, the Prime Minister flew to Moscow for Andropov's funeral. She met and was profoundly unimpressed by his surprise successor, Konstantin Chernenko. Her next move was to invite Gorbachev and his wife Raisa to visit her at Chequers, which they did for the first time in December. It was their first visit to a west European country. The elegant Raisa Gorbachev appeared in a smart grey suit of a kind which, Margaret Thatcher commented, she would have thought of wearing herself. A huge fire was burning in the hearth. Several Cabinet ministers were present at the lunch. From the outset, Gorbachev appeared completely different from other Soviet leaders. He was relatively young, open and expansive, smiling and acting like a western-style politician.

After lunch, the Prime Minister and Gorbachev spent three hours meeting in the library. He did not, she found, depend on advisers or any notes prepared for the meeting. The conversation soon turned into a 'vigorous two-way debate' about the issues that concerned her and the nature of the Soviet and western systems. He described the reforms he was trying to make to the Soviet economy She said that it would do better if it operated on a free enterprise basis! He insisted on the superiority of the Soviet system in which, he claimed, people lived 'joyfully'. She criticised the restrictions on Jewish emigration. He claimed, she knew falsely, that those prevented from leaving had been work- ing on national security. She complained about Soviet funding of the National Union of Mineworkers, about which he claimed that he knew nothing.

If she had paid attention only to the content of his remarks, she would scarcely have found it encouraging. But she was impressed by the free and open manner in which he debated issues. She felt that it was the style more than the rhetoric that defined his personality. When he waxed eloquent about the dangers of a nuclear holocaust, she was unimpressed, contending that it was nuclear deterrence that had preserved the peace since the war. It was clear that the Russians were extremely concerned about Reagan's strategic defence initiative (SDI). They wanted it stopped at almost any price. She pointed out they had already deployed an anti-ballistic missile system around Moscow. She would not be separated from Reagan on this.

The other participants in this encounter felt that something special had happened. The normally unemotional Denis Thatcher saw it as a lunch that changed history. Margaret Thatcher had always prided herself on her instinctive judgements about people, telling the BBC the next day that she felt this was a man she could do business with. The Americans, towards whom this remark was in part directed, were not particularly impressed. They had yet to see Gorbachev deviate from the Soviet line on any matter of substance.[140]

When she went back to Moscow in March 1985, it was for Chernenko's funeral. Her meeting with Gorbachev was impaired by the silent, sardonic presence of the veteran hard-line Foreign Minister, Gromyko. Gorbachev spoke openly of the terrible state of the Soviet economy. The defection to Britain of the senior KGB officer Oleg Gordievsky resulted in the expulsion from Britain of a number of Soviet spies.

A meeting between Reagan and Gorbachev in Geneva in November yielded little of substance, but a good personal relationship had started to develop between them. Gorbachev continued to play skilfully on European nuclear anxieties.

In October 1986 there was a summit meeting of an entirely different order between Reagan and Gorbachev in Reykjavik, causing an appalled Margaret Thatcher to swiftly take corrective action in Washington (see Chapter X), aided by the US chiefs of staff as well as Shultz and Weinberger who all agreed with her.

When Gorbachev invited her to visit Moscow in February 1987, she held another preparatory seminar at Chequers. The sceptics considered that, despite the reformist language, Gorbachev was still pursuing orthodox objectives. Studying his speeches, she noted that in local party elections, party members were being given a limited choice as to who to elect. She familiarised herself with the key concepts of *perestroika* (restructuring) and *glasnost* (openness). There was little sign of the Soviet economy functioning better, but there was much greater freedom of expression, with dissidents like Andrei Sakharov now supporting Gorbachev. She too was convinced that he deserved support.

Having also consulted the KGB defector Oleg Gordievsky, she sent a message to Reagan about the need to do something to moderate Soviet concerns about SDI. She consulted Mitterrand, who felt that by changing the form, Gorbachev could end up changing the substance of the Soviet system, and Chancellor Kohl, who was worried about Gorbachev's chances of survival. In a speech on 21 March, she saw in his reforms 'a clear admission that the communist system is not working'.

She then set off for Moscow. When she inspected the present the Foreign Office had chosen for her to give to Gorbachev, she found that it consisted of two silver-handled hairbrushes. 'But he's completely bald,' she raged.

On the Sunday morning, she visited a monastery outside Moscow, accompanied by the communist 'minister for religious affairs'. Impressed by the intensity of the worshippers, she reflected that it would take more than limited reform of the communist system to contain the power of this Christian revival. In the afternoon, as she walked around a housing estate in a bleak Moscow suburb, the accompanying press could not believe the size of the crowd that gathered to meet her. Adam Boulton described her careering about the outer Moscow tenement blocks in her brand new Aquascutum suit as the most impressive demonstration of political canvassing he had ever seen. In the evening she attended a performance of *Swan Lake* at the Bolshoi with the Gorbachevs. Gorbachev told her about the intense unpopularity of the campaign he was trying to wage against alcoholism.

In the meetings on the following day, he complained that her recent statements about the Soviet Union had sounded like Churchill's 'iron curtain' speech. She replied that, despite his reforms, she had seen no evidence as yet that the Soviet Union had given up its expansionist policies in Ethiopia, Angola, Nicaragua or Afghanistan. She wanted to know whether the internal changes he was making, which she applauded, would lead to changes in foreign policy as well, in particular an end to the Brezhnev doctrine aiming for communist dominance worldwide. Gorbachev's National Security Adviser, Anatoly Chernyaev, described her in the meetings as being 'attractive, earnest but determined, stubborn, sometimes didactic. He was ironic, sarcastic, at times even abrupt.' The discussion became so passionate that they started interrupting one another. She had not expected so much heat to be generated so early in the meeting, but Gorbachev took it well.

There followed a philosophical argument about what differentiated the western and communist systems of government. He said that the Conservative Party represented the haves against the have-nots. A disquisition by him about his reforms brought the rejoinder: 'But, Mr First Secretary, you do realise that communism will never work, don't you?'

On arms control, he blamed her for opposing a world free of nuclear weapons. She said it had long been the Soviet objective to denuclearise Europe, leaving them with a preponderance of conventional weapons. But she was glad that he had broken the link the Russians had been making between SDI and an INF agreement. Chernyaev observed that the more heated the argument between them, the better they seemed to get on. She then went off to a lunch with the Sakharovs and other dissidents, whom she found supporting Gorbachev.

On her return to the Kremlin, she pressed him on allowing more Jewish emigration and on Afghanistan, where he seemed to be looking for some way out. By now guests were arriving for the dinner in her honour. Having no time to return to the embassy, she had to attend the dinner in the short woollen dress she had been wearing all day, feeling, she said, like Ninotchka in reverse.

On the following day, she gave a remarkable, unprecedented interview on Soviet television. Asked by three Soviet correspondents why she opposed nuclear disarmament, she went through every weapon in the Soviet nuclear arsenal, which she knew by heart, emphasising their superiority in conventional forces and then explained that an anti-ballistic missile (ABM) system had been deployed around Moscow, while none existed in the US. The interview went out uncut on Soviet television, which she regarded as proof that her belief in Gorbachev's integrity was not misplaced. The interview had a dramatic effect. In the words of the *Guardian* correspondent in Moscow, Martin Walker, her style, appearance and frankness made her appear like a creature from another planet. She very clearly had wiped the floor with her interviewers and Russian audiences had never been exposed directly to most of these facts or arguments or a performance of this kind before.

This was followed by a private dinner with the Gorbachevs. She asked how the 'working class' was defined in the Soviet Union. Raisa Gorbachev thought that anyone who worked, whatever their profession, was working class. Her husband at first argued that only blue-collar workers qualified, but then acknowledged that this did not do justice to the structure of modern society.

On the next morning, she had breakfast with refuseniks at the

British embassy, who had suffered severe persecution at the hands of the regime. She flew on to Tbilisi in Georgia, where she saw at the time no evidence of the nationalities problem that was to engulf the regime. But she returned convinced that the ground was shifting under the communist system and that, in de Tocqueville's words, 'the most dangerous moment for a bad government is generally that in which it sets about reform'. Despite their quite fierce exchanges, she had developed a real affection for Gorbachev and his wife. She never underestimated the risks he was taking in pressing for increasingly far-reaching reforms.[141]

Chernyaev felt that, self-evidently, Thatcher had got the better of the argument about free market reforms. She also had exposed the contradiction, which Gorbachev acknowledged to the politburo after their meeting, between his internal reforms and the continuance of old-style Soviet foreign policy, which he proceeded to set about changing, having become convinced that it was unaffordable anyway. According to Chernyaev, Gorbachev told the politburo that 'the fact that Thatcher supports *perestroika* is very important. The Americans regard this as her biggest mistake!'

In December 1987 Gorbachev accepted her invitation to stop over at the RAF base of Brize Norton on his way to Washington to sign the INF Treaty. The Americans had asked her to press him on Afghanistan, where there were signs that he was looking for a way to disengage. Gorbachev had fallen out with Boris Yeltsin, head of the party in Moscow. Within the politburo, only the Foreign Minister, Eduard Shevardnadze, and Gorbachev's close adviser, Alexander Yakovlev, were thought to be fully committed to his reforms.

Gorbachev found Margaret Thatcher 'not an easy partner

for us', given her fierce anti-communism. But he enjoyed their exchanges about economic policy, knowing what she had achieved for the British economy. As for her criticisms, he acknowledged that 'she was able to substantiate her charges with facts'.[142]

Gorbachev described the difficulties he was facing. She told him how infuriated she was that the Soviet and especially the western media kept describing his opponents as 'conservatives'. Discussing the negotiation to reduce strategic nuclear weapons (START), she made clear that Britain would retain Trident, which Gorbachev described as like 'sitting on a powder keg'. On Afghanistan, he said that a solution would be easier if the West stopped arming the rebels. On human rights, he argued that these were a matter for the countries concerned. She asked him privately if Oleg Gordievsky's family could be allowed to join him in London. Gorbachev pursed his lips and gave no reply. By February 1988, he was indicating that Soviet troops would indeed be leaving Afghanistan.

☞

In November 1988 she visited Poland, a country for which she had always felt affection, then still under General Jaruzelski. To welcome her, the government announced the closure of the Gdansk shipyards, home of Solidarity, on the 'Thatcherite' grounds that they were, supposedly, uneconomic. Jaruzelski even congratulated her on her trade union reforms! In preparing for her visit she had consulted the Pope, who had made his own historic visit to Poland the year before. She visited the church where Father Jerzy Popiełuszko had preached sermons against communism, before being murdered by the security police. As the congregation broke into a Polish hymn on her arrival, she had no doubt that it was his creed and not that of those who killed him that would prevail in Poland.

The next day was one she would never forget. The scenes on her arrival at the Gdansk shipyard were 'unbelievable'. She met Lech Wałęsa, under a form of house arrest. She gave him some fishing tackle, having heard he was a keen fisherman. Thousands of shipyard workers greeted her cheering and waving Solidarity banners. It struck her that the Solidarity leaders did not have a specific set of objectives. Characteristically, she set about trying to formulate these. They decided together that what she must impress on Jaruzelski was the need to legalise the movement. When they visited a church nearby, the congregation rose and sang the Solidarity anthem, 'God give us back our free Poland'. She could not keep the tears from her eyes.

Unlike Gorbachev, Jaruzelski had imposed a news blackout on her visit to Gdansk. She told him that she had been impressed by Solidarity's moderation. Any attempt to ignore them would court disaster.

Gorbachev accepted her invitation to make an official visit to Britain in April 1989. He was uncertain about the intentions of the incoming Bush administration and counting on her to use her influence with them which, he noted, she proceeded to do. She understood that he had reached a difficult and unpopular phase in his reforms, with the old order being demolished and people not knowing what would take its place.

Some of President Bush's advisers, including the National Security Adviser, Brent Scowcroft, and Robert Gates, head of the CIA, were still at the time very sceptical about Gorbachev. Scowcroft regarded him as a new and more dangerous type of Soviet leader, precisely because of his ability to influence European opinion. He suspected, as he put it, that they were still dealing with 'a Brezhnev system with a humanitarian paint job'.[143] Astonishingly, in retrospect, it was not until December 1989, over a year after his election, that George Bush held his first meeting as President with Gorbachev in extraordinarily unsuitable circumstances on board US and Soviet ships in storm conditions in the harbour of Valletta, Malta.

In June 1989, Solidarity had won the elections in Poland and Jaruzelski had to accept the result. Demonstrations led to the fall of the hard-line Erich Honecker in East Germany in October. The demolition of the Berlin Wall began on 10 November. By the end of the year, Václav Havel had been elected President in Czechoslovakia and Ceauşescu had been overthrown in Romania. She did not believe that it would be easy to establish democracy and free enterprise in these countries. The changes around her were happening much faster than she or anyone else had anticipated because, by this stage, Gorbachev had indeed renounced the Brezhnev doctrine. She had been proven right in her judgement about him. He wanted to reform communism, rather than abolishing it, which she considered to be impossible. But she felt him to be 'humane'. In the crises of the late 1980s, she did not believe that he would use force to bring East Germany or any of the other countries in eastern Europe back into line, despite the intense pressures on him to do so. Her concern was that the permanence of these changes depended on the survival of a reformist government in Moscow. It was vital to avoid actions by the West that could appear provocative to the Soviet leadership or military. In her view, that applied particularly to the prospect of German reunification.

She had always been an ardent advocate of freedom for the Baltic states, though, conscious of the need to avoid making things impossible for Gorbachev, she urged caution on President Landsbergis of Lithuania when she saw him in London in November 1989. Ukraine already had a special status as a separate member of the United Nations, but she was cautious about encouraging other parts of the Soviet Union to secede.

It was, she felt, one thing to expect a military superpower, even a sickly one, to change its policies, another to expect it to commit hara-kiri. Gorbachev told her at a meeting in Paris that his 'stopping point' was the external perimeter of the Soviet Union. She did not accept this, but took the warning seriously. Over lunch in the Kremlin, Gorbachev had recalled General de Gaulle's complaint about the difficulty of governing a country which had 200 types of cheese. Gorbachev said how much more difficult it was with over a hundred nationalities. 'Especially when there is a shortage of cheese,' added Deputy Prime Minister Albakin.[144]

She told George Shultz: 'Gorbachev thinks there are problems with the way the system works; he thinks he can make changes to make it work better. He doesn't understand that *the system is the problem.*'[145]

The emergence of Boris Yeltsin as a radical reformer ought to have strengthened Gorbachev's position, but the two were bitter rivals. By now she felt protective towards Gorbachev but, she acknowledged, he remained a communist to the end. There was a tendency in the West, particularly in Washington, to write off Yeltsin as a buffoon. She doubted this and wanted to see for herself. When he asked to see her in London in April 1990, she agreed enthusiastically, having first cleared this with Gorbachev. Yeltsin had been the only member of the politburo to declare that it was the Communist Party that was responsible for the crisis in Russia and had driven millions into poverty. Democratic centralism should be rejected and replaced by genuine democracy. He also wanted an end to the special status of the Communist Party.

She found him to be far more of a typical Russian than Gorbachev. But he had thought through some of the fundamental problems more clearly. She said that she supported Gorbachev. He said he knew that she did and that he had started by doing so as well. But *perestroika* had been intended to make communism more efficient. This was impossible. It was necessary to go much further, including the introduction of a market economy. Unlike Gorbachev, he had escaped the communist mindset. They had to decentralise and give more power to the republics. She was impressed, but when she reported to George Bush on her favourable impressions she was told that the Americans did not share them, which she regarded as a serious mistake. He and Scowcroft were at the time deeply sceptical about Yeltsin, following a spectacular display of drunkenness on a visit by him to the United States.[146]

She made her final visit to the Soviet Union as Prime Minister in June 1990. She found Gorbachev less ebullient than usual, but still good-humoured. She promised him her continuing support. She tried to convince him that it was in Soviet interests that a unified Germany should be part of NATO. To her surprise, he did not rule this out. He was more difficult about Lithuania. She gave him evidence that the Soviet Union still had an active biological weapons capability, about which he claimed to know nothing. It was only when Yeltsin took over as President that effective action was taken to terminate the biological weapons programme.

She did, however, persuade Gorbachev to put a stop to Russian efforts to remove the British embassy from its historic site on the Moskva River opposite the Kremlin. Stalin had been upset to gaze out of his window and see the Union Jack flying there every morning. The British government previously had agreed to move but she persuaded Gorbachev that it should remain as the ambassador's residence. When a member of her entourage asked about the cost, 'You cannot put a price on prestige' was the reply.

She had asked to see the Soviet generals, who she met at the Defence Ministry. They were, according to Rodric Braithwaite, British ambassador at the time, tickled pink at the prospect of meeting her but apprehensive, no doubt remembering how she had dealt with the Soviet defence correspondents on television three years before. Mrs Thatcher said that it was nuclear weapons that had kept the peace; their great advantage was that once you had them no one wanted to attack you. The generals nodded sagely, but said that while they might have kept the peace in Europe, they were dangerous elsewhere. She went on to visit Leninakan, one of the cities hit by an earthquake in Armenia. Braithwaite could not believe the reception she received, with over 100,000 people turning out to meet her.[147]

She went on to visit a British exhibition in Kiev, portraying the house of a British working-class family. This was a hit with the Ukrainians but, to her distress, the teenager's bedroom was a mess. She was persuaded with some difficulty that it was more authentic not cleared up. Everywhere she went, she was confronted by blue and yellow flags and demands for Ukrainian independence. She did not think Gorbachev would give up Ukraine without a struggle. Summoned to meet the Ukraine Parliament, she felt unable at the time to promise a British embassy in Kiev, though she did feel subsequently that an independent Ukraine was strategically advantageous for Europe and the West. She felt doubtful that the Soviet Union could ultimately be held together.

She visited Prague to congratulate President Havel whom, although well to the left of her, she liked and admired, and Václav Klaus, whom she found to be a kindred spirit. She got an equally warm reception from the new regime in Budapest.

Attending the Conference on Security and Co-operation in Europe (CSCE) summit in Paris on 20 November, she had her last meeting as Prime Minister with Gorbachev. They discussed the situation in the Soviet Union where he observed that, as an experienced politician, she understood the dangers he was facing. She said a quiet 'God bless you' to him, before returning to the British embassy to find that she had not won an adequate majority in the first round of the Conservative Party leadership election.

In his memoirs, Gorbachev waxed lyrical about her. 'Margaret Thatcher did much to support our perestroika.' She had her own views on his reforms, which she saw as going in the same direction as hers. 'She genuinely wanted to help us and to mobilise the efforts of the western nations in support of her policies.' During the attempted August 1991 coup, she spoke out in defence of democracy and of him and his family. One must also give her credit, he added, for her services to her own country. 'Mrs Thatcher took over at a time when the United Kingdom was lagging behind the other major western nations and she succeeded in changing both the domestic and the international situation of her country.' He deplored her authoritarianism and 'rough methods' in the run-up to the Gulf War but, 'All in all, she was a strong advocate of western interests and values indeed. Margaret Thatcher had much of what I would call the "Old English Spirit", at least as we Russians usually understand it.' As for her resignation, 'It was a noble act. Nevertheless, I regretted it.'[148]

She continued, even after her downfall, to enjoy a special status in Russia. 'You can have Gorbachev and we'll have Thatcher', was the reaction of many in Moscow.

XII

'THE WHOLE WORLD WILL BE
AGAINST YOU, LED BY ME'

In the morning of 1 April 1989, a small party waited on the tarmac at Windhoek airport for an improbable visitor to arrive. The RAF VC10 touched down exactly on time. The Prime Minister marched down the steps, showing no signs of having spent a night on the plane, with Denis Thatcher, Charles Powell and Patrick Fairweather of the Foreign Office in tow. The accompanying press descended in her wake, blinking in the sunlight, bemused at arriving in remote and beautiful Namibia instead, as they had expected, at Heathrow.

Her visit to Namibia had been decided at the very last minute, a ceasefire between the South Africans and the guerrilla forces of the South West Africa People's Organization (SWAPO) having come into force a few hours before. This was day one of the implementation of the UN plan to hold elections and bring Namibia to independence, as we had done in Rhodesia nine years before. She wanted to show support for the peace process now under way.

The Prime Minister was greeted by the last South African governor of the territory, Louis Pienaar, and met the very pukka

Sandhurst-trained Indian head of the UN force, General Prem Chand. She was whisked off to have lunch in their tented camp with the British military contingent. The rest of us were offered fizzy water but, thoughtfully, they had provided an otherwise indistinguishable glass of gin and tonic for Denis Thatcher. We then set off for the British-owned Rössing uranium mine, on which Namibia depended for the majority of its exports. There had been fierce pressure on Rio Tinto to close down the mine, which would have been a disaster for Namibia, as it would have been extremely difficult ever to open it up again. Instead it had set an example to the rest of the territory by developing housing, health, pensions, safety and other standards far superior to those anywhere else in the country.

As we boarded the plane for Rössing, the first reports were coming in of large-scale SWAPO incursions and clashes on the Angolan border. By the time we returned to Windhoek, it was clear that the entire agreement was threatened. Louis Pienaar reported that large armed SWAPO columns, crossing the border in direct contravention of the terms of the ceasefire, had been intercepted by the South African forces. Both sides already were behaving as if the agreement was no longer in existence.

The large, rotund and extremely tough Martti Ahtisaari, who later was to become President of Finland, was in an impossibly difficult position as the UN representative in charge of a settlement that was falling apart around him. The Prime Minister told Ahtisaari that he must get agreement from the UN Secretary-General, Pérez de Cuéllar, to authorise South African ground forces to stop the SWAPO incursions which were a clear breach of the ceasefire. Otherwise the settlement would be lost.

The scene shifted to a long and extremely difficult meeting at the airport with the South African Foreign Minister, Pik Botha. With a thick lock of black hair falling down across his forehead, built like a buffalo and habitually clutching a large glass of whisky in his hand, he was one of the world's great theatrical performers. But on this occasion, though extremely overwrought, he was not play-acting. He and his outstanding deputy, Neil van Heerden, had invested much personal credit in negotiating an honourable way out for South Africa from Namibia. He now had every hawk in the South African security Establishment, led by President P. W. Botha, chomping at the bit to resume the fight against their foes in SWAPO. Under pressure from his President, he was adamant that the South Africans would have to take the law into their own hands and call in air strikes against the SWAPO columns, whether the UN authorised these or not.

Mrs Thatcher said that she had told Ahtisaari that he must call Pérez de Cuéllar and get him to authorise the local South African forces to deal with these incursions. Pérez de Cuéllar, with whom we had many dealings over Rhodesia and the Falklands, was an exceptionally stalwart Secretary-General, who, unlike most of his predecessors and successors, was unafraid to take decisions, and we believed he would respond. But she warned Pik Botha in no uncertain terms that if the South Africans took unilateral action and used their air force, 'the whole world will be against you – led by me!'

This argument went on for two hours, with frequent calls by Pik Botha to Pretoria, until at last, fearing it might go on forever, Denis Thatcher put his foot down. 'Enough of this, we are going home,' he declared. This was not a style in which anyone else was accustomed to addressing the Prime Minister, but she got to her feet as instructed. As I returned to Windhoek, I was told by Ahtisaari that the UN had authorised action to deal with the incursions and by Pik Botha that the air strikes had been called off.

Margaret Thatcher boarded her plane extremely reluctantly. She clearly was attracted by the prospect of continuing to conduct the affairs of Namibia. In the midst of this crisis, Martti Ahtisaari and Prem Chand had badly needed her support. Pérez de Cuéllar, who had supported us in Rhodesia, did so on this occasion as well. Within a couple of days, the ceasefire was restored. As Margaret Thatcher put it in her memoirs, she had been the right person in the right place at the right time.[149]

☞

Following the resolution of the Rhodesia conflict, Margaret Thatcher had enjoyed a brief honeymoon with the other Commonwealth leaders. She understood that this was simply a prelude to addressing the issues of Namibia and South Africa, but her ideas on how to do so were very different from theirs. The UN Security Council resolution calling for independence for Namibia was not supposed to be subject to any conditions at all, but the western 'contact group' had made no progress in persuading South Africa to withdraw. Instead a proxy war was being conducted in southern Angola between Angolan government forces, bolstered by 30,000 Cuban troops supplied by the Russians, and the National Union for the Total Independence of Angola (UNITA) rebels led by Savimbi, supported by South Africa. The South West Africa People's Organization kept trying to push forces across the border from their camps in Angola, but militarily the South Africans remained very much in control.

As she recorded in her memoirs, she did not share the established Foreign Office view of Africa. Given that fundamental
change was indeed required in South Africa, the question was
how best to achieve it. It seemed to her that the worst approach
was to further isolate South Africa, as isolation contributed to
a siege mentality on the part of the Afrikaners. They would
not relinquish power without safeguards. The South African
economy was run mainly on free enterprise lines and most of its
neighbours depended on it – a fact regarded as too inconvenient
to mention at Commonwealth meetings.

She reacted with genuine indignation to any suggestion
of racism. In my own discussions with her, there was never
any doubt about her opposition to apartheid. She regarded any
racially based legislation as totally incompatible with her meri-
tocratic vision of society in which, if someone had the merit and
capacity for hard work, they deserved to get on, irrespective of
race and creed and so much the better if they came from modest
origins.[150] She saw the apartheid laws as inhuman and absurd,
understanding very well that the people they alienated most
were the entire black elite on which the future of the country
would depend.

She did, however, feel a good deal of sympathy for the white
population of South Africa, whom she credited for the country's economic development. She was unimpressed by what she
regarded as the 'half-baked socialist policies' being pursued by
many African governments at the time and unconvinced about
their competence. As she observed to me, she also feared that
most African governments did not understand that it was in
their own interests to limit their own power, preferring instead
to try to suppress the opposition and control the press and

judiciary. She wanted to see South Africa progressively reinte-
grated into the international community through step-by-step
reform and did not regard this as an ignoble objective.

Having been introduced to him by the author Laurens van
der Post, she was an admirer of Chief Buthelezi, whose Inkatha
Freedom Party movement, based in rural Zululand, was the chief
internal rival to the African National Congress (ANC). I too was
impressed by Buthelezi, who consistently had refused to negotiate with the government until Mandela was released. He and the
ANC were engaged in a bitter and bloody power struggle in the
province of Natal. I discovered that in Michael Caine's film *Zulu*,
the role of King Cetshwayo was played by Buthelezi himself. He
had a much better grasp of economics than the ANC and a low
regard for the achievements of the 'armed struggle'.

Visiting Buthelezi in his stronghold in Ulundi was like stepping back in time on the African continent. On ceremonial
occasions he was to be found brandishing a battleaxe and wearing
a necklace of lions' teeth, disguising a formidable intelligence. In
an attempt to broaden Laurens van der Post's contacts, I arranged
for him to meet the ANC deputy leader, Thabo Mbeki. But this
was not a success, as Laurens dismissed the pipe-smoking Thabo
as unacceptably westernised.

Within South Africa, President P. W. Botha had started by
presenting himself as a modernising reformer, though none of his
changes gave any effective representation to the black community. His Foreign Minister Pik Botha, however, had negotiated
the Nkomati Accord, contributing to a relaxation of tension with
Mozambique. In June 1984 President Botha visited Europe for
the fortieth anniversary of the Normandy landings (ironically, as
he had been a Nazi sympathiser during the war). Being a believer

in engagement rather than ostracism, the Prime Minister invited him to visit her at Chequers. The veteran anti-apartheid campaigner, Bishop Trevor Huddleston, met her to urge her not to see Botha. She replied that she wanted to tell Botha face-to-face that South Africa must change. The opponents of apartheid never seemed to her to grasp that capitalism itself was a force for reform and political change, eroding the apartheid laws and creating a black middle class which ultimately would insist on a share of power.

President Botha complained that he never received any credit for improvements that had been made in the conditions of black South Africans. In return he got a forthright lecture about the continuance of forced removals of black people from areas reserved for the whites, and about the need to release Nelson Mandela. She did not believe that any long-term solution could be achieved without his cooperation. There was no progress in discussing Namibia, where the South Africans were determined to remain in control so long as the Cubans remained in Angola.

She found P. W. Botha charmless and inflexible, but she remained convinced of the importance of a continuing dialogue with other members of his government. As unrest spread across South Africa, in 1985 a state of emergency was declared. Foreign banks led by Chase Manhattan refused to roll over South African loans. Under pressure from Congress, President Reagan agreed to limited sanctions; the European Community was moving in the same direction.

At the Commonwealth heads of government meeting in the millionaires' playground of Lyford Cay in the Bahamas, she said that she had accepted the European sanctions but would go no further. Over dinner she was attacked by the Australian Prime

Minister, Bob Hawke, and replied with vigour. She was urged by the Commonwealth Secretary-General, Sonny Ramphal, to compromise and show goodwill.

On the next day, she was lectured on her lack of political morality, her perceived preference for British jobs over black lives and her lack of concern for human rights. The accusations became more vitriolic and personal until she exploded. 'To their palpable alarm, I began to tell my African critics a few home truths.' She pointed out the extent to which most of them were trading with South Africa, while urging others not to do so. They were reminded of their own 'less than impressive' records on human rights. When the Ugandan representative accused her of racial discrimination, she recalled the expulsion of the Ugandan Asians to Britain.

Over lunch, she decided to make small concessions by accepting a ban on the import of Krugerrands and on official support for trade promotion to South Africa. 'As I entered the room they all glared at me ... I had never been treated like this and I was not going to stand for it.' She told them that she had never been so insulted and this was no way to conduct international business. They all protested that it was not personal. She replied that it clearly was. She then announced her two concessions, which were accepted.[151]

The heads of government agreed to send a group of 'eminent persons' to South Africa, which she saw as a way of fending off sanctions and enabling her to press the South Africans for further reforms. She sought to persuade Geoffrey Howe to become one of the eminent persons, but he resisted, no doubt calculating the chances of success as low. When he protested that he was Foreign Secretary and could not do both jobs, she untactfully suggested that she could do his while he was away.

In a press conference she described the concessions she had made on sanctions as 'tiny', to the dismay of Geoffrey Howe and the Foreign Office.

The 'eminent persons' visit to South Africa was, she acknowledged, a disaster. Having met Mandela and the South African government and been encouraged by Pik Botha to believe that they could play a positive role, the mission was torpedoed when P. W. Botha ordered the South African forces to launch raids during their visit on ANC targets in Botswana, Zambia and Zimbabwe.

When a Commonwealth mini-summit convened in London to review policy towards South Africa, she knew that, with the ANC banned, Mandela still in prison and the government having imposed a state of emergency, there was no prospect of political progress. The US Congress was pressing for tougher sanctions and, later in the year, overruled President Reagan's veto against them. There was much talk in the press of the Commonwealth breaking up. She did not believe that the pro-sanction views of most of the commentators were really representative of British opinion and there were indeed many who shared her irritation at being lectured on human rights and sanctions by African Presidents who never hesitated to lock up their own political opponents or trade with South Africa.

In an atmosphere every bit as unpleasant as that at Lyford Cay, she found Kenneth Kaunda, President of Zambia, arguing that if more sanctions were not imposed, South Africa would go up in flames. Robert Mugabe was equally intransigent, with the Canadian and Australian Prime Ministers, Brian Mulroney and Bob Hawke, playing in her view to the African gallery. The list of sanctions they wanted included cutting off air links; banning investment and agricultural imports, the promotion of tourism, new bank loans, imports of uranium, coal, iron and steel; and the withdrawal of consular facilities. She was particularly irritated by Australian demands for a ban on South African agricultural exports which, self-evidently, would benefit their own farm lobby. She pointed out that these measures, if enforced, would cause mass unemployment in South Africa, putting millions of black South Africans out of work. This argument made no impression. She did, however, agree to go along with a ban on coal, iron and steel imports, if the European Community went ahead with one later in the year, and to ban new investment and the promotion of tourism. In the event, the Germans blocked a European ban on the import of coal.

As Britain was taking over the Presidency of the European Community, it was agreed that Geoffrey Howe should visit South Africa to press for political change and the release of Mandela. He was once again reluctant to go and, as she acknowledged, his reluctance proved justified. In Zambia, he was berated on television by President Kaunda and would have done his political prospects at home more good if he had walked out of the meeting. He then found it impossible to make any progress with P. W. Botha, who lectured him against foreign interference in South African affairs. She learned later that he felt he had been set up for an impossible mission. She had, again, underestimated the intransigence of P. W. Botha.

I was despatched by her to be ambassador to South Africa in 1987 because she wanted to play a more activist role than the embassy had been doing, having been instructed by the Foreign Office to keep a low profile and engage in damage limitation. We had more at stake there than any other country – by far the largest investments and, in that and many other respects, the most to lose. Of the 1.5 million English-speaking white South Africans, nearly a million either had or were entitled to British passports. The Home Office had begun to worry what might happen if all or half of them decided to migrate to Britain. Important British economic interests were at stake; she had no intention of throwing them away.

In a first meeting with P. W. Botha, in September 1987, I told him how infuriated the Prime Minister had been by the cross-border raids that had destroyed the Commonwealth negotiating mission. She would, a few weeks later, be facing another Commonwealth conference and South Africa needed to avoid any actions that could further increase its isolation. I did not know how much longer it would take finally to see the end of apartheid. But we were determined to contribute to resolving the Namibia problem, which would be very much in South Africa's interests.

Neither I nor anyone else I knew warmed to P. W. Botha on this or any other occasion. His domed head and tinted glasses gave him the appearance of a B-movie villain. He was in the habit of receiving me in a study lit only by his desk lamp, conjuring up images of what it must have been like calling on Hitler in his bunker. He was prone to furious rages and his ministers were terrified of him. On one occasion, infuriated by the television news, he telephoned the South African Broadcasting Corporation to get it changed in the middle of the programme. When Hendrik Verwoerd was assassinated in Parliament, brandishing his fist in her face, he had yelled at apartheid's most ferocious critic, Helen Suzman, that she was responsible for what had happened.

My close friend and colleague, Chester 'Chet' Crocker, Reagan's negotiator on Namibia, was being criticised by the

European Foreign Ministries, including our own, for linking South African withdrawal from Namibia to the withdrawal of the 30,000 Cuban troops in Angola. This was a good example of the bizarre positions diplomats, from time to time, get themselves into. Personally I thought the linkage entirely justified and so did the Prime Minister. I did not see how, otherwise, we were going to persuade the South Africans to withdraw from Namibia. As the Americans had no embassy in Angola, we were able to give them some very effective help in the negotiations through our embassy in Luanda, headed by Patrick Fairweather.

A major tank battle won by the South Africans in October 1987 in southern Angola was followed by a counter-move by the Cubans, pushing tanks up to the Namibian border. The war was becoming increasingly dangerous for both sides. It also had become extremely unpopular in Cuba. The new Soviet Foreign Minister, Eduard Shevardnadze, disconcerted the Angolans by informing them that in future Russia's relations with them and other African governments were going to be conducted on the basis of cost–benefit analysis!

In January 1988 the Angolans indicated that they might, after all, accept the principle of Cuban withdrawal. In June there was a further clash between the Cubans and South Africans on the Namibian border. In July the Cuban negotiator, Carlos Aldana, showing himself to be more realistic than the Europeans, told his South African counterpart, Neil van Heerden, that the linkage with Cuban troop withdrawal was accepted. In December the agreement was signed on the implementation of the process leading to Namibian independence – a triumph of persistence by Chet Crocker, but also by Pik Botha and van Heerden.

But, with Reagan's departure, Crocker by now was close to

leaving the scene. The new Secretary of State, James Baker, felt that he had become too much of a liability with the black caucus in Congress, who wanted the administration to side more openly with the liberation movements. My experience in Rhodesia led me to suspect that implementing the agreement would be no less difficult than negotiating it. Crocker told me that we were going to have to take on much of the burden of helping to ensure that it was in fact implemented.

Mrs Thatcher was due to make a visit to Nigeria, Zimbabwe and Malawi. I wanted her to end this tour in Namibia, arriving there on 1 April 1989 – the day on which the UN plan, to which the South Africans now had agreed, began to be implemented. But we would not know until the last moment what the situation would be in the Namibian capital, Windhoek, on that day. I went ahead to Windhoek and it was agreed by Margaret Thatcher that a decision should be taken only as she was about to leave Malawi.

Having talked to the South African Administrator, the UN representatives, Martti Ahtisaari and General Prem Chand, the British military signals contingent who were providing communications for the UN force and a number of black Namibian friends, I sent a message urging her to come. Foreign Office officials, understandably concerned that the Prime Minister might find herself in a difficult situation, felt that this was a risk not worth taking. As always, she took pleasure in overruling them. The press accompanying Mrs Thatcher on her plane were told only on take-off that they were heading for Namibia, not Heathrow. It was, as I have described, just as well she got there when she did.

The crisis passed and when the SWAPO leaders returned from exile to Windhoek, I invited them to lunch at the Kalahari

Sands hotel. We had kept in touch with them through their years of exile. I said that I did not expect them to feel any particular affinity with a Conservative government in Britain – or vice versa. We did not agree with their Marxist economic views and hoped that they would change them. But we were determined to see that they were given a fair chance in free elections and I expected them to win. If they did, we would help the new government to get established, just as we had in Zimbabwe and elsewhere.

I was told not to take too much notice of the rhetoric. They were determined to preserve the Namibian economy. I urged them to visit Rössing, which they did, telling me on their return how impressed they were by what they had found there. They already were turning out to be a great deal more pragmatic than the World Council of Churches, which had flatly refused even to visit the mine they were trying so hard to close.

As the elections, due in November, drew closer, I had no doubt that we would witness a further attempt to disrupt them. One day in Pretoria I suddenly was summoned to an urgent meeting with Pik Botha and General Geldenhuys, head of the South African Defence Force. Pik Botha read out intercepted radio messages intended to convince us that another massive SWAPO incursion was planned, with the connivance of the Kenyan battalion of the UN force. As we controlled the UN's communications in Namibia, it did not take me long to discover, and to warn van Heerden, that these messages were false. A furious Pik Botha had been deceived by his own intelligence services. The crisis passed, SWAPO winning the elections by a large margin.

Douglas Hurd and I attended the celebrations in Windhoek of Namibia's independence. It was a chaotic evening, with Peréz de Cuéllar and various heads of state barely able to get into the stadium, and a decidedly scruffy and unshaven Yasser Arafat attempting to accost Jim Baker, who was determined not to meet him. But there was no doubting the relief among the immense crowd gathered there at the end of a long and bitter war. In September 1990, meeting her for the first time, President Sam Nujoma thanked Margaret Thatcher for the role she had played at a critical time.

XIII

'A VERY POWERFUL LADY – SOMEONE I WOULD RATHER HAVE AS AN ALLY THAN AN ENEMY'

At midnight on 1 February 1990, President F. W. de Klerk telephoned me at the British embassy in Cape Town. He had been working until then on his speech at the opening of Parliament next day. I could tell Margaret Thatcher, he said, that she would not be disappointed.

And so we gathered next day, in our morning suits, the ladies all in hats, for the opening of Parliament. Andries Treurnicht and his Conservative Party cohorts walked out as de Klerk announced the removal of the ban on the ANC and the South African Communist Party, the freeing of political prisoners, the suspension of capital punishment and the lifting of many of the restrictions imposed under the state of emergency. De Klerk was proclaiming nothing less than a constitutional revolution. One of my friends in the African National Congress, Cheryl Carolus, was at that moment making a fiery speech to a huge crowd in Greenmarket Square urging them to march on Parliament, an idea that had to be abandoned when she heard, to her utter surprise, what de Klerk had done.

De Klerk had told me that he would not be announcing on

that day the release of Nelson Mandela, as practical arrangements had to be made for this, on Mandela's own insistence. Eight days later he gave me a few hours' notice of the announcement of Mandela's release.

A few weeks later I received a message from Nelson Mandela asking me to see him in a small private clinic in Johannesburg, where he had been admitted suffering from exhaustion. It was by then my umpteenth meeting with him. At the end of each one of these, he would urge me to consider joining the ANC. It was, he contended, a broad church and 'you think like us'. This was a debatable proposition. Each time I reminded him that, as Mrs Thatcher's envoy, I would not be able to accept his invitation. He kept insisting that I was his adviser and by now I realised that, just as he had co-opted his warder, who ended up as his batman, and the Minister of Justice, who had kept asking me to help get him released, so I too was being co-opted onto the Mandela team.

His next target for co-option was more ambitious: it was in fact the Prime Minister. The rest of the ANC held against Margaret Thatcher her opposition to further sanctions. They wanted to fight with her. Mandela held the opposite view. She was, he said, a very powerful lady, 'one I would much rather have on my side'.[152] He wanted to know: how was he going to get her there?

The world since then has chosen to regard Mandela as a saint and he has indeed some saintly characteristics. I was no less impressed, however, by his extraordinary political cunning and adroitness in seeking to ensure that even those who appeared to be his most determined potential adversaries were brought over to his side.

He was about to leave on his first visit to the United States, to be followed by a meeting in London with Margaret Thatcher. I told him that we were extremely worried about his schedule in the US, where he was expected to visit seven cities in ten days. If he allowed this, his US hosts would end up killing him. To give him some rest beforehand, we were arranging for him and Oliver Tambo, the ANC President, to spend a quiet weekend together in the English countryside on his way to America, a gesture enormously appreciated by Mandela.

Amidst much hilarity, we then agreed to conduct a dress rehearsal for his meeting in Downing Street, with Mandela playing the role of Mandela and me that of Mrs Thatcher – one I had by then got to know quite well. 'You must stop at once all this nonsense about nationalising the banks and the mines,' I told him, on her behalf. 'But it was your idea,' Mandela replied, referring to the influence of the London School of Economics and others on budding African politicians in the 1950s. 'It was fashionable then,' he added with a smile. I replied that it definitely was not fashionable now. This was not a policy he should try defending in Downing Street. Mandela thanked me warmly for these 'tips' for his meeting with the Prime Minister.

Once in England, Mandela telephoned Mrs Thatcher before departing for the United States to thank us for arranging the weekend with Tambo, only to receive a stern lecture about his programme.

Mandela arrived back in London, as I had feared, suffering from a chest infection and utterly exhausted. I saw Mrs Thatcher before the meeting. Mandela, I told her, was no Marxist and it was the regime that had forced him to threaten violence. His own activities in that regard had been limited to trying to blow

up a few electricity pylons. He was, I told her, very different in
character to any other political leader I had ever encountered.
Asked if he bore any resemblance to Mugabe, I was able to
assure her that I had never met two political leaders who bore
less resemblance to each other than Nelson Mandela and Robert
Mugabe. I reminded her that he had waited twenty-seven years
for the chance to tell her and other heads of government his
story. 'You mean I mustn't interrupt him?' she enquired.

Mandela was accompanied by his deputy, Thabo Mbeki.
The meeting lasted three hours. The Prime Minister was very
concerned about Mandela's state of health, and attempted to
revive him with a small glass of port. As he put it, 'she chided
me like a school-ma'am for not taking her advice and cutting
down on my schedule'. Displaying, for once, exemplary patience,
she listened, asking no more than a couple of questions, for over
an hour as he explained to her the history of the ANC and the
difficulties he was facing in negotiations. He thanked her for
the support he was receiving from us, but made no headway with
a half-hearted plea for more sanctions.

Over lunch, there was an intense discussion of the sort of
constitution which ought to emerge and which we could support.
She found him 'supremely courteous, with a genuine nobility
of bearing' and – to her amazement as well as that of others –
devoid of any trace of bitterness. But she also found him very
outdated in his attitudes, 'stuck in a kind of socialist time warp',
hardly surprisingly, she acknowledged, given the three decades
he had spent in prison.[153] Her attempts to correct this resulted in
a hilarious exchange on basic economics.

The meeting lasted so long that members of the press wait-
ing outside began to chant: 'Free Nelson Mandela!' Mandela felt

that it had gone very well and, to the dismay of her domestic opponents, emerged on the doorstep of 10 Downing Street to pay tribute to the Prime Minister for the role she had played in helping to secure his release. Margaret Thatcher, for her part, had proved no less susceptible than others to Mandela's courtliness and charm. Her insistence that the ANC should announce an end to the 'armed struggle' was answered by Mandela when they did so four weeks later.

☞

After meeting P. W. Botha and his ebullient Foreign Minister, Pik Botha, the next senior government minister I had met on arriving in South Africa in 1987 was the supposedly deeply conservative leader of the National Party in the Transvaal and Minister of Education, F. W. de Klerk. At the end of a long and friendly conversation, he said to me: 'I want you to know that, if I have anything to do with it, we will not make the same mistake they made in Rhodesia.' What was the mistake, I asked? 'Leaving it much too late to negotiate with the real black leaders,' said de Klerk.

Believing in evolutionary change, the Prime Minister had resisted further sanctions at the 1987 Vancouver Commonwealth summit, where she felt the Canadians were trying to be more African than the Africans. When Kenneth Kaunda irritated her by saying that Africa was not at all her area, she reminded him that her government had brought Rhodesia to independence. She flatly opposed any sanctions that would cause mass unemployment, telling Mugabe that 80 per cent of Zimbabwe's trade passed through South Africa and one million Zimbabweans lived and worked there. Her Canadian hosts were embarrassed by the undiplomatic revelation that their trade with South Africa had been increasing.

At the end of the conference she was asked by a journalist about a statement by the local representative of the ANC that if she continued to oppose sanctions, British businesses in South Africa would become legitimate targets for attack. Understandably irritated, she replied that this showed what a typical terrorist organisation it was. Meanwhile, through a systematic programme of visits to the townships and support for organisations and projects in them, I and the younger members of the embassy, led by John Sawers, were in touch with virtually the entire internal leadership of the ANC.

Another colleague, Anthony Rowell, was in regular contact with Thabo Mbeki and Jacob Zuma in Lusaka and I was also in touch, when on leave, with the leader of the African National Congress Oliver Tambo and his family in Muswell Hill, who always welcomed me with great kindness and courtesy. On the Prime Minister's return from Vancouver, I told Charles Powell that we intended to continue all these contacts, and there was never any opposition to my doing so. In fact, throughout four years in South Africa I received no instructions but plenty of encouragement from her. There were no instructions from the Foreign Office either, as they were afraid she might not agree with them.

In February 1988, P. W. Botha attempted to suppress what resistance remained by banning the United Democratic Front (UDF), which was the internal wing of the ANC. This was the moment to make a very undiplomatic speech. In the 1960s, I pointed out, South Africa had been able to maintain apartheid and still have economic growth. That was not possible any longer.

South Africa was approaching a further turning point in its relations with the outside world. 'We do not believe in our isolation;
but we cannot prevent you isolating yourselves ... If you want to
get out of a hole, the first thing to do is to stop digging.'

This was splashed across the front pages of the South African
press. I was accused of interfering in South African politics,
which certainly was the case. Any ambassador who made such a
speech in any other African country would have been expelled
forthwith. But there was support from the Johannesburg business community, increasingly alarmed at P. W. Botha's disregard
for the economic consequences of his actions and, more signifi-
cantly, from most of the Afrikaans press.

To broaden the Prime Minister's horizons about South Africa,
I arranged for her to meet my closest South African friend and
ally, the redoubtable anti-apartheid campaigner, Helen Suzman.
These two formidable ladies got on extremely well. Helen said
that she was right to oppose comprehensive sanctions and to
work for peaceful change, but she must not expect anything
positive from P. W. Botha. We had to work on those likely to
succeed him.

The next task was to try to save the lives of the Sharpeville six,
condemned to death for the murder of a black town councillor.
Helen Suzman, who had refused to speak to P. W. Botha, except
for her stinging attacks on him in Parliament, for twenty years,
Professor Heyns of the Reformed Church and I all arranged
to see him separately, on the same day, to spell out the consequences for South Africa if they were executed. P. W. Botha
blustered about foreign interference, but the six were reprieved.
The liberal *Weekly Mail* wrote that they had much to thank us –
and Margaret Thatcher – for.

Willem (Wim) Wepener, editor of *Beeld*, the main Afrikaans paper in the Transvaal, which increasingly represented enlightened (*verligte*) Afrikaner opinion, asked if I could arrange an interview with her. I encouraged him to ask the question: what is the difference between the IRA and the ANC? *Beeld* carried the interview with the banner headline: 'The IRA have the vote; the ANC do not.' I arranged for her to give a similar interview to Aggrey Klaaste, the equally independent-minded editor of *The Sowetan*, by far the most widely read newspaper.

In January 1989, P. W. Botha suffered a stroke while preparing for the state opening of Parliament. He invited the National Party to elect a new leader in Parliament, though he had no intention of standing down as President. The succession was decided between two politicians – F. W. de Klerk and the Finance Minister Barend du Plessis – with whom I was on friendly terms. The securocrats led by General Magnus Malan were sidelined. The result was a narrow victory for de Klerk.

He followed up his victory by making a reformist speech. There were some who believed this still to be play-acting. His brother, Wimpie, who was playing an active part in private discussions with the ANC, told me that F. W. was far too conservative to be a good President. I said that he knew his brother better than I did, but I thought de Klerk would prove him wrong.

A couple of days after his election I went to see de Klerk on his own, in a small office in Parliament. The most extraordinary feature of F. W. de Klerk was his apparent ordinariness – completely belied by a display of extraordinary political courage in steering his country on a completely new course to which the security forces at the time were strongly opposed. Devoid of any trace of arrogance or pomposity, sitting behind his desk, chain-smoking at the time, the affable and unflappable de Klerk was always to be found reacting calmly to the turbulence and violence around him and was always focused on getting to the next stage.

I assured him that if he was able to take South Africa in a different direction, we would try to help him. But if the security police and military intelligence were allowed to continue their activities, including murder squads, unchecked, there was no way any of us were going to be able to help South Africa. South African military intelligence was continuing to support the insurgency by the Renamo rebel movement in Mozambique. Other elements of the security forces were engaged in murdering opponents of the regime. De Klerk told me that he had never been involved in authorising these activities (which we knew from our own intelligence sources to be true). He was determined to deal with them. But, he added, as I would understand, he would have to deal with the security forces with a velvet glove.

As a friend of his, but also, and far more importantly, as Margaret Thatcher's envoy, throughout the year leading up to Mandela's release in February 1990 I was able to establish a regular pattern of meetings with de Klerk, who I saw on his own and who had convinced me of his intention to make major changes. De Klerk's friends were not the security chiefs, but the business community of Johannesburg, and precisely those leading Afrikaners who had felt alienated under P. W. Botha. The greatest Afrikaner business leader and philanthropist, Dr Anton Rupert, and his son Johann were encouraging him along the path of reform. Gerhard de Kock, Governor of the Reserve Bank, a golf-playing friend of de Klerk, explained to him what would happen to South Africa, with the population increasing by a million people a year, if the capital outflow continued. Only disaster could result from continuance on the existing course.

Nelson Mandela, meanwhile, in the Victor Verster prison in Paarl, had heard about the support we were giving to community groups in the townships. Through one of his lawyers, he sent me a message of thanks for this and asked for his regards to be passed to the Prime Minister. I was astonished to receive a hand-written letter on prison notepaper from Mandela, emphasising his disagreement with Mrs Thatcher about sanctions and saying that he would have liked the opportunity to express his views directly to her. Nevertheless, 'I am happy to request you to pass my very best wishes to the Prime Minister.'

This gave me the opportunity to reply direct to Mandela in prison, telling him that we were intensifying our efforts to secure his release. There was a debate within the South African government as to whether this letter should be passed on to him but, in the end, it was.

The next step was to arrange for de Klerk to visit Mrs Thatcher at Chequers. At the time this was still an unpopular thing to do: we were accused of colluding with the apartheid regime and the meeting was picketed by the Anti-Apartheid Movement. In fact Mrs Thatcher made clear to de Klerk, with her customary lack of ambiguity, the need to get on with the Namibia settlement and to release Mandela. She found de Klerk open-minded and a refreshing contrast to P. W. Botha, but his replies enigmatic. As we stood on the steps of Chequers watching de Klerk's motorcade depart, she told me that she still was uncertain how far he would be prepared to go. I told her that I thought he would go further than she expected.

The meeting was important to de Klerk, as the Americans

still were unwilling to invite him to Washington and, with the administration's hands bound by the Congressional sanctions legislation, were unable to offer him any practical encouragement even if he did set out on a new course.

As P. W. Botha attempted to cling on to power, in August de Klerk and his senior colleagues told him that he would have to resign as President. De Klerk succeeded in beating off the challenge from the right-wing Conservative Party in new elections. His first acts as President were to ban the use of the *sjambok* – the whips the South African police had employed for decades as their favourite method of crowd control – and to authorise a series of mass demonstrations.

He followed this by making a remarkable speech, in private, to most of the hierarchy of the South African police. The police, he said, for too long had been asked by South Africa's politicians to solve the country's political problems for them. More fighting would lead not to victory, but to racial conflagration. 'For if this Armageddon takes place – and blood flows ankle-deep in our streets and four or five million people lie dead – the problem will remain exactly the same as it was before the shooting started.'

The security chiefs were told that the politics of repression were getting South Africa nowhere. As de Klerk put it, they were trying to stamp out a bush-fire which then simply flared up elsewhere on the veld. These problems had to be tackled at their political source.

With the United States, we redoubled our efforts with the new regime to get South Africa to terminate its military nuclear programme, centred on the uranium separation plant at Pelindaba. The Finance Minister, Barend de Plessis, turned out to be an ally. He could not understand what use South Africa could possibly make of nuclear weapons. 'We can', as he put it, 'hardly drop them on Lusaka or Soweto.' De Klerk ordered the closure of the plant at Pelindaba, thereby terminating any further development of the military nuclear programme. Orders subsequently were given by him to decommission the seven nuclear devices the South Africans already had produced. South Africa thereby became the only country ever to develop a nuclear weapons capability and then renounce it. For this act alone, de Klerk deserved the Nobel Prize.

The central issue, however, was what was to be done about Mandela and the ANC. De Klerk had told me that he had to create the right climate before he could consider releasing Mandela. I argued hard, for many weeks, for the release of Walter Sisulu and all the other ANC leaders except Mandela as the next step. In October 1989 they were released. It was an emotional homecoming as these by now elderly gentlemen, all wearing waistcoats and looking remarkably unrevolutionary, invited us to meet them in Soweto.

We were now on the verge of another Commonwealth conference in Kuala Lumpur in October 1989. I had used its proximity, unashamedly, to accelerate the release of Walter Sisulu and his companions. Given these positive moves by de Klerk, Margaret Thatcher was determined to support him and more than ever disposed to resist any further sanctions. In this, she was fully justified; if the release of the senior ANC leaders had been followed by more punitive actions, this would have played into the hands of de Klerk's conservative opponents within the Afrikaner community.

She enjoyed the ensuring fracas with most of the other heads of government, determined to ignore what actually was happening in South Africa, rather more than her new Foreign Secretary John Major. Hawke, Kaunda and others argued for more sanctions. The Foreign Ministers came up with a communiqué John Major and the Foreign Office officials felt they could 'live with'. Considering that it paid no regard whatever to the positive developments in South Africa, she proceeded to issue a statement of her own, paying tribute to those changes and suggesting that the Commonwealth should concentrate on encouraging them, rather than on further punishment. Hawke and Mulroney protested at this appalling breach of etiquette. She got a terrible press in Britain, suggesting that she had disavowed John Major, though he had in fact approved her statement, and noting that, once again, she was 'isolated'. Given that within four months de Klerk was to announce the release of Mandela, the stand she made and the statement she issued made a great deal more sense than theirs did.

There was no doubt that de Klerk wanted to release Mandela, but he was going to need some support and encouragement. In November 1989, I returned to London to see Douglas Hurd, who had taken over as Foreign Secretary. I explained that while I continued to urge de Klerk to release Mandela and remove the ban on the ANC, he was going to want to know what we would do if he did take those steps. An obvious response would be to rescind the ban on new investment, enabling de Klerk to demonstrate that this fundamental step had produced a response, at any rate from us. There would be a storm of criticism from others. Nor would anyone else follow us immediately, though I was sure some would do so in due course. Douglas Hurd was undismayed by the idea of doing this on our own – a position strongly endorsed by Margaret Thatcher.

So, on my return to South Africa, I was able to tell de Klerk that if he took these steps, there would be a response from us. De Klerk relayed this to the members of his Cabinet in their meeting on the eve of the opening of Parliament, before his midnight call to me.

Mrs Thatcher had a final meeting with de Klerk at Chequers six weeks before she resigned. Once she had left office, de Klerk regarded it as a debt of honour to invite her to visit South Africa – which to her great regret, she had been unable to do as Prime Minister. He gave a state banquet for her in Cape Town. We took her to Soweto, where she got a warm reception at the Baragwanath Hospital and from Aggrey Klaaste and his staff at *The Sowetan*.

We spent two days with de Klerk and his wife at the Mala Mala game reserve. As de Klerk records in his memoirs, Mrs Thatcher kept insisting on seeing a lion. As dusk fell, we came upon a lion and lioness mating furiously, accompanied by tremendous roaring.

I accompanied Mrs Thatcher on the last leg of her visit, to meet Buthelezi at Ulundi. She was greeted by the usual array of Zulu warriors with their *assegais* and shields, and visited the battlefield on which the British army finally had managed to defeat the Zulus.

When, shortly afterwards, I left South Africa, the *Financial Times* unkindly described me at my farewell party as struggling in the embrace of Winnie Mandela, while Nelson Mandela was delighted to meet Professor Johan Heyns, head of the Dutch Reformed Church, who had denounced apartheid as a heresy.

In a fit of hyperbole the paper claimed that since Sir Alfred Milner had started the Boer War, 'no British envoy has had such an impact on South Africa'. The tribute was undeserved, for it ignored the fact that the influence we were able to exert derived essentially from Margaret Thatcher. De Klerk was far more disposed to listen to her than to any other foreign leader, and the ANC, once reassured of our commitment to genuine majority rule, looked to us to help overcome obstacles with the South African government.

During Margaret Thatcher's visit to South Africa and on subsequent occasions, Mandela stated publicly that 'we have much to thank her for', despite her disagreements with the ANC about sanctions. Though she was no friend of the liberation movements, it was thanks to her willingness to take the necessary risks that we had been able to end the Rhodesian war, and no head of government had tried harder to secure his release. She had in fact helped to achieve more in southern Africa than her predecessors combined.

When Mandela made his state visit to Britain as President of the new South Africa, he insisted on meeting her to thank her again for her assistance in helping to secure his release from prison. On several of his subsequent visits to London, he took time out to keep in touch with her. Whenever I have seen him, he has always asked me to pass his regards to Margaret Thatcher.

XIV

'IF YOU TRY TO BUCK THE MARKET, THE MARKET WILL BUCK YOU'

In the summer of 1987 Jacques Chirac, who had become Prime Minister of France in uneasy 'co-habitation' with President Mitterrand, launched a campaign for an oil and fats tax to be imposed on agricultural imports into the European Union. Margaret Thatcher denounced this as outright protectionism. Noting that in France he was called 'le bulldozer', she intended to demonstrate that the lady was not for bulldozing. One meeting between them concluded with her observing that she and Chirac could argue all day, but she would not accept such a tax. Nor did she.

Her campaign to control agricultural expenditure was less successful. Chirac wanted the EU to aim for self-sufficiency in agricultural production, dispensing with the need for imports. If she did not agree, he would challenge Britain's budgetary abatement. She advised him not to threaten her. At the Brussels European Council in February 1988, with Chancellor Kohl literally thumping the table and Chirac shouting and throwing papers around, her only effective ally, the Dutch Prime Minister Ruud Lubbers, abandoned her. Shedding a few tears of rage, she had to accept an outcome on agricultural spending a long way short of what she would have wished.

She was rather more successful in her constant campaign for the European Community to play a constructive role in international trade negotiations, despite the constraints imposed by the Common Agricultural Policy. Here she could count on support from the Dutch and Danes and, from time to time, from the Germans. When she urged on Mitterrand the need to reduce trade barriers, he replied that of course the Community was protectionist: that was the point of it!

In September 1988, Jacques Delors annoyed the Prime Minister by giving an address to the Trade Union Congress extolling the benefits of 'social' Europe. The Foreign Office had been keen that she should make a speech about Europe, and a battle ensued with No. 10 about the content of the speech. The Foreign Office Under-Secretary, John Kerr, reported to Geoffrey Howe that damage limitation had been successful: 'No. 10 have (largely) come to heel on this.'[154]

Notwithstanding the fuss it caused at the time, in many respects the speech she made in Bruges was a classic exposition of British views and very similar to one delivered by Tony Blair in Oxford eight years later. She insisted that Warsaw, Prague and Budapest also were great European cities. Closer European cooperation did not require more and more power to be centralised in Brussels, with decisions taken by an appointed bureaucracy. 'We have not successfully rolled back the frontiers of the state in Britain, only to see them re-imposed at a European level with a European super-state exercising a new dominance from Brussels.'

As opinion in Britain has come to feel that the country has had

about as much European integration as it can stand, and Lord
Denning described the impact of European law as like a tidal
wave 'flowing inland over our fields and houses, to the dismay
of all', it is hard to find much fault with this statement either.
But it was a direct challenge to the European Commission and
its view of Europe then and now, thereby provoking a furore in
the European and parts of the British press, and causing much
pain to Geoffrey Howe, who would have preferred her to be
more conciliatory.

When Ted Heath took Britain into the first attempt at
European currency coordination – the so-called 'snake' – in
1972, the pressures on sterling caused the abandonment of this
experiment within six weeks. At the end of 1978, when the other
eight member states of the EC signed up to a fresh attempt at
currency coordination through the European Monetary System
(EMS), as Leader of the Opposition she did not react viscer-
ally against this. Her approach was to adopt a positive general
attitude to the EMS while avoiding any specific commitments.
At her first European Council in Strasbourg in June 1979, to
display the new government's European credentials, she said
that although Britain was not in a position to join the European
Exchange Rate Mechanism (ERM), she was prepared to swap
some of the Bank of England's currency reserves into the new
European currency units (ecus).

In October 1979, she held an initial meeting to discuss the
ERM. The Foreign Office saw this as a question of European
relations, the Treasury as an economic issue. Geoffrey Howe as

Chancellor was against joining, in part because of uncertainties about abolishing exchange controls. The Governor of the Bank of England was a bit more favourable. No one suggested they should join immediately. They agreed to stick to the formula that they would consider this when 'the time was right'.

As she was being pressed by Helmut Schmidt to join, she reopened the issue in 1980. The Treasury was firmly against joining. If they had joined the previous year, it would have required massive intervention in the currency markets to hold sterling down. She had opened the discussion by saying that domestic monetary policy must remain paramount. They concluded that they should stick to the line about joining when conditions permitted.

There was a further discussion in the autumn of 1981. Within the Treasury, Geoffrey Howe and Leon Brittan (as Chief Secretary) still were against joining. Nigel Lawson's position (he was then Financial Secretary) was less clear. Margaret Thatcher's own caution was reinforced by advice from her economic adviser, Alan Walters. He pointed out that under the existing system, the participating currencies fluctuated within bands, triggering periodic realignments, which were the subject of political horse-trading. In Walters's view, in determining currency rates, the market did a better job.

At a further meeting in January 1982, Geoffrey Howe remained against joining. The Prime Minister feared it would restrict their freedom of manoeuvre in domestic economic policy. She did accept, however, that when inflation and interest rates in Britain moved closer to those in Germany, the case for joining would be more powerful.

When Nigel Lawson became Chancellor in 1983, the exchange rate was just one factor in assessing monetary conditions. Attention still was focused on the growth of the money supply. But they were finding it harder and harder to read the monetary aggregates. The narrow measure of monetary growth MO, measuring essentially cash, moved very differently to the broader measure M3, which included various forms of savings. As Lawson increasingly lost confidence in the monetary measurements, he sought an alternative standard in the exchange rate.

In February 1985, he told Mrs Thatcher that maintaining financial discipline in his view could be achieved either by monetary targets or by a fixed exchange rate. The financial markets were having difficulty understanding the government's policy on the exchange rate. Joining the ERM would provide clarity on this. M3 was becoming increasingly suspect as a monetary indicator (she agreed). He also believed that joining the ERM would be popular with Conservative MPs.

The Prime Minister was serious about the control of inflation and of public spending and deficits, but disliked committing herself to economic targets, especially those involving the exchange rate, which she thought ultimately could not be controlled. In the course of her political career, she had seen both the Wilson and Heath governments come to grief when they had tried to do so. The division between her and Lawson in this regard was never reconciled and grew steadily deeper over time. Nevertheless, she agreed to another seminar on the subject.

Alan Walters could not attend but warned her that, in his view, membership would increase the pressures on sterling. Nigel Lawson did not argue that they should join straight away, but clearly was in favour of doing so in due course. Geoffrey Howe by now had been converted to the Foreign Office view that Britain should join, but they would need to build up foreign exchange reserves if they were to do so. She agreed that the Treasury and Bank of England should look into this.

In September 1985, Lawson returned to the charge on the ERM, which she felt was becoming an *idée fixe* with him. He sent her an extraordinary paper about what might happen if they were in the ERM and the markets thought they might lose an election. In that event, they would need to exit the system temporarily, while declaring that they would re-join immediately at the same parity if they won.

Not surprisingly, this reinforced her worries about the whole project. She doubted Lawson's central premise, which was that defending a fixed exchange rate was compatible with taking the right decisions in terms of management of the domestic economy. She could see no good reason to allow British monetary policy to be determined largely by the German Bundesbank unless they had no confidence in their own ability to control inflation. She was extremely sceptical that the commercial lobbies pressing them to join the ERM would remain enthusiastic when this started to make British exports uncompetitive. She doubted, presciently, if the public would welcome what could turn out to be the huge cost of defending sterling within the ERM which, anyway, might prove to be impossible in the run-up to an election. Over the previous five years, sterling had fluctuated dramatically against other European currencies. It would have required massive intervention in the currency markets to have tried to keep sterling within the ERM. These arguments, however, made no impression on Nigel Lawson and Geoffrey Howe.

There followed a quite dramatic meeting on 13 November 1985 at which Lawson argued that their anti-inflationary policy needed a shot in the arm, which would be provided by joining the ERM. She realised that, by now, she was close to being opposed to joining in principle, not just because the timing was not right. Lawson was supported by Geoffrey Howe as Foreign Secretary and Robin Leigh-Pemberton, the Governor of the Bank of England. Even Norman Tebbit, as Conservative Party chairman, appeared to be in favour. She continued to question how membership of the ERM could be compatible with setting interest rates at the levels required to manage the domestic economy. It could instead enclose the government in a strait jacket. Willie Whitelaw, trying to sum up the discussion, said that if the Chancellor, Governor and Foreign Secretary all were agreed that they should join the EMS 'then that should be decisive. It certainly has decided me.' The Prime Minister brought the meeting to an abrupt conclusion by saying that she did not agree: 'If you join the EMS, you will have to do so without me.'[155] Lawson returned to 11 Downing Street and seriously considered resigning, but was talked out of it by colleagues.

In the run-up to the Luxembourg European Council in December 1985, Lawson warned that she must avoid any new commitment to monetary union, with which of course she agreed. 'Economic and monetary union', however, had been an official EC objective since the days of Heath in October 1972. In a discussion with Chancellor Kohl, she got it agreed that the treaty language in the Single European Act would add the important gloss 'cooperation in economic and monetary policy'.

She asked the Treasury Permanent Secretary, Peter Middleton, why he was so set on joining the Exchange Rate Mechanism. He said that she would not be there forever. Europe was the only way of instilling fiscal discipline in the longer term.[156]

From March 1987, though she did not know it at the time, Nigel Lawson decided to pursue a policy of shadowing the deutschmark, setting interest rates at a level intended to keep the pound at or below three deutschmarks. Part of the purpose was to demonstrate that sterling could enter the ERM at that level without adverse consequences. Extraordinarily, she only learned about the systematic shadowing of the deutschmark at a meeting with the *Financial Times* in November 1987, when they showed her a chart demonstrating this. Infuriated by her Chancellor pursuing a policy not disclosed to her, she was convinced that the attendant exchange rate interventions had resulted in importing inflation. Her relationship with Lawson never recovered from this. In March 1988, so much intervention was required to hold down sterling that Lawson accepted that it must be allowed to rise above the three deutschmark 'cap'. Commenting on this in Parliament, she said: 'There is no way in which one can buck the market.' Lawson, on the other hand, was still saying that he did not want to see the exchange rate appreciate further.

From this time on, it was clear that Geoffrey Howe and Lawson were aligned against her. In May, Howe said in a speech that they could not go on forever qualifying the commitment to join the ERM by saying 'when the time is right'.

Following the Hanover European Council in June 1988, a committee of central bank governors was set up to report on monetary union. While Lawson favoured joining the ERM, he was just as strongly opposed as she was to monetary union. They hoped that the Governor of the Bank of England, Robin Leigh-Pemberton, would be able to make common cause with Karl Otto Pöhl, President of the Bundesbank, to oppose the project. She could not believe that the Bundesbank or the German people really wanted to trade the deutschmark for the euro. But, under pressure from Chancellor Kohl, Pöhl's opposition was never expressed.

In May 1989, Lawson again pushed to join the ERM. Alan Walters suggested that the conditions for doing so should include the abolition of exchange controls by all the other member states and complete freedom to provide financial services across the EC. While this would put a more positive aspect on joining, it did not actually deal with her and his more fundamental objections to doing so. Nevertheless, she realised, it might be the only way to defuse the differences with her Chancellor and Foreign Secretary.

On 14 June 1989, shortly before the Madrid European Council, Howe and Lawson mounted what she regarded as an ambush. They sent her a joint minute – a very unusual procedure on a contentious subject – arguing that to deflect Delors's proposals for a monetary union, she should accept a 'non-legally binding reference' to sterling joining the ERM by the end of 1992. Again, she doubted the central premise, which was the idea that the others would be deflected from pursuing EMU if she agreed to join the ERM. This was a truly bizarre thesis, since the French and Chancellor Kohl intended to pursue monetary union whether or not Britain was in the ERM. She questioned this argument when she saw them on 20 June, only for her then to receive another joint minute demanding a further meeting.

She was convinced that Howe had put Lawson up to this. The European elections had gone badly for the Conservatives. Quietly ambitious, he had always hoped to become Prime Minister one day. He did not enjoy being attacked by her in front of others.

They went to see her at 8.15 on the Sunday morning she was due to leave for Madrid. In a dramatic encounter, Geoffrey Howe insisted that she must speak first at the European Council, setting a date by which Britain would join the ERM. This would check the progress toward monetary union. If she did not agree, they would both resign.

She was not prepared to be blackmailed into a policy she believed was wrong. She told them that she had a paragraph spelling out the conditions under which sterling could enter the ERM. But she was not prepared to set a date. That would be a gift to speculators, as they must know. 'They left, Geoffrey looking insufferably smug. And so the nasty little meeting ended.'

As a result, the atmosphere in the British delegation in Madrid was, in the words of Stephen Wall, 'electrically awful'. In the European Council she set out the 'Madrid conditions' for sterling's entry into the ERM. She reaffirmed the intention to join once inflation was down and exchange controls in Europe were abolished. But she did not set a date to do so. Her statement was received quite positively. In Cabinet Nigel Lawson observed that Madrid had gone rather well, hadn't it?[157]

She was determined never again to suffer an ambush of this kind. Geoffrey Howe was moved from the Foreign Office to become Leader of the House of Commons with, in addition, what she regarded as the meaningless title of Deputy Prime Minister, with John Major – to his surprise – appointed to succeed him. Nigel Lawson continued as Chancellor, but the tension with him soon exploded again, this time terminally, over the independent advice she was receiving from Alan Walters, who had been reappointed as her special adviser in May 1989. The overheating of the economy in 1988 and surge in inflation had resulted in interest rates having to be doubled in a matter of months from 7.5 to 15 per cent and both she and Lawson were beleaguered. Walters had publicised trenchant views in numerous articles and these were frequently quoted by the press against the Chancellor. In October the press republished an article by him, written eighteen months before, describing the ERM as 'half-baked'. On 26 October Lawson told her that Walters must go, or else he would resign. She said she needed Walters's frank advice and was not prepared to sack him: he was an adviser; Lawson was in a far superior position as Chancellor. Lawson returned after lunch to say that he had decided to resign. John Major, who had served only a few months as Foreign Secretary, was told that he must succeed Lawson as Chancellor. To compound the embarrassment, Walters then decided that he must resign as well.

Douglas Hurd, an Old Etonian and former member of the Foreign Service, was appointed to succeed John Major as Foreign Secretary. He had been promoted steadily by her, notwithstanding his prior very close association with Ted Heath. His ideas were not very different from those of Geoffrey Howe, but she trusted him and he was much better at managing her. She did, however, worry that he was too much of a gentleman to deal with some of his European counterparts, not all of whom, in her opinion, merited that description.

On the subject of the ERM, she found that John Major's main preoccupation was not with the fundamental arguments for or against but, as a former Chief Whip, with the need to do whatever was necessary to hold the parliamentary party together. He agreed that to set an advance date for joining would simply encourage speculation. But he was in favour of joining and felt that to do so would help to bring interest rates down. Having lost confidence in the monetary targets, the Treasury had been converted to a belief that the best way of enforcing financial discipline would be via membership of the ERM which, in John Major's words, had become the new 'lodestar'. On monetary union, she still hoped that if they made clear that Britain did not intend to join, under pressure from the Bundesbank, Germany might not do so either.

In April 1990 Major reported that he had been startled by the determination of the other EC Finance Ministers to commit to a full monetary union. There had been no support for the British alternative approach of allowing a European currency unit, the so-called 'hard ecu', to circulate alongside the existing currencies, instead of replacing them. Whatever the intrinsic merits of this idea, it never had the slightest chance of being accepted by the other member states, bent as they were on establishing a currency union. By now she was resigned to sterling joining the ERM, not because she had any real belief in this course of action but because she could not afford another clash with her most senior colleagues.

They decided to join on the basis of the broader band, enabling the currency to appreciate or depreciate by up to 6 per cent either way within the system. Nigel Lawson was subsequently to claim that sterling eventually joined the ERM 'at the wrong rate, in the wrong way and at the wrong time'. It would, she observed, have tested the wisdom of Solomon to determine the 'right' rate at which to join; 'I doubt if Solomon in his wisdom would ever have set himself such a task.'[158] Sterling, she noted, had been at DM3.75 in November 1985 and DM2.85 a year later. More recently, it had been oscillating between DM3.16 and DM2.87.

When they joined, they did so at DM2.95, the rate at which the London market had closed on the evening before. She was no longer able to stand out against what virtually every other member of the Cabinet, the majority of the parliamentary party and the leading business organisations all were urging the government to do. On 5 October 1990 the government announced that sterling was joining the ERM, a decision greeted with a brief burst of euphoria. She insisted on a 1 per cent reduction in interest rates being announced at the same time, also declaring that she was not prepared to run down the currency reserves to support sterling. If such a situation arose, they would have to realign.

In April 1990 she had received a paper from John Major about EMU, raising the prospect of a 'two-tier Europe', which she was quite prepared to contemplate, and of the other member states all pressing ahead with a treaty on EMU. He favoured subscribing instead to a treaty allowing Britain to 'opt in' if and when it chose to do so. She was still resisting this. Nicholas Ridley, Trade Secretary at the time, contributed to a paper before the June 1990 European Council in Dublin arguing that they should accept a multi-tier Community, in which not all member states would participate on the same basis.

By this time she was about to be overtaken by events. Having attended two of the meetings on the ERM in the mid-1980s, I had been more impressed by the questions she was asking than the answers she was getting. While the Governor of the Bank of England, Robin Leigh-Pemberton, seemed inclined towards joining on broad political grounds, she was paying more attention to the more sceptical views of his deputy, Eddie George, who was much more closely involved with the financial markets. As a firm believer in floating exchange rates, I was supposed to be alone in the Foreign Office in doubting if it was in Britain's interest to take sterling into the ERM. This was not quite true: one of the economic advisers agreed with me! The Foreign Office institutionally, however, was in favour of the ERM and so by now was Geoffrey Howe. I could not understand how everyone could have forgotten so quickly the horrendously distorting effect exerted on economic policy for decades in Britain after the war by the futile efforts to defend the sterling exchange rate against the dollar. Far from believing that defending a fixed exchange rate could help to reinforce domestic economic policy, it seemed self-evident that sooner or later it could lead to our having to raise interest rates in the depths of a recession, which is exactly what happened two years after we joined the ERM, leading to our exit from it on Black Wednesday.

XV

'AN UNAMBIGUOUS FAILURE'

Mrs Thatcher had breathed a sigh of relief when George Bush defeated Michael Dukakis in the US presidential election in November 1988. But with Bush as the new President and James Baker as Secretary of State, she found herself dealing with a team which tended to see Germany as its key partner in Europe and which paid lip service at least to the goal of European integration. To some extent this was a deliberate reaction by the Americans to what they felt was the excessive influence she had enjoyed with Reagan, resulting in decisions being skewed in favour of the British. More importantly, however, with the dramatic changes in the Soviet Union, it was because Baker and Bush saw Germany as being at the centre of events in Europe.

She had always found George Bush easy to get on with and admired the role he had played in keeping the Reagan administration in touch with European opinion. She regarded him as one of the most decent, honest and patriotic Americans she had met. 'But he had never had to think through his beliefs and fight for them when they were hopelessly unfashionable', as she and Ronald Reagan had been obliged to do.[159] She learned later that he was sometimes exasperated by her habit of talking non-stop about the issues that interested her, when he felt he should have been leading the discussion. He also wanted to show that his administration was different from that of Reagan. George Bush kept in mind the importance of the US–British relationship and the need to consult her. But he was determined that the US must lead the alliance.[160]

As Nigel Lawson observed, despite their forthright private arguments, there always was an element of deference in her attitude to Ronald Reagan. With George Bush, she was much less deferential, if at all.

To her dismay, she discovered that the State Department was inclined to brief against her policies in Europe, until the Gulf crisis caused a volte-face by them. She was not as close to Baker as she had been to George Shultz. She found the State Department enamoured of the view that it was in everybody's interests that Germany should be bound more tightly into a more united Europe.

While Shultz, like her, saw politics as about the pursuit of broad principles, Baker saw diplomacy as about getting things done, an art in which he had few equals. Shultz had used her to help moderate Reaganite positions. George Bush's policies did not need toning down. They were in some respects too moderate for her. The Bush adviser closest to her way of thinking was his outstanding National Security Adviser, the tough and ascetic General Brent Scowcroft. Famous for sleeping through Cabinet meetings on the grounds that nothing of interest ever happened in them, Scowcroft all the rest of the time was the lynchpin of the Bush foreign policy team.

Despite her liking for George Bush, she was right in not considering him a kindred spirit. As Vice-President, George Bush told me, he had arrived one weekend at Chequers with his golf clubs, only to find himself immersed for twenty-four hours in discussions about world affairs, with no time allowed by her for golf! Having served as ambassador to China and the UN and as head of the CIA, he was a great public servant and a statesman, rather than a political leader, which cost him dear when it came to seeking re-election. Despite a keen sardonic sense of humour, he never had any pretentions to eloquence. In contrast to Reagan, as he declared himself, he did not do 'the vision thing', a handicap in a country that looks for that in its leaders. It was fortunate for the world that he became President at a time when his international skills were most badly required, though his preoccupation with international affairs was to prove costly in causing him to lose traction domestically.

George Bush was a great believer in the importance of cultivating close personal relations with other world leaders. Henry Kissinger argued to him that these were no substitute for deep national interests: the leader of a country was not going to change his country's policy simply because he liked another leader. But George Bush persisted in his efforts to woo his counterparts, luring a series of foreign dignitaries to the Bush family holiday home in Kennebunkport, Maine. Margaret Thatcher was not one of them. As she had no small talk or leisure interests, she was never going to be easy to schmooze.

Following the signature of the agreement eliminating land-based intermediate-range nuclear weapons in Europe (INF), Margaret Thatcher was worried about pressure to reduce short-range nuclear forces (SNF), which she saw as potentially weakening deterrence. She was conscious that NATO had only eighty-eight Lance missile launchers; the Warsaw Pact had 1,400 equivalent weapons. Gorbachev had launched a very successful propaganda drive to win over German opinion against the modernisation of NATO's short-range nuclear weapons.

Chancellor Kohl by now was becoming decidedly lukewarm about NATO plans to modernise the shorter-range nuclear forces by replacing the obsolescent Lance missiles in Germany. To the Americans' dismay, he suddenly announced with no consultation that a decision on this should be postponed. The US and British position was that cuts must be made to redress the imbalance in conventional forces before engaging with the Russians on SNF. When James Baker saw Margaret Thatcher at Chequers, she favoured NATO making unilateral reductions in SNF, rather than getting involved in negotiations. Baker was more concerned about how German sensitivities were to be managed. In a further meeting with Kohl, she argued the case against negotiations on this subject. In a speech at the Guildhall in London, Gorbachev predicted dire consequences for East–West relations if NATO went ahead with SNF modernisation.

Kohl was conscious of the need to deal with press stories about their poor personal relations. To try to improve matters, in April 1989 he invited her to meet him at his home in the village of Deidesheim. Despite this friendly gesture, the discussion became quite heated, as she found him shifting his ground on SNF. Kohl said that he did not need any lectures about NATO. He was opposed to zero SNF. But Germany was more affected than anyone else by SNF. If the weapons ever were used, it would be on German territory; therefore, German interests should be given priority. Once the INF agreement had been reached, it was no longer possible to reject negotiations on SNF.

The atmosphere was otherwise friendly and *gemütlich*. A huge lunch of potato soup, pig's stomach, liver dumplings and sauerkraut was devoured by the Chancellor. When they visited the nearby cathedral, Kohl took Charles Powell, who accompanied her, aside to say that now that he had seen him on his home territory, close to the border with France, surely she would see that he was as much European as German. Could he please help to persuade her of that? Rather ungratefully, on the plane back to London, her reaction was to complain that he was 'so German!'[161]

Kohl's Foreign Minister, Hans-Dietrich Genscher, whom she had always distrusted (as did the Americans), suspecting him of neutralist views, made a statement in the Bundestag about cuts in SNF in advance of any agreement on this in NATO. This triggered a telephone call from her to Bush which he described as 'vintage Thatcher'.

Bush and Brent Scowcroft shared her concern at the extent to which Kohl was shifting his ground. They sensibly rejected, however, a suggestion that they should leave it to her to deal with him. George Bush observed that while Reagan had usually set the tone at international meetings, he often turned the rest of the discussion over to her. She was 'never without an opinion, forcefully stated'. But Bush intended to speak for himself.

When the Germans unilaterally announced that they wanted negotiations on SNF, Bush was as irritated as she was. She urged Bush to be firm with the Germans. The way Bush and Baker set about finessing these intra-Alliance differences was to hold a series of meetings with Kohl and his colleagues to convince them that SNF talks could not begin until cuts in conventional forces had actually been achieved, and that some short-range nuclear weapons must remain after the negotiations. To brief her about the US proposals for cuts in conventional forces, they sent to London two of her favourite US officials, Larry Eagleburger and

Bob Gates, whom she greeted as 'Tweedle-dum and Tweedle-dee'. Though they found her still very wary, she said, 'If the President wants it, of course we will do it.'

At the NATO summit, Bush proposed equal limits for US and Soviet forces in Europe, entailing much bigger cuts for the Russians, plus limits on each side's tanks and artillery, warmly greeted by Mrs Thatcher. She was, however, still urging Bush not to 'give in'. Baker secured agreement that once the conventional force reductions were being implemented, NATO would engage negotiations on a partial reduction in SNF. The Prime Minister, having helped to secure priority for conventional force reductions and no zero-SNF, 'waxed enthusiastic'. She regarded this as a crucial victory for her point of view. The agreement, however, had been engineered by Bush and Baker, and over her initial objections to any SNF negotiations at all.

Bush then made a speech in Mainz describing the Germans as 'partners in leadership', giving the press a field day at her expense. The Americans could not for the life of them understand the fuss made by the British press about Bush's statement which, Scowcroft observed, was simply intended as a rhetorical flourish and not to downgrade the relationship with Britain.[162]

☞

Attending an encounter between Margaret Thatcher and Mitterrand at Chequers in 1989, John Major described it as 'not so much a meeting as a flirtation', which they both clearly enjoyed. They were very different characters. Mitterrand had little interest in economics, but was as keen as she was to play a role on the world stage. Where they disagreed, they circled warily around one another in a far warmer relationship than she was ever able to establish with Helmut Kohl.[163]

The demolition of the Berlin Wall began on 10 November 1989. This put Germany more than ever at the centre of American calculations. The triumph of Solidarity in Poland and Havel in Czechoslovakia, and the downfall of Ceauşescu in Romania and of the regime in East Germany represented the most important and welcome political changes of her lifetime. But she continued to worry about the survival of the reformist regime in Moscow which had permitted these changes to take place, expecting at some point the hardliners there to try to stage a comeback. She feared that the emergence of a much more powerful reunited Germany could imperil the reformers in Moscow as well as alter fundamentally the balance of power and influence in western Europe.

There was, she believed, a tendency to regard the 'German problem' as a matter too delicate for political leaders to bring up. She was a convinced believer in national character and no one who attended, as she did, countless European meetings in Brussels and elsewhere could fail to be struck, and amused, by the extent to which the various delegations seemed determined to compete with one another in near-caricature of their real or reputed national characteristics. The people who did acknowledge the 'German problem', she found, were the modern-day Germans themselves, who did not want their country ever again to find itself in too dominant a position. That was one reason many of them wanted to see Germany locked into a federal Europe. She feared that a reunited Germany would be simply too big and too powerful to be just another player in Europe.

At this stage it seemed that the Soviet Union would be strongly opposed to the re-emergence of a powerful Germany, reunited on the West's terms. She had a frank discussion with Gorbachev in Moscow in September 1989. She said that although NATO had always called for German reunification, in reality Britain and other west European countries were apprehensive about it (a clear reference to Mitterrand). The post-war frontiers must not be changed. The West would not interfere in the developments in eastern Europe: the changes there must be the result of internal pressures. Gorbachev said that he did not want German reunification either. This encouraged her to believe that it might be possible to slow things down. She believed it would be best for East Germany in the first instance to become a separate free-standing democracy, posing less of a problem vis-à-vis Russia. Scowcroft was as cautious as she was about the wisdom of pursuing reunification in the near term. It was, he observed, popular in the two Germanys, but not anywhere else in Europe.

At this point, events started accelerating at a vertiginous pace. Kohl telephoned her on 10 November as the Berlin Wall was being dismantled. She urged him to keep in touch with Gorbachev, which he promised to do. Kohl's call for the people of East Germany to be allowed to decide their own future triggered an EC summit meeting in Paris. Kohl spoke passionately for forty minutes. Mrs Thatcher urged caution. To talk about border changes or German reunification could undermine Gorbachev and, with him, the prospect of democracy in the Soviet Union.

In his memoirs, Kohl described her as 'ice-cold in pursuit of British interests', which she considered a compliment. He added that 'even Margaret Thatcher could not prevent the German people from following their destiny', denouncing her opposition to German reunification as well as that, more subterranean, of Mitterrand.[164]

Scowcroft also feared that the loss of East Germany could bring down Gorbachev, and could not see anything wrong with two democratic Germanys as an interim solution. Bush found that the Dutch and Italian Prime Ministers, as well as Mitterrand, shared Margaret Thatcher's concerns, but she was expressing them more openly than they did. So far Gorbachev had accepted the changes in eastern Europe and had overcome resistance to them among his military and the party. But the Americans were expecting the Soviet military to fight unification tooth and nail. The US focus at this stage still was on promoting East German self-determination.

George Bush, however, had decided to back Helmut Kohl. In a meeting with him at Camp David on 24 November 1989, Margaret Thatcher said that talk of reunification or changing the borders could only frighten the Soviets. The objective was to secure democracy throughout eastern Europe. They had decided not to pursue independence for the Baltic states at this stage because this would undermine Gorbachev's efforts, she reminded Bush. She pulled a map out of her handbag, showing the pre-war boundaries of Germany. She still believed that reunification could mean the end of Gorbachev, though they could not prevent it happening eventually if the Germans wanted it. She found Bush distracted and uneasy. He asked if her approach was giving rise to difficulties with Kohl, and about her attitude to the EC. She urged him not to cut defence spending, which he said he was going to have to do.

Kohl, meanwhile, was ploughing ahead towards his objective of reunification, though at this stage even he was still talking of it being accomplished over a number of years. At the NATO summit in Brussels in December, Bush again laid emphasis on 'European integration'. As this was exploited by the press against her, Bush telephoned her to say that his remarks were meant to refer to the single market, and not to political integration. Although this was rather disingenuous, in my own dealings with George Bush, Baker and Scowcroft, I never found any of them showing any interest in European integration, enthusiasm for which was confined to officials in the European bureau of the State Department. Baker wholeheartedly approved of her position on monetary union.

The only hope of slowing down reunification now lay, she believed, in an Anglo-French initiative. Mitterrand was continuing his flirtation with her and was to prove a true ally in the Gulf, as he had in the Falklands. When he invited her to attend the 200th anniversary of the French revolution, he was amused rather than irritated when she asked, in effect, what is there to celebrate? In an interview with *Le Monde* she pointed out that human rights did not begin with the French revolution; they had been developed over the preceding centuries in England. At the ceremonies, she presented Mitterrand with a copy of Dickens's *A Tale of Two Cities*.

At the Strasbourg European Council in December 1989, she and Mitterrand had two private discussions about the German problem. She found him as concerned as she was, observing that in history the Germans had been a people in constant movement and flux. She again pulled out of her handbag the map showing the various configurations of Germany in the past, which neither of them found reassuring. He said that Britain and France should draw together. She felt that they both wanted to try to check the

German juggernaut. He was, however, a far more feline politician than her. His public stance did not correspond to his private thoughts. He was not, he said publicly, one of those who were 'putting on the brakes'.

She saw him again at the Elysée in January 1990. He complained that the Germans regarded any talk of caution as anti-German. In reality there was no force in Europe that could stop reunification happening. She still wanted to delay the process to the extent possible. She realised, however, that he was unwilling to alter the entire direction of his foreign policy, which had been constructed around cooperation with Germany.

She told the former head of Radio Free Europe, George Urban, that she had never believed that German nationalism was dead, and that a united Germany inevitably would dominate Europe. In March 1990 she organised a Chequers seminar about Germany, attended by several well-known historians – Lord Dacre, Norman Stone, Timothy Garton Ash and Fritz Stern. They tried to convince her that the dangers were much less than she feared, with limited success. Lord Dacre (Hugh Trevor-Roper) pointed out that if anyone had told them in 1945 that there was a chance of a Germany united in freedom, a solid member of the West, 'we would not have believed our luck – and we should welcome it, not resist it'. This, he felt, did make an impact on her. The seminar reached the generally sensible conclusion that, though Germany would become more dominant within the European Community, history was unlikely to repeat itself and 'we must be nice to the Germans'. Charles Powell's note on the seminar, containing some colourful language about supposed German 'angst, aggressiveness, assertiveness, bullying, egotism, inferiority complex and sentimentality', subsequently was leaked to the press, causing quite a furore.[165]

Not long after the Chequers seminar, her confidant Nicholas Ridley, Transport Secretary, told Dominic Lawson, as he believed off the record, what he thought of the Germans. Monetary union, he said, was 'a German racket to take over the whole of Europe'. Mrs Thatcher felt that this remark represented 'an excess of honesty', but since he threw in a reference to Adolf Hitler, to her regret, he had to resign.

The Americans considered that her distrust of reunification was rooted in Britain's history as the keeper of the European balance of power. This was not a worry for them. What they did worry about, like her, were the implications this could have for Gorbachev. Kohl told Bush that it was 'a great mistake on Maggie's part to think that this is a time for caution'. Gorbachev, however, still was adamantly opposed to reunification. The US concern was that, united or not, Germany must remain within NATO.

George Bush observed that while Mrs Thatcher, Mitterrand and others feared that Germany might yet cause more trouble and tragedy, he did not. He was not worried about the ghosts of Germany's past. He became the first member of his own administration to support the cause of German reunification as a near-term objective, rather than over a period of time, thereby earning the lasting gratitude of Helmut Kohl. He did so ahead of all the other European leaders, who all were worried about the Gulliver effect of a reunited Germany.

By this stage Margaret Thatcher regarded reunification as inevitable. She agreed that a united Germany must be part of NATO, but she objected to the Bush/Kohl idea that this should be as part of an 'increasingly integrated European Community'. She feared they could find they had not attached Germany to Europe, but Europe to Germany! The EC 'might become Germany's new empire: the empires of the future will be economic empires'.[166]

She did not see Helmut Kohl as a benign bear-like Europhile, but as a heavyweight German Chancellor literally thumping the table and pursuing German interests as ruthlessly as, in his position, she might have done. She saw, however, that there was by now little chance of slowing down the process, particularly as, despite his private concerns, Mitterrand was not prepared to join her in doing so. As Mitterrand said to Bush, 'there is not much we could do'. Scowcroft doubted if the French could continue an equal partnership with the Germans, an opinion shared by the Quai d'Orsay.

The Americans saw 1990 as a very difficult year for Gorbachev, with no real improvement in the Soviet economy and increasing trouble with the nationalities. They worried as much as she did about Gorbachev's chances of survival.

In a telephone call with Bush in February, Mrs Thatcher stressed the importance of US troops remaining in Europe. Looking into the future, to Bush's surprise, she saw Russia as a counterweight to Germany in Europe. Kohl had alarmed the Poles by his vagueness about the eastern border. While as committed as ever to NATO, she had begun to see the CSCE process as a way of embracing the Russians into an 'alliance for democracy from the Atlantic to the Urals and beyond'.

At this point, the US proposed further cuts in US and Soviet forces in Europe, to 200,000 on each side. Eagleburger and Gates were sent across the Atlantic once again to persuade Mrs Thatcher. 'Take your usual seats,' she said to them. Scowcroft felt that her caution on this subject was justified, reflecting her 'strategic cast of mind' and fears that reform in the Soviet Union was not yet irreversible. She wanted to know whether Soviet forces really would be withdrawn beyond the Urals. Once reassured on this essential point, she acquiesced in what was proposed. Tweedle-dee and Tweedle-dum were told that they would always be welcome, 'but never again on this subject!'

There followed in March a crisis over Lithuania, with the Soviet military leaders determined that the country should not be allowed to leave the Soviet Union. On 28 March Margaret Thatcher told an alarmed George Bush that Gorbachev had been evasive when she had urged him, in a telephone conversation earlier in the day, not to use force in Lithuania, as the Soviet military were urging him to do. He had sounded sombre, pessimistic and solitary. Bush sent him a message expressing concern that Gorbachev had told Thatcher that his options were narrowing and joined in her remonstrance that a crackdown in Lithuania would be fatal to the cause of reform. While a major crisis was narrowly averted, when Margaret Thatcher and Bush met in Bermuda in April, they agreed that the pressures on Gorbachev were increasing: the military were withdrawing their support.[167]

Scowcroft saw that they were underestimating the speed at which East Germany was disintegrating, though the Soviet Foreign Minister, Shevardnadze, still was insisting that a united Germany must be neutral. Bush assured Kohl that he would support reunification, provided a unified Germany remained within NATO.

By this stage, Douglas Hurd was describing Margaret Thatcher to George Bush as a 'reluctant reunifier – not against, but reluctant'. She wanted further thought to be given to what this would mean for the EC, NATO and East–West relations.

She continued to worry that the appearance of NATO moving east would destabilise Gorbachev. She remained fiercely loyal to the man who had rendered eastern European freedom possible. Her foreign policy adviser, Percy Cradock, felt that, by this time, she had become overprotective of Gorbachev. The very real alternative, however, looked to be a reassertion of power by the Soviet old guard. Scowcroft and the French were as concerned as she was about this. They all feared the sort of coup that was in fact attempted against Gorbachev in August 1991. Scowcroft, though, was dismayed that she seemed to support a demilitarised East Germany, alternatively suggesting that Soviet forces might stay there for a while. She continued to press for clarity on German intentions about the border with Poland.

George Bush's priority was to get a firm commitment from Kohl that he would seek full membership in NATO for a united Germany.

In a meeting at Camp David, Kohl said that Europe must now press ahead with monetary union. To Bush's alarm, he envisaged a semi-detached relationship with NATO. He was told that one France in NATO was enough. He thought that Soviet acquiescence in a united Germany might turn out to be a question of cash. To both Bush's and Margaret Thatcher's concern, Kohl still was ducking recognition of the Oder–Neisse border with Poland on the grounds that this must be a matter for a united German parliament. In March, Genscher speculated that both NATO and the Warsaw Pact might soon wither away.

Realising that the relationship with Bush was in need of repair, Mrs Thatcher arranged a more relaxed meeting with him in Bermuda in April 1990. By now she had learned to wait for him to set out his own views before explaining hers. Denis

Thatcher was dragooned by the always hyperactive George Bush into playing eighteen holes of golf in a near-hurricane and pouring rain, described by her as 'a very British occasion' and by her husband as the worst golfing experience of his life.

Bush found her more optimistic about a united Germany in NATO, but still suggesting that Soviet troops might stay for a while. Bush disagreed: 'I want the Soviets to go home.'[168]

Despite the differences of view between the principals, in particular about Germany, a very special relationship did exist in this period between General Brent Scowcroft, Bush's National Security Adviser, and Charles Powell, who spoke on the telephone almost every day. Scowcroft felt that by this time Powell was 'the only serious influence on Thatcher's views on foreign policy'.

More often than not, he alone was present with her at meetings with other heads of government, highlighting in his often brilliantly written memoranda what appeared important in these exchanges. He thought like her and was exceptionally close to her, leading Percy Cradock to observe that 'it was sometimes difficult to establish where Mrs Thatcher ended and Charles Powell began'. Scowcroft regarded his exchanges with Powell as representing the embodiment of the special relationship.

The Foreign Office, which distrusted his eurosceptical views and feared that he did not always act as a moderating influence on her, had tried in vain to despatch Powell as ambassador to Switzerland or to Spain, only for both appointments to be vetoed by the Prime Minister. For he had become her closest and most trusted adviser, matching her in energy and stamina and making a major contribution to her success, as he did subsequently in helping her successor, John Major, through the Gulf War. In the tribute to him in her memoirs she wrote that, although he could be very diplomatic, he 'recognised, as I did, that there was more to foreign policy than diplomacy'.[169]

On 31 May, Gorbachev arrived in Washington. In the private talks, Bush persuaded him that they must leave it to the Germans to decide if they wanted to be in NATO, to the visible consternation of the other members of his delegation, who showed virtually open rebellion against him. They shared a helicopter to Camp David, both of them, ironically, accompanied by a military aide carrying the codes that would authorise a nuclear attack on the other's country.

Mrs Thatcher had agreed to host a NATO summit in London in July. Bush circulated a draft statement intended to help Gorbachev by offering an olive branch to the rapidly disintegrating Warsaw Pact.

She was alarmed at the US proposal to declare that nuclear arms were 'weapons of last resort', which she regarded as getting dangerously close to the Soviet doctrine of 'no first use' of nuclear weapons. In the run-up to the summit she made a speech looking ahead, in which she urged that NATO must give more thought to threats to its security from other directions. NATO, she argued, must transform itself by being prepared to act in the future outside the European theatre.

At the summit, further cuts in nuclear weapons were firmly linked to agreement on conventional forces and the US text was watered down to express the pious hope that NATO would reach a state of affairs that would mean that nuclear arms would become 'truly weapons of last resort', thus satisfying her. It also stated that NATO was moving away from 'forward defence', a change with which she wholeheartedly agreed.

Following the summit, she was definitively outflanked when Kohl met Gorbachev in the Caucasus. They agreed that Germany would take over all East Germany's debts to the Soviet Union, massively subsidise the withdrawal of Soviet forces and offer other economic assistance. In return, Gorbachev accepted publicly that a united Germany would be in NATO if the German people so decided, a statement Bush and Baker regarded as marking the end of the Cold War.

She recognised subsequently that Bush and Baker managed the difficult and dangerous transformation with great skill. If there was one area of foreign policy, she wrote later, in which she met with unambiguous failure, it was her policy on German reunification. In the event, the desire for unity among the German people proved irresistible. Yet she believed that, over time, Europe would find it hard to cope with the Gulliver of Germany, that increasingly the Franco-German relationship would be dominated by Germany and that the eurozone would turn out to be a deutschmark zone.

As George Bush told me, he never found it easy to deal with Margaret Thatcher, but this did not stop him admiring her. Not surprisingly, he found it easier to get on with John Major, both being pragmatists and neither being a devotee of what Bush described as the 'vision thing'. Partly, this was because Bush had been a number two for eight years while Margaret Thatcher was a number one and she failed to adjust when that relationship changed. He did not enjoy, and Baker was at times exasperated at, being lectured by her. Yet he acknowledged that, while completely mistaken on German reunification, on some other issues she was right, notably no zero option for SNF, the need to achieve deep cuts in Soviet conventional forces in Europe and preservation of the doctrine of flexible response. It was for this reason that he described her with a smile as his 'anchor to windward'.

She was remarkably unfazed by the signs of tension in the relationship, remarking that, in the first serious crisis, the Americans would soon rediscover who their real friends were. This was not long in coming and, when it did, the Gulf crisis brought her and George Bush much closer together than they had ever been before. He was never to forget the impact she made when members of his own administration were divided as to how to respond to the invasion of Kuwait.

XVI

'NO TIME TO GO WOBBLY'

A few years before, when asked who might succeed Margaret Thatcher if she were run over by a bus, Peter Carrington had replied: 'What bus would dare?'

But in April 1990 he invited her to dinner at his house in the country to persuade her to consider stepping down. He told her that the party wanted her to leave office with dignity and at a time of her choosing. She interpreted this as a message from the Conservative Party Establishment, alarmed at the party's poor standing in the opinion polls due mainly to high inflation and high interest rates and the general unpopularity of the poll tax. There was a feeling that she was no longer in touch with opinion, as she had been in her early years, and that she was in very obvious danger of going on too long. This opinion was not shared by her, as she made clear to Carrington. There was, she felt, no successor she could trust to safeguard her legacy, except possibly John Major who was, however, untested. She intended if necessary to go down fighting for her beliefs. 'Dignity' did not come into it.[170]

At around this time, the Conservative Party chairman, Kenneth Baker, attended a dinner with Tim Bell and Gordon Reece who, with Maurice Saatchi, were both personal friends and her favourite media advisers. They agreed that it was time for her to go. 'You must tell her', Tim Bell said to Reece. Reece said that he couldn't because 'I love her'. Denis Thatcher, who agreed with them, interjected: 'Steady on. She's my wife!'[171]

☞

On 1 August she flew across the Atlantic to meet George Bush in Aspen, Colorado. She was aware that the Iraqis had sent troops to the border with Kuwait, but this was generally believed to be sabre-rattling. At 2 a.m. on 2 August, the Iraqi army invaded Kuwait. Charles Powell telephoned to tell her the news and she instructed two British naval vessels in the Indian Ocean to head for the Gulf. The Arab League failed to agree a statement, with King Hussein defending the Iraqi action. The Gulf rulers were very alarmed, as were the Saudis. The UN Security Council passed a resolution condemning Iraq and calling for withdrawal. The immediate question was whether Saddam Hussein would next cross the border to seize the Saudi oilfields. In his initial comment to the press that morning, George Bush said that he was not contemplating intervention. This was an off-the-cuff remark, but Brent Scowcroft was alarmed at the tone of the first discussion in the National Security Council, which he regarded as implying acceptance of the Iraqi invasion of Kuwait as a fait accompli, with the focus on the implications for Saudi Arabia.[172]

In Aspen, Margaret Thatcher was staying at the summer ranch owned by the US ambassador in London, Henry Catto Jr. She was told that George Bush was still coming to Aspen to talk to her, which was of itself a tribute to her importance in a crisis of this kind. He began by asking her what she thought. She said that it was a clear case of aggression and aggressors must never be appeased. There was little to stop Saddam Hussein seizing the Saudi and Gulf oilfields if he wished to do so. George Bush had been speaking to President Mubarak and King Hussein. They had asked for time to find an Arab solution. He said that this must involve Iraqi withdrawal. He had imposed sanctions against Iraq and ordered US ships into the area. She wanted the Security Council to impose a full trade embargo. They agreed that they could send troops to protect Saudi Arabia, but only at the request of the King.

At their subsequent press conference, Bush was asked if he ruled out the use of force. He said that he did not, which was interpreted as a strengthening of his position, as indeed it was, though in her memoirs Margaret Thatcher observed that she had not detected any weakness in it from the first.

She then spoke to Mitterrand, who took a firm line against the Iraqi aggression. He showed throughout the crisis that the French were the only other European country 'with the stomach for a fight'. In her speech at the Aspen Institute she said:

> Iraq's invasion of Kuwait defies every principle for which the United Nations stands. If we let them succeed, no small country can ever feel safe again. The law of the jungle would take over … a vital principle is at stake: an aggressor must never be allowed to get his way.

The European Community imposed a general trade embargo. She asked the Foreign Office to prepare plans for a blockade and suggested that thought should be given to precise military guarantees for Saudi Arabia.

On the White House lawn on 5 August, George Bush said: 'This will not stand, this aggression against Kuwait.' Colin Powell believed that this did owe something to his meeting with Mrs Thatcher. 'This will not stand', he felt, had a Thatcheresque ring to it.[173] But Bush was heading in that direction already, even though other key members of his administration, including James Baker and General Powell, were not as yet planning for anything more than the protection of Saudi Arabia.

The Prime Minister flew from Aspen for a further meeting with Bush in Washington. She found him much more self-confident than in any of their previous meetings – firm, cool and decisive. She had always liked him; her respect for him now soared. Iraqi tanks had moved right up to the Saudi border. She feared that Iraq might attack Saudi Arabia before the King formally asked the US for help.

At this point, the US Defense Secretary, Dick Cheney, telephoned Bush from Saudi Arabia. King Fahd was fully behind the US plan to send the 82nd Airborne Division with air support to Saudi Arabia. But he wanted no announcement until the forces were actually in place.

The meeting, however, also saw the beginning of an argument with the Americans, particularly Jim Baker, about what UN authority was needed to deal with Saddam Hussein. The Prime Minister felt that the resolution already passed by the UN Security Council demanding Iraqi withdrawal was sufficient, together with the right of self-defence under Article 51 of the UN Charter. Although firmly considering herself to be a strong believer in international law, she did not like unnecessary recourse to the UN, where resolutions could get blocked or watered down. Too often, the UN was rendered powerless by Russian or Chinese obstruction. She believed that in such circumstances the US and its allies must be prepared to act anyway.

The UN Security Council had voted unanimously to impose sanctions against Iraq. The Prime Minister said that these would not work without a blockade. Bush agreed with her, but a blockade was an act of war. Scowcroft suggested they call it quarantine.

Also in the meeting, they discussed the need to respond to any Iraqi use of chemical weapons. She was determined that they must keep Israel out of the conflict. She undertook to use her influence with the Gulf rulers to mobilise support for what they were doing. On return to London, she had an hour-long telephone conversation with King Fahd to secure his formal request for British aircraft and forces to be stationed in Saudi Arabia. He was incredulous that King Hussein should have come out in support of Iraq.

From 9 August, her government sent Tornado and Jaguar squadrons to Saudi Arabia. She kept in frequent touch with Bush by telephone. It looked as if Saddam would not move into Saudi Arabia once US forces were there, but she did not want any repetition of the mistaken assessment about Kuwait. She regarded the Syrians as especially unsavoury allies, but reluctantly agreed to restore diplomatic relations as they too were opposed to Iraq. Saddam, meanwhile, held a televised meeting with terrified British hostages in Baghdad.

There was a continuing argument as to whether the UN resolution authorised the use of force. In mid-August this came to a head as five tankers en route to Iraq headed for Yemen and resisted being boarded or turned back. When the Americans talked to the Prime Minister about it, 'of course Thatcher said go after the ships'. Baker persuaded Bush to delay so that he could try to get Eduard Shevardnadze on board. Bush telephoned her at three in the morning London time to tell her this – a conversation he was not looking forward to. It was on this occasion that she famously told him: 'Well, alright George, but this is no time to go wobbly!' Both Bush and Scowcroft were amused. After this, said Scowcroft, they used the phrase among themselves almost every day.[174] On 25 August they got the UN Security Council to pass a fresh resolution authorising 'all appropriate measures' to enforce the embargo against Iraq.

When King Hussein saw her on 31 August, she expressed her bitter disappointment that one of Britain's closest friends in the region appeared to be siding with the enemy. When he sought to defend the Iraqi action, he was told that he was defending a blatant act of aggression. Saddam was an international brigand who had used chemical weapons against his own people. She could not have been more direct, but the King did not appear to believe that he could come out against Saddam and survive.

A vote in the House of Commons on 6 September produced a huge majority in support of the government's position. She was increasingly convinced that a military campaign would have to be fought. The Foreign Secretary, Douglas Hurd, believed that sanctions might work if they could convince Saddam that he would be defeated militarily if he stayed in Kuwait. She insisted on looking at dates on which military action could be taken. She feared that, otherwise, the coalition against Saddam could start to crumble and even that Israel might intervene.

The Americans asked her to send an armoured brigade with Challenger I tanks. She was concerned that these had a poor reputation for reliability. The Ministry of Defence and the manufacturer, Vickers, were subjected to a merciless inquisition and she insisted that they must be despatched with a large cache of spares. She wanted the force commander to be someone in whom she and his troops could have full confidence. General Sir Peter de la Billière, commander of the SAS, was her choice for the post. The Defence Secretary, Tom King, objected that de la Billière was within a week of retiring, but was overruled.

She telephoned Bush to confirm that she was sending the 7th Armoured Brigade with 120 tanks, a regiment of field artillery and a battalion of mechanised infantry to the Gulf. He described this to her as a 'marvellous commitment, this is really something'.

She saw Bush again in New York on 30 September. He told her that he thought there would be an Iraqi provocation and they could launch a huge air strike to devastate Iraq's military and strategic facilities. Both she and Scowcroft were sceptical about this: they had to plan for ground forces as well.

With Baker joining the meeting, they discussed his wish for a further UN resolution specifically authorising the use of force to secure Iraqi withdrawal. As always, she would have preferred to rely on Article 51, the right to self-defence, though it was far from clear how exactly this applied. It was very clear, however, that sanctions alone were not going to bring about an Iraqi withdrawal.[175]

Baker was worried about Congressional support. Finding Mrs Thatcher more warlike than he was and conscious that 90 per cent of the military effort would have to be made by the Americans, Baker wrote amusingly in his memoirs that much had been written about the special relationship between the United States and Great Britain, and the bilateral ties forged over two centuries were every bit as durable as advertised. 'We have no better friends than the British. And the relationship *is* special. This gives the British a license others don't have – the license of occasionally flexing *our* muscles.'[176]

She felt, as in the case of the Falklands, that there was never any lack of people anxious to avoid the use of force, no matter how slight the chances of any negotiation succeeding. On this occasion, the task of last-ditch diplomacy fell to Gorbachev's representative, Yevgeny Primakov. Having seen Saddam Hussein in Baghdad, he met the Prime Minister at Chequers to say that some way must be found, for instance an initiative on the Arab–Israeli dispute, to save his face. He got very short shrift. In his own account of the meeting Primakov claimed that, when asked what Russia could do to help, she replied that what Russia could most usefully do was get out of the way.

In mid-October she told Bush that she was concerned about holding the coalition together. Once they had the necessary forces in place, they should act at the latest by mid-February. Otherwise the Arab governments would start to lose confidence. He assured her that they would return to the UN only if confident they could get the resolution they needed, but it would be the better course if they could get one. He raised the idea of a mission to rescue embassy personnel in Kuwait which, wisely, she opposed as too risky. It was around this point, according to Scowcroft, that George Bush finally resolved that a land war was going to be necessary to liberate Kuwait.

On 23 October, she had a meeting with the Defence Secretary, Tom King, and Douglas Hurd to give guidance to the Chief of Defence Staff for talks in Washington with General Colin Powell. The object was the liberation of Kuwait, not to remove Saddam, though that might be an admirable side effect. Further work on targets in Iraq was needed, including possibly power stations and dams. There was no intention to occupy any part of Iraq, but allied forces must be able to cross into Iraq to achieve the liberation of Kuwait. They must get the Americans to accept that military action probably would have to be initiated before year end. They should be weaned away from seeking prior authorisation for the use of force from the UN.

She had a further argument about this with Baker on 9 November. But he was not to be moved. He said that UN authority was vital to sustain the support of US opinion for military action.[177]

In the Gulf, General de la Billière was told by the Defence Secretary, Tom King, that there was a real chance of a coup against Mrs Thatcher in the Conservative Party. For someone working flat out to plan a military campaign, the news was extremely disconcerting. He deplored what he regarded as the 'shenanigans' in the Conservative Party at a time when British forces were about to go into action. The news that Margaret Thatcher was indeed being forced to stand down sent a shock wave through the coalition. Arabs and Americans alike 'all had the highest regard for her and simply could not understand how it was possible for a leader of international stature, who had done so much for her country, to be evicted from office by a vicious party squabble just as Britain was preparing to fight a major war'. The Gulf rulers, he had found, were not merely pro-British, but even more pro-Thatcher.[178]

De la Billière felt strongly that this, to him, unseemly party squabble should have been settled once the war was over, not as it was about to begin. To his immense relief, however, he was told that at her last Cabinet on 22 November – the one at which she resigned – the decision was taken to double Britain's military commitment by sending a further armoured brigade, forming the 1st Armoured Division, with over 30,000 British troops committed to the campaign.

Bush and Scowcroft found her downfall amazing, 'so fast and almost unforeseen'. Both were astonished at the suddenness and ruthlessness of this very British coup. While they had not been as close as she was to Reagan, George Bush felt that their relationship had grown steadily warmer through his time as President. It was, he thought, typical of her that her farewell letter as Prime Minister should have informed him of a doubling of the British military commitment.[179]

In her memoirs, she wrote with understandable bitterness that she 'was not allowed by the Conservative Party to see through the campaign to throw Saddam Hussein out of Kuwait'.[180] There is no doubt that she contributed more than any world leader except George Bush to that objective, though John Major was equally steadfast in support of the Americans when the conflict began.

Although it would have saved her from the ignominy of being ousted by her own party, it was perhaps as well that Carrington's advice, which she never was likely to have heeded anyway, was not followed at the time. For this was the kind of crisis in which she excelled. The Americans could not have valued more highly her support from the outset and the major military commitment she made, though they felt that she was getting carried away in her demands for more immediate action and Baker, through skilful diplomacy, did in the end get the UN resolution he needed. He was able to do so, however, only because the Russians, under Gorbachev at the time, were prepared to be a great deal more accommodating than has usually proved to be the case, before or since. Margaret Thatcher had every reason to be proud of her part in securing the liberation of Kuwait.

XVII

'A SINGLE CURRENCY IS NOT THE POLICY OF THIS GOVERNMENT'

The sequence of events that led to her downfall had started many years before, with the abrupt departure from the government of Michael Heseltine in 1986, in protest at her refusal to promote a European defence industry merger to save the Westland helicopter company. Although Heseltine had no support from other members of the Cabinet at the time and it was never clear that he was right about Westland, he was, as she acknowledged, one of the most charismatic and talented figures in British politics, who had been a darling of the party conferences and who, as Defence Secretary, had led with brio her government's successful battle against the Campaign for Nuclear Disarmament and their supporters. His exit left on the back benches a figure who undoubtedly did have leadership qualities and ambitions of his own.

Following her 'ambush' by Geoffrey Howe and Nigel Lawson about the ERM before the Madrid European Council, she had concluded that she must never allow anything of the kind to happen again. Yet as she prepared for a government reshuffle one month later in July 1989, Geoffrey Howe still felt confident that he would continue as Foreign Secretary. It came as a complete shock and surprise to him to be told that she wanted to remove him from the Foreign Office and make him Leader of the House of Commons. She offered him the Home Office, which she knew he would not accept. She also knew that he had become extremely fond of Chevening, the Foreign Secretary's country house. So, with Lawson's agreement, she offered him the Chancellor's country house, Dorneywood, and finally, with reluctance and at his insistence, the title of Deputy Prime Minister.

Details of the protracted negotiations leaked to the media, with Geoffrey Howe getting a bad press about the country houses, which he blamed on her. In some further unpleasant briefing, 10 Downing Street indicated that the title of Deputy Prime Minister was essentially meaningless. The result of all this was an outpouring of sympathy and support for Geoffrey Howe. When he rose in Parliament to answer his first question as Leader of the House, with the Prime Minister in her place on the front bench, he was greeted with a roar of approval from both sides of the House. Had she been more Machiavellian, she could have portrayed Howe's new role in a more constructive way. But that was not in her nature. Nor was she prepared to create any impression that he might succeed her.

She had intended Nigel Lawson to continue as Chancellor, but three months later he too was gone. The boom which had helped to win the 1987 election had resulted in an overheated economy. Nigel Lawson later acknowledged that interest rates were cut too far in response to the October 1987 stock market crash and should have been raised earlier.[181] His reluctance to do so was influenced by his effort to maintain the DM3 parity between the pound and the deutschmark. Inflation had reached levels she had never expected to see again. As interest rates had to be hiked to 15 per cent, the government had lost its reputation for economic competence. In common with the 'teenage scribblers' in the press denounced by Lawson, Margaret Thatcher held him partly responsible for this state of affairs. The reappointment of Alan Walters as her special adviser had triggered a spate of press stories contrasting his views of the ERM with those of the Chancellor, precipitating Lawson's resignation and that of Walters.

Following Lawson's resignation and the ousting of Geoffrey Howe from the Foreign Office, a 'stalking horse' candidate appeared to challenge her for the leadership of the parliamentary party in the form of Sir Anthony Meyer, a little-known pro-European backbencher. He won only thirty-three votes to her 314. But a further twenty-seven MPs spoiled their ballots or abstained. Many of these dissenters, in now her third term in office, either never had been appointed to the government or had been dismissed from office by her. Her campaign manager, the Defence Secretary George Younger, warned her that this reflected discontent in the parliamentary party.

She continued to trounce in single combat interviewers like Robin Day, who had terrorised both her ministers and opponents but was reduced to apologising to his viewers for his failure to make any impression on her. To the commonest charge against her, she offered a characteristic response: 'The very leadership and style you criticise has in fact done a great deal for this country.' Accused of being domineering in an interview with Brian Walden, she told him that 'the only person trying to be domineering in this interview is you!'

Her position in the party and the country was being fatally undermined by her unflinching advocacy of the poll tax, or the community charge, as she preferred to call it. John Major had to keep reminding himself never to call it the poll tax in front of her. There was a good deal of logic to the original concept. It seemed to her unreasonable that so much of the burden of funding local government should fall on the ratepayers, when a much wider range of people benefited from local services. If the burden were spread more widely, there would be more incentive to control local government spending.

Nigel Lawson had opposed the idea flatly, telling her from the outset that a poll tax would be 'completely unworkable and politically catastrophic' and that what was required instead was reform of the rating system.[182] Yet several of the best and brightest members of her government, starting with Kenneth Baker and William Waldegrave and then Chris Patten, were involved in both formulating and implementing it. The new charge turned out to be far higher than originally estimated, just as unpopular with Conservative supporters as it was with the rest of the population and exceptionally difficult to levy. Her dogged pursuit of this new system of local taxation was taken as a sign by many of her supporters that she was simply out of touch.

Yet it was Europe that lit the fuse that finally exploded beneath her. Returning from the European Council in Rome in October 1990, she stated that a 'single currency is not the policy of this government'. In reply to questions, she doubted if the 'hard ecu' would become widely used in the Community. She was entirely right about that, but this caused John Major almost to fall off his seat beside her, as this was the concept the government had been advocating in a futile attempt to head others off from pursuing a common currency. She added that 'this government believes in the pound sterling'. By now she was being egged on by her backbenchers. As for Jacques Delors's concept of a federal Europe, where the European Parliament would be the legislature, the Commission the executive and the Council of Ministers the Senate, 'no, no, no' was her response.

What she was stating was British policy, then and now. It was the way in which she said it that was the final straw for Geoffrey Howe.

Later in the week at a Cabinet meeting, she chastised him in front of his colleagues about the legislative programme. That afternoon, he resigned. On 3 November, Michael Heseltine published a letter about the need for the government to chart a new course on Europe. The opinion polls were showing Labour over twenty points ahead. Her advisers then made a series of errors. The date for a leadership challenge was brought forward to a point at which the day of the vote coincided with the Conference on Security and Co-operation in Europe (CSCE) summit she was due to attend in Paris. The No. 10 press office appeared to be goading Heseltine to stand against her.

In his resignation letter, Geoffrey Howe had said that 'the risks of being left behind on EMU are severe'. He was 'deeply anxious' that the mood she had struck made it more difficult for Britain to influence matters. He felt that more than one form of monetary union was possible, without explaining how.

When Parliament reopened, she claimed that Neil Kinnock would be hard pressed to find any significant policy difference on Europe between her and Howe, who was further infuriated by this. In press interviews over the weekend, she denounced Heseltine's commitment to corporatism and state intervention in the economy.

On 13 November, with her in the Chamber and Nigel Lawson

sitting beside him on the back benches, Geoffrey Howe began his resignation speech in his usual low monotone. Denis Healey had once described being attacked by him as like being savaged by a dead sheep. But on this occasion there was no mistaking the passion with which he was speaking. He revealed that he and Lawson had been urging Britain to join the ERM since 1985 and argued that inflation would have been lower if they had done so. Britain could not afford once again to be left out of developments in Europe. He described her remarks about the hard ecu as undoing the work of the Chancellor and the Governor of the Bank of England, like sending batsmen to the crease only for them to find that their bats had been broken by the team captain. It was time for others also now to consider where their loyalties lay.[183]

Nigel Lawson and many others regarded it as the most devastating speech they had heard in Parliament and an indictment of her whole style of government, the more devastating because of the measured way in which it was delivered. She recognised it herself as Howe's finest parliamentary performance. She was hurt and shocked, despite the irritability of their relations over the years, regarding it as an act of 'bile and treachery', forgetting her own offensive treatment of him.[184]

Two days later, Heseltine announced his candidature, promising a fundamental review of the community charge. Douglas Hurd and John Major proposed and seconded her. In press interviews she declared that a referendum would be needed before there was any question of joining a single currency. This was not just an economic issue: it had profound constitutional implications. On 18 November she left for the CSCE summit in Paris, signing the historic agreement on the reduction of conventional forces in Europe. She had the usual rounds of talks with Gorbachev, Mitterrand and others and dinner at the embassy with Kohl. Hurd was full of admiration for her composure at the summit.[185]

Her campaign team which, from the outset, had been hopelessly overconfident and very poorly led by Peter Morrison MP, had continued to believe she would win. On the afternoon of 20 November, Charles Powell received the news by telephone and gave a sad thumbs down. She had defeated Heseltine by 204 votes to 152, with sixteen abstentions. Under the complex rules, if she had secured just two more votes, she would have won outright, with no need for a second round of voting. She immediately walked outside to the press and on the embassy steps announced that she would be contesting the next round. She had not intended to go to the grand dinner at Versailles, until she was told that Mitterrand was holding it up until she got there. She did not yet realise that this was the point at which many of her government colleagues were planning to abandon her.

On her return to London, she went up to the flat in 10 Downing Street to see her husband. 'Affection never blunted honesty between us.' His advice was that she should withdraw. 'Don't go on, love,' he said.[186] She was not persuaded.

When she asked Douglas Hurd to re-nominate her, he agreed unhesitatingly, even though he told her he was by now finding her difficult to work with, 'though some of us want to try', because of her tendency to argue her case so passionately that it could be offensive to others. John Major's hesitation was palpable. 'If that is what you want, I will.' The polls by now were suggesting that if Heseltine were elected leader, the Conservative Party would move ahead of or level with Labour again.

She had already been told by a group of her colleagues that there were fears that she would be humiliated if she faced a second vote and that Heseltine might easily prevail. Norman Tebbit, Kenneth Baker and Cecil Parkinson supported her to the end.

But when, over two hours, she consulted the members of her Cabinet one by one in her room in the House of Commons, nearly all of them used the same formula which they clearly had concerted between them. They would back her, of course, but they did not believe she could win. This message, which she was to describe as 'treachery with a smile on its face', was delivered with particular gusto by Ken Clarke. She had not expected support from Chris Patten ('a man of the left') or Malcolm Rifkind, neither of whom had ever been political soulmates. But the same message was delivered with sadness by her long-time supporters. She was told that the only way to prevent Heseltine becoming leader was for her to release Hurd and Major to stand against him.

She spent the evening working on her speech in the 'no confidence' debate. At 7.30 the next morning she telephoned the Cabinet Secretary, Andrew Turnbull, to tell him she was resigning. Hurd and Major were informed. She told the Cabinet she was resigning to give the Conservative Party the best chance of winning the next election. She felt as if she were sleep-walking, at times overcome by emotion and giving way to tears. When Cabinet members started paying tributes to her, she brought them to a halt by saying that she found business easier to cope with than sympathy.[187] She told the Cabinet they must unite to back the candidate most likely to defeat Michael Heseltine. Later in the Cabinet meeting, she secured their agreement to send a second armoured brigade to participate in the campaign to liberate Kuwait. She sent messages to her fellow heads of government, then had a brief meeting with the Queen, before setting off for the House of Commons. There followed one of the truly great performances of her parliamentary career.

In response to a not very effective speech by Neil Kinnock, she started by reminding the House of Nicholas Henderson's despatch of 1979 chronicling Britain's economic decline and loss of influence in world affairs. Conservative government, she claimed, had reversed all that. The government had 'given power back to the people' by curbing the trade unions, with wider home and share ownership, more choice in health and education, privatisation, lower taxes, two million more jobs, an enterprise economy and higher living standards overall. As for Kinnock, he did not know whether he was in favour of the single currency or not, because he 'does not know what it means'. When he interjected that it was a hypothetical question, she said that it most certainly was not. She rejected the idea of a European Central Bank accountable to no one, least of all national parliaments.

> The point of that kind of Europe ... is no democracy, taking powers away from every single Parliament, and having a single currency, a monetary policy and interest rates which take all political power away from us. A single currency is about ... a federal Europe by the back door.

'I am enjoying this', she added, noting that, ten years before, the whole of eastern Europe had been under totalitarian rule. Now they had a Europe in which democracy, the rule of law and human rights were spreading widely; the threat to security from the overwhelming conventional forces of the Warsaw Pact had been removed. The Berlin Wall had been torn down and the Cold War was over. 'These immense changes did not come about by chance. They had been achieved by strength and resolution in defence and a refusal ever to be intimidated.' Western governments had kept alive the hopes of the eastern Europeans that one day eastern Europe too would enjoy freedom. She concluded with: 'There is something else which one feels. That is a sense of this country's destiny: the centuries of history and experience which ensure that, when principles have to be defended, when good has to be upheld and evil has to be overcome, Britain will take up arms.'

Her government had never flinched from difficult decisions and that was why the House and the country could have confidence in it. She had, she believed, 'restored Britain's reputation as a force to be reckoned with in the world'.[188]

This tremendous performance more than trumped that of Geoffrey Howe, causing some of her backbenchers to wonder what on earth they had done.

She remained extremely bitter at what she regarded as the treachery of the Cabinet, but proceeded to campaign harder for her chosen successor, John Major, than she had done for herself. She preferred Major to Hurd, she said, because she did not want old-style Etonian Tories to succeed her. John Major had been obliged to make his own way and would have more appeal to the voters. Major won the election with fewer votes than she had received, but Hurd and Heseltine then withdrew.

She spent a sad last weekend at Chequers, then visited Conservative Central Office, where she unwisely suggested she would be 'a very good back-seat driver'. George Bush telephoned her about Kuwait. 'He won't falter,' she concluded with satisfaction. Overwhelmed by saying goodbye to her Downing Street staff, she left No. 10 in tears en route to their house in Dulwich.

In the end she had lost the instinctive feel for what the electorate wanted that had served her so well through three election victories. Her third term was in every respect less successful than her first two. There was, intellectually, a hardening of the arteries, far less of the questioning attitude which had been a hallmark of her before, and more prolonged attacks of dogmatism. Her legendary ability to function on only four or five hours' sleep a night and her demonic energy were fading away. She was showing signs of cumulative exhaustion, no longer welcoming argument as she had done before and finding it instead an irritating distraction. After more than a decade as Prime Minister, she found it harder to remain the best-prepared leader in any international meeting, as she invariably was in her earlier years. Officials called in to brief her, she felt, had less knowledge of the issues, and far less experience of the personalities involved, than she did. Following the removal of Geoffrey Howe as Foreign Secretary, the resignation of Nigel Lawson, and unremittingly bad economic news, a bunker mentality had taken hold in 10 Downing Street. Yet, once her fate had been decided, she had delivered a performance in the House of Commons that none of her opponents, before her or behind her, could ever have achieved, leaving her supporters and many other observers with the impression that a great leader had been overthrown by relative Lilliputians.

The Lilliputians had their reasons, not least a desire to get re-elected. John Major, attempting the near-impossible task of following in her shoes, was a much underestimated Prime Minister, who left the country and its economy in remarkably good shape when it was handed on to his successors.

John Major regarded her 'warrior characteristics' as profoundly un-Conservative. Yet he felt that it would have been more fitting if a leader of her stature had been overthrown by the British people in an election, rather than by her Cabinet and parliamentary colleagues.[189] The last word on this subject should be left with her. Invited by Lord Carrington to retire with dignity, she replied that dignity had nothing to do with it. She intended to go down fighting and that is what she did.

XVIII

'THE UNITED STATES CAN BE RELIED UPON TO DO THE RIGHT THING IN THE END, HAVING FIRST EXHAUSTED THE AVAILABLE ALTERNATIVES'

As an inveterate workaholic whose only real interest was in politics, Margaret Thatcher found it extremely difficult to adjust to life after 10 Downing Street. She kept herself occupied making visits to and speeches in the many parts of the world in which she continued to be held in high esteem, especially the United States, eastern Europe and Asia. As a passionate conviction politician, there were bound to be issues on which she was going to disagree with her successors, a classic case being that of Bosnia.

In the autumn of 1991 she denounced the aggression by the Serbian-dominated Yugoslav National Army against Croatia and called for the recognition of Croatia as an independent state. The lack of any western response encouraged the Serbs to believe that they could do the same in Bosnia. In August 1992 the Bosnian Vice-President Ganic saw her in Switzerland to tell her at first hand about the horrors of life under the Serb bombardment in Sarajevo. Aiming her remarks at US opinion, she wrote in the

New York Times on 6 August that, if the Serbs did not cease their aggression, there should be air strikes against bridges, military convoys, Serb gun positions and supply depots. She denounced the UN arms embargo as penalising only the Muslims, as the Serbs were supplied by the Yugoslav National Army.

She was a firm believer in the dictum attributed to her hero Edmund Burke that for evil to triumph, it was sufficient for good men – and women – to do nothing.[190] She had little faith in the 'international community', which she found a nebulous concept. She did not believe that it or the United Nations were capable of dealing with really menacing regimes, a task which she saw as falling, typically, to the United States and its allies, led by Britain, preferably under UN auspices.

But there was no appetite on the part of George Bush, facing an election, to get involved militarily in Yugoslavia. In an internal meeting, Baker had declared that 'we do not have a dog in this fight'. John Major convened a conference in London at which he announced that British troops would be sent to Bosnia, under UN auspices, but their mission would be restricted to helping to get humanitarian supplies through.

The despatch of British and other European forces undoubtedly helped to save thousands of lives. But, from the outset, it seemed doubtful if a role restricted to a humanitarian mission could possibly be viable in the midst of a raging war. As she pointed out, the UN forces in Bosnia were hopelessly vulnerable if NATO got serious about dealing with the Serbs.

Bill Clinton came into office determined to be a domestic-policy President. He did not want any entanglements in the Balkans. I found him trying to quote to me Bismarck's statement about the whole of the Balkans not being worth the bones of a single Pomeranian grenadier. There followed a truly shameful period in which the United Nations declared Sarajevo and other enclaves 'safe areas', only for them to be mercilessly shelled by the Serbs.

When Douglas Hurd said that lifting the arms embargo on the Bosnian Muslims would simply create a 'level killing field', she denounced this as a disgraceful phrase: Bosnia already was a killing field, the like of which she had thought they would never see in Europe again.

By June 1995, the position of our forces had become so precarious that I had to warn the US Chairman of the Joint Chiefs of Staff, Shalikashvili, that we might need the assistance of a US airborne division to help in extricating them. When this was reported by Shalikashvili to the President, it helped to bring home to a still very cautious Bill Clinton that US forces might have to become involved anyway, and in the worst of circumstances. John Major took the courageous decision to send two artillery batteries to Bosnia to increase the ability of our forces to defend themselves.

Serb aggression, and the failure to do anything to stop it, culminated in the surrender and humiliation of the Dutch UN contingent at Srebrenica, while General Mladic organised a massacre of the surviving male inhabitants. The small British military contingent at Goražde very clearly was next in line.

As Malcolm Rifkind arrived during this crisis in Washington, having taken over as Foreign Secretary from Douglas Hurd, I told him that the Americans would agree that, this time, we should give Mladic a real ultimatum, to be delivered not by the useless UN representative, Mr Akashi, but by NATO air force commanders, as to what would happen to Mladic and his forces if he attacked Goražde. I received an extremely satisfying account of Mladic's reactions when confronted with this message by the head of US Bomber Command in his aviator jacket and dark glasses, and the very pukka head of RAF Strike Command. Margaret Thatcher was absolutely right that this was a message that should have been delivered long before.

Shortly afterwards, I went to see President Clinton, who agreed to see me on his own. In personal terms, we had always got on extremely well. I argued that if, following Srebrenica, we permitted the Serbs to go on attacking and enter Sarajevo, the reputation of no western leader would survive, including his own. I found to my relief that Bill Clinton by this time had reached this conclusion himself.

At the end of August, a mortar bomb fired into Sarajevo killed thirty-seven people. Our forces had been withdrawn from their exposed position in Goražde. NATO aircraft finally launched a sustained two-week bombing campaign against all identifiable Bosnian Serb military targets, paving the way for the Dayton Peace Accords.

My farewell dinner in Washington in July 1995 coincided with a visit by Margaret Thatcher. I recalled that, in sending me there, she had exclaimed: 'At least you are not a diplomat.' The Defense Secretary, Bill Perry, replied by reminding me of my favourite Churchill quotation: 'The United States can be relied upon to do the right thing in the end, having first exhausted the available alternatives.'

XIX

'THE CONVEYOR BELT TO FEDERALISM'

On 16 September 1992, the British government suffered the crushing setback of 'Black Wednesday'. The former Governor of the US Reserve Bank, Paul Volcker, had asked me at a dinner in Washington what we intended to do in response to the pressures on sterling. When I replied that he should not underestimate the determination of the Prime Minister and Chancellor to defend the parity etc., Volcker looked down from his considerable height at me as if I had taken leave of my senses. Three days later, working in my office at the embassy, I was told that the government had raised interest rates to 12 per cent, in the depths of a recession, to defend sterling. Two hours later, I learned that the intention was to raise them to 15 per cent. It was with immense relief that I greeted the news, which followed not long after, that we had left the European exchange rate mechanism (ERM).

Norman Lamont, Chancellor of the Exchequer, flew straight from this disaster to the IMF meetings in Washington. It was in the Washington embassy that he claimed, subsequently, to have been singing in his bath, following our expulsion from the ERM.

As I also had staying with me in the embassy Margaret Thatcher, making one of her frequent visits to Washington, while, at the weekend, Geoffrey Howe came to dinner, the embassy took on the character of a Feydeau farce, as efforts had to be made to prevent all these dignitaries bumping into one another – an experience which, though all belonging to the same party, they would not at the time have enjoyed.

Throughout the crisis, she had remained silent, despite her well-publicised views on the ERM. Once we had left it, I urged her to avoid saying in her speech to the CNN economic conference 'I told you so.' Leaving the embassy, she handed me a copy of her speech. She had, instead, quoted Kipling: 'We have had no end of a lesson. It will do us no end of good!'[191]

During Margaret Thatcher's visit, I accompanied her to the White House to see George Bush. As she entered the Oval Office, instead of enquiring about his health or how his re-election campaign was going, she opened with the words: 'George, why on earth don't you change your position on abortion?' The President, understandably flustered, announced that his pollster had advised that it was only the seventeenth most important issue. There followed a 'you just don't understand' exchange, with Thatcher pointing out that he was level among men and ten points behind among women, for many of whom it was *the* most important issue. The younger ones simply would not vote for a party that still pledged to amend the Constitution to make abortion illegal. As Baker commented to me afterwards, she was absolutely right.

The issue on which she was most seriously at loggerheads with her successors was that of Europe, where her attitude caused great difficulties for John Major, driving him to distraction. To distance himself from her on this subject, John Major had declared in March 1991 his intention to place Britain 'at the very heart of Europe'. This seemed to her an impossibility in more than the purely geographical sense.

In a Commons performance of 'primal force' in June 1991, she rejected any extension of majority voting, the idea of a common defence and security policy, the notion that Britain should join the 'narrow band' of the ERM and any possibility of joining a single currency which, she said, would be the 'greatest abdication of parliamentary and national sovereignty in our history'.[192] In October 1991, she made an appearance at the Conservative Party conference, earning a seemingly endless standing ovation.

In November, on the eve of the Maastricht European Council, she made another storming speech, her last in the House of Commons, denouncing the 'conveyor belt to federalism'.[193] This was felt to be rhetorical exaggeration at the time, but any country planning to stay in or join the eurozone today is being required to subscribe to precisely that. She concluded by calling for a referendum if there were to be any question of joining a single currency – a position adopted subsequently by both the main parties, but which both still were resisting at the time.

At Maastricht, John Major succeeded in negotiating 'opt-outs' for Britain from the planned economic and monetary union and the 'social chapter' of the treaty. Charles Powell was convinced that, if she had still been in office, she would have done the same. The others would have gone ahead with their plans in any event.

She supported Major's successful re-election campaign in April 1992, though worried about the size of the budget deficit. She had by now been persuaded to leave the Commons for the Lords, but she would not support the Maastricht Treaty, causing John Major terrible difficulties in getting it ratified, which he only managed to do by a majority of three votes in the Commons. Maastricht, she said, was 'a treaty too far'.

Whatever view may be taken of her position on Maastricht

– her argument being that she would have preferred to make the others proceed on their own, outside the existing European treaties – in a good many other respects her views on Europe were as relevant as ever today. She worried from the outset about the tendencies towards statism and bureaucratic centralism of the European Commission – 'socialism by the back door'. She understood better than most others the incessant drive of the Commission to issue new regulations and directions as a way of asserting its 'competence' i.e. authority, at the expense of the national governments. Furthermore, nearly every one of these new EC-wide regulations tended to increase the burdens on European business. So far as she could see, no attention was ever paid to job creation and keeping Europe competitive. She regarded all the talk of deregulation and 'subsidiarity' as gobbledygook, as she never saw any evidence of it being put into practice, with Douglas Hurd protesting vainly at the tendency of the Commission to want to interfere in the 'nooks and crannies' of British life.

When David Hannay, at the time Britain's envoy in Brussels, suggested that negotiating there was like a game of snakes and ladders, he was told that he was wrong: 'In Brussels, they are all snakes!' This was not meant to be taken literally. While he felt, with some justice, that in Europe 'she did not know when to stop', she considered that those who wanted Britain to join the monetary union for fear of being 'left out' did not know where to start in terms of protecting the country's interests.[194]

As Prime Minister, in the mid-1980s she led a campaign to review all existing EU legislation to determine whether it was beneficial or not and what burdens it imposed on enterprise. She also insisted that all new proposals for legislation must be accompanied by an impact assessment indicating the cost to business. Although these initiatives, in which I was involved, were formally endorsed by Jacques Delors, President of the Commission at the time, they never had any practical effect. The raison d'être of the EU institutions generally was to regulate and legislate, thereby increasing their authority. They had no intention of deregulating anything.

In an illustration of absurdity, in the Foreign Office at the time I could hardly believe it when the Commission produced a proposal to harmonise the British sausage. I sent them the *Yes Minister* video of how Jim Hacker became Prime Minister (by defending the UK sausage) in a successful attempt to persuade them to drop this. It was followed by a proposal that all pint glasses should be phased out and replaced by half-litre measures, which reluctantly they also were persuaded to drop.

As Prime Minister, Mrs Thatcher would open meetings from time to time with the observation that we must find a way to exit the European Union, yet while in office she never displayed any intention of doing so. She accepted that our influence with the United States and elsewhere in the world depended on our playing an active role in Europe. She was clear also that the EU, for all its defects, offered a very important beacon of hope and magnet of attraction for the newly emerging democracies of eastern Europe, which she had always wanted to see one day incorporated into it. In her speech on Europe in Bruges she said that 'Britain does not dream of some cosy, isolated existence on the fringes of the European Community. Our destiny is in Europe, as part of the Community.'

Once she left office, her attitude hardened. In her last book, *Statecraft*, she forecast that we would regret incorporating the

European Convention on Human Rights into UK law through the Human Rights Act, as this would give rise to aberrant judgements, and to 'government by the judges', irrespective of the views of Parliament.[195] As, in her view, Britain invented human rights, she did not consider that the country needed the help of a court in Strasbourg in adjudicating them. As the European Court of Human Rights falls outside the EU treaties, these were powers that could be repatriated.

Her frustration with Europe derived not from rank prejudice, though she certainly was prejudiced against further major transfers of sovereignty, but from a sentiment on her part that the sort of Europe she hoped for – enterprise-friendly, decentralised and outward-looking, promoting growth and employment – was not the direction in which the EU was heading. Instead she found that the response to events was not to adopt new policies or change direction, but to tinker further with the institutions and the treaties so as to increase centralism, statism, bureaucracy and centralised regulation, on a basis she regarded as constantly further infringing national sovereignty but also as inimical to enterprise and growth. She saw this as increasingly frustrating the ability of individual member states to create an enterprise culture themselves. How then could Europe expect to compete with the rapidly developing Asian economies with much lower government spending, borrowing and taxation?

No less a believer than de Gaulle had been in a Europe of the nation states, with the drive towards monetary union she saw the EU as heading in the direction of a supranational and highly bureaucratised continental system, with authority progressively ebbing away from the member states. While she always had been prepared to cut deals with her counterparts in Europe, she was not prepared to be ruled by the Brussels and Strasbourg institutions.

She had told George Bush that rather than attaching Germany to Europe, they could find that they had attached Europe to Germany: 'The empires of the future will be economic empires.' She saw Helmut Kohl as bulldozing through German reunification, coupled with the creation of a monetary union in which Germany was bound to be the dominant partner. In the process, he ignored the advice of the Bundesbank and his own finance ministry that the southern member states were not ready to join a monetary union or to respect the disciplines involved in doing so.

She understood with crystal clarity that a monetary union dominated by Germany would benefit mainly the Germans, protected from competitive devaluations, and could never really work with countries as economically divergent as Greece and Germany. The effect was bound to be a huge transfer of sovereignty, great hardship for the weaker member states no longer able to devalue, and immense pressure on the Germans to bail out the rest of the Community, in return for which they would press for control over their budgets and full political union. She foresaw that membership of the monetary union would be bound in some countries to lead to 'national resentment, because the accompanying single currency and single centralised economic policy will leave the electorate of a country angry and powerless to change its conditions'.[196]

While her objections could have been expressed in a less abrasive manner, her opposition to Britain joining a European monetary union and to further major transfers of sovereignty to the European institutions reflected the views of the majority of the British electorate, then and now. She was surely right in insisting, long before either of the major political parties accepted this, that such a transfer of sovereignty would require the assent of the British people in a referendum. Events to date have justified her view that a monetary union cannot succeed without a massive transfer of fiscal sovereignty as well. Angela Merkel has been sounding like the Thatcher of our era in insisting that indebtedness cannot be cured by more debt and growth cannot be achieved by ever more government spending. The eurozone, which always has been an essentially political project, will have to move much closer to a fiscal union for its survival, with Germany more than ever the dominant partner.

XX

'SIGNPOSTS AND WEATHERVANES'

On Margaret Thatcher's departure from government, most of her colleagues breathed a sigh of relief. Chris Patten felt that, suddenly, they had all been liberated. They found it much easier to get on with each other than they had with her. Instead of introducing each item of the Cabinet agenda with a clear statement of his own views, as she had been accustomed to do, John Major acted as a chairman, summing up the conclusions of the meeting, rather than as an imperious CEO.[197]

Yet I missed her clarity of purpose and, above all, her absolute contempt for any semblance of wishful thinking, which often turned out to be a stock-in-trade of most of the other governments I had known. She had an innate ability to get to the heart of any really difficult or unpleasant problem and not to try to wish it away. On Bosnia she understood, well before the government did, that we were engaged in a peace-keeping mission in the absence of a peace to keep and that this was not sustainable in the absence of more forceful action to bring peace about. The crisis of sterling in the ERM would have come as much less of a shock to her than it did to the Major government and she would, as she made clear on joining, have sought to insist on a realignment of sterling rather than engage in a futile attempt to defend an unsustainable exchange rate.

She was conscious of the fact that, in her attitude to Europe, she constantly was accused of being narrow, parochial, insular and backward-looking. She indignantly denied this, as she did have a vision for Europe in terms of what she saw as the historic role it must play in embracing and helping to bolster democracy and economic prosperity in the fledgling democracies of eastern Europe.

She also considered it her role to represent the views and interests of ordinary people in Britain, rather than the European Foreign Ministry mandarinates or intelligentsia. When *Der Spiegel* reported to her Chirac's accusation that she had been acting 'like a housewife' over agricultural subsidies, her response was: 'It's a shame that more politicians don't act like housewives … Housewives of the world unite!' As Stephen Wall, later Britain's ambassador to the EU, observed: 'It was hard not to cheer Margaret Thatcher at her rambunctious best.'[198]

Her Canute-like opposition to German reunification was, as she put it herself, an unambiguous failure, leaving it to John Major to restore relations with Helmut Kohl. Yet with her customary disdain for wishful thinking, she was right that it would be no use France or Britain trying to pretend that, henceforth, they would be co-equal with Germany in Europe, and ignoring the increasing dependency on Germany that would result from monetary union.

Her critique of the failure of the European institutions to promote enterprise and help create jobs for the millions of young people entering the labour market each year has become commonplace today. Robert Zoellick, as outgoing President of the World Bank, observed that Europe's leaders have failed to comprehend just how rapidly Europe's stature is seen as diminishing in the rest of the world. Europe, he added, is looked upon as an example of a continent in deep trouble, while a project (monetary union) that was supposed to bring Europe together has actually been creating more and more fissures.[199]

The issues Margaret Thatcher was raising – hyper-bureaucracy, lack of accountability, over-regulation and their stifling effect on job creation and enterprise – ought to be of concern to all member states and recently have been complained about by the Dutch Prime Minister. Chancellor Angela Merkel has stated that Europe's ability to withstand the challenge of globalisation will depend on spending more on research and education and overhauling its tax and labour markets to restore competitiveness. Europe, she points out, which accounts for 7 per cent of the world's population, is currently financing 50 per cent of global social spending. These challenges are more severe with an ageing population. An economy that is no longer competitive will deny people prosperity. It is wrong to assume any longer that Europe is regarded as a model for others. She has been seeking to persuade the Commission and the other member states to commit to 'binding contracts for competitiveness and growth'.[200] It will be interesting to see if she will have more success in this enterprise today than Margaret Thatcher did in her campaign for deregulation in the 1980s.

In his speech on 23 January 2013, promising a referendum on Europe in 2017, David Cameron referred to a crisis of European competitiveness, much of which, he argued, was self-inflicted through complex rules restricting labour markets, excessive regulation and a desire to 'harmonise everything'.

Europe, as Margaret Thatcher anticipated, has evolved in a way that has settled for the foreseeable future the question of whether Britain can or would wish to be at the heart of it. There is no appetite to join the monetary union or the fiscal union that will result from it. The real European Union increasingly will be the eurozone. Countries in the outer circle of this system may find it hard to avoid being marginalised in decision-making and to maintain their rights under the treaties to ensure that there is no discrimination against them by those in the core grouping. The discussion over Britain's place in Europe over the next few years is likely to be influenced as much by practical developments as by theoretical debate.

It remains to be seen how this new structure will evolve. Margaret Thatcher never called in her public statements for Britain to leave the Community, save in the very last of them, but in later years she demanded a restoration of parliamentary sovereignty over and above the EU treaties. In private, she did advocate exiting the EU as the only way of recovering sovereignty and of escaping what she regarded as the enterprise-stifling effects of EU regulation. Given the common interest in free trade access, with the EU members exporting substantially more to Britain than we do to them, she would not accept that the British economy could not thrive outside the EU: that would depend on the policies British governments then pursued. She would and did accept, however, that Britain's influence would be less outside the system, both in Europe and beyond it, including with the United States which, historically, has counted on Britain to help overcome transatlantic differences and to ensure that the European Union is less protectionist and more outward-looking than it otherwise would have been.

Government is different. If reincarnated as Prime Minister today, it would be totally uncharacteristic of her to fail to make a huge effort to change the EU, before contemplating abandoning it. She would be sceptical about the chances of repatriating powers, except in areas like justice and policing, the whole EU system being designed to prevent that happening. She would be certain, however, to seek to launch a crusade with Angela Merkel, the Dutch and Swedish Prime Ministers and some of the eastern Europeans to change the direction of EU policy in order to foster growth and jobs and restore competitiveness, and to safeguard the rights of the EU member states outside the eurozone, only then deciding whether enough had been achieved to render continuing membership worthwhile.

☞

How was this opinionated, uncompromising, at times unnecessarily abrasive leader able to make a greater impact on world affairs than her predecessors or, to date, successors have done? Henry Kissinger, who considered that under Reagan she had won an influence on American policy not seen since Churchill's day, attributed the impact she made to 'above all, courage and character'.[201] A remarkably nerveless risk-taker, she performed better in crises than in normal times, not hesitating to take difficult or unpopular decisions.

Her approach was the polar opposite of that of Harold Macmillan, for whom politics were governed by events. For her, politics were governed by ideas. The idea she espoused most passionately was that of reducing the role of the state in the economy. She became an icon for those around the world who wished to do the same in their own countries. The concept was simple and far from new. Executing it, however, required a sustained, focused and ferocious burst of energy which she was ideally equipped to provide.

She thereby achieved a following beyond British shores far greater than that she enjoyed in the United Kingdom. She understood the rising power of Asia, to which she was a frequent visitor, and was by far the European leader best known and most admired there.

In terms of the war of ideas, she was convinced that the Cold War was there not just to be fought, but won. She 'had always believed, during the long struggle with the Soviet Union, that my firmest allies were the people of the eastern bloc'.[202]

Another core conviction was that aggressors must be confronted and, wherever possible, defeated. Of course her counterparts around the world would all claim to agree with that – in principle. But in her case, as she showed in the Falklands and the Gulf, there was never any doubt that she really meant it.

Her intellectual curiosity led her in some unforeseen directions. One of the features of her prime ministership was her ability to surprise. She might seem an unlikely early forecaster of climate change. But she noted the discovery by the British Antarctic Survey of a hole in the ozone layer protecting life from ultraviolet radiation as well as evidence that chlorofluorocarbons (CFCs) were responsible for ozone depletion. In a speech to the Royal Society in September 1988, prompted by the British ambassador to the UN, Sir Crispin Tickell, she said:

For generations we have assumed that the efforts of mankind would leave the fundamental equilibrium of the world's systems and atmosphere stable. But it is possible that with all these enormous changes (population, agricultural, use of fossil fuels) concentrated into such a short period of time, we have unwittingly begun a massive experiment with the system of this planet itself.

In March 1989 she chaired a conference of well over a hundred nations to strengthen the UN protocol for the reduction of CFC emissions by aiming to eliminate them within a decade. She also committed Britain to cutting carbon dioxide emissions, but condemned what she regarded as the politicisation of climate change, insisting that solutions must be founded on good science and were more likely to be found through technological innovation than massive state intervention.[203]

Other world leaders, whatever their differences with her, admired her sheer political courage, as epitomised in the Falklands conflict and her struggles with the unions at home. They also noted her transformation from, apparently, a classic Cold War warrior into the western leader closest to and most influential with Mikhail Gorbachev, despite US misgivings about him at the time. She had shown resolution in dealing with the Soviet Union in its still menacing and expansionist phase, facing down opposition to the deployment of intermediate-range nuclear weapons, and more imagination than other western leaders in exploiting the opportunities offered by a new leadership in Moscow. Proven correct in her judgement that Gorbachev would not use force to preserve the Soviet empire in eastern Europe, she had every right to state in her farewell message to Gorbachev her belief that 'together we really did contribute to changing our world'.

In her ostensibly cosy relationship with the United States, she showed an implacable and effective determination to protect British interests when she thought they were being ignored. In southern Africa, this supposed friend of apartheid made a greater contribution to the resolution of the Rhodesia and Namibia conflicts and to political change in South Africa than her more apparently Africa-friendly predecessors had done. On the world stage, she was a figure who simply could not be ignored.

She prided herself on being no diplomat, because she could not stand the pious platitudes which, to her, seemed to be the stock-in-trade of diplomacy. Rather than calling for the umpteenth time on the Serbs to cease attacking UN 'safe areas' in Bosnia, she was more interested in what could be done to stop them. One of the many paradoxes about this right-wing lady is that she did believe, more strongly than most of her more progressive counterparts, in intervening decisively in cases of this kind.

She had some important blind spots, rejecting in November 1988 Nigel Lawson's proposal to restore independence to the Bank of England and, thereby, de-politicise interest rate changes. She did not seem to Lawson to appreciate that there was going to be another government one day and that it was in the national interest to entrench anti-inflationary policy for the future.[204] Lawson, who did not really expect her to accept his proposal, described this as the ERM argument all over again – except that, this time, he was right and she was wrong. My farewell despatch from Washington, after she left office, carried with it two graphs illustrating British and US inflation and interest rates since the war – the first showing a relatively benign picture save for the surge in inflation and interest rates during the Carter administration, the latter an exercise in bungee jumping, including in her own last two years in government. The idea of restoring to the Bank of England the power to set interest rates, thereby reinforcing the credibility of monetary policy in the United Kingdom, as against handing it over to the European Central Bank, was one she should have embraced as squarely in the line of her own reforms. But she was not prepared to give up the power to set interest rates so long as she was still Prime Minister.

☞

Nigel Lawson concluded his memoir by describing her as a leader who 'will go down in history as one of the greatest Prime Ministers this country has known'.

Geoffrey Howe, who genuinely believed that he could have achieved the same results in a more emollient and far more pro-European manner, conceded that she was 'beyond argument a great Prime Minister', before arguing that in her final years no distinction was to be drawn between person, government, party and nation. 'She was breaking with Europe and I had to break with her.' Douglas Hurd felt that she had accomplished 'amazing things for this country', but, by the end, had ceased to listen to the advice of others.[205]

While John Major sought to escape from her shadow, talking of Thatcherism with a human face, she exerted a particular fascination on Tony Blair. When, at the Conservative Party conference, she quoted from the 1944 Keynesian paper on employment, he unwisely accused her in Parliament of not having read it, whereupon she pulled a heavily marked copy from her handbag and, brandishing it about, used quotes from it to prove that Keynes was a Thatcherite, to roars of laughter in the House of Commons. Blair described her as 'undoubtedly a great Prime Minister', vowing himself to preserve 'the best of Thatcherism'. When, however, she suggested to him that 'together' they had defeated socialism, he said he would have to give the exclusive credit for that to her![206]

Some of the greatest tributes to her came from those who had fought hardest against her. Tony Benn observed that politicians are either weathervanes or signposts. Indisputably, she was a signpost, pointing in the opposite direction to him. In the words of one of her critics, Andrew Marr, hers was 'the most extraordinary and nation-changing premiership of modern British history'. As another, Francis Pym, observed, the general sentiment was that she was 'the first Prime Minister in decades to have the guts to do what was necessary to put the country back on its feet'.[207]

In her dealings with other heads of government, she was the beneficiary of Nicholas Henderson's dictum that Britain's influence would be measured by our own economic success or failure. She had succeeded in reversing Britain's economic decline, pretty well invented privatisation against near-universal resistance at the time, then spread it around the globe, shifting the British political landscape irreversibly in her direction. She had won the battle of ideas about the role of the state in the economy, and not only in her own party or her own country. While her colleagues contributed to this transformation, few of them believed that they could or would have succeeded without her implacable determination.

In his book *Thatcher and Sons*, Simon Jenkins observes that no part of the British political class was left unaffected by her. He described her as a truly revolutionary leader who, far from being conservative, set about changing everything around her. Unafraid to be unpopular, instead of running before the wind, she headed straight in to the oncoming gales and, against all expectations, prevailed.[208]

She had made far more of an impact in world affairs than any post-war British Prime Minister. The huge crowds that greeted her in eastern Europe and the former Soviet Union in the late 1980s felt that she represented something important to them. Her faults were of the same dimensions as her virtues. In his most famous book, *Le Fil de l'Epée* (*The Edge of the Sword*), written in the run-up to the Second World War, de Gaulle described the kind of leader to emerge in a real military or national crisis as not at all likely to be pleasant, accommodating, conciliatory or easy to get on with, but solitary, intractable, difficult to deal with, yet able to provide leadership and direction in such a crisis, based on inner certainty. De Gaulle was later to claim of his compatriots that, 'Everyone has been, is or will be a Gaullist'. It was fortunate for the British people that this extraordinarily determined, intransigent, uncompromising, at times impossible lady arrived on the scene when she did. She brought about no less a transformation in Britain's fortunes than de Gaulle achieved in 1960s France. The changes she wrought went some way beyond his, exporting a generally successful new concept – privatisation – to large areas of the world and helping to ensure that, in the words of President Thabo Mbeki and many other world leaders around the globe: 'We are all Thatcherites now.'

ACKNOWLEDGEMENTS

I am especially grateful to Christopher Collins of the Margaret Thatcher Foundation, who has given me invaluable help not only as a guide to the source materials available from the Foundation, but in his very perceptive comments on and contributions to the manuscript more generally. The superbly organised website is an extraordinary resource, including all relevant material released by the Cabinet Office under the thirty-year rule, most recently in relation to the Falklands War. The Cabinet minutes and minutes of the War Cabinet in relation to that conflict are now available in the National Archives at the Public Record Office, Kew (CAB148 and OD (SA) 82). The PREM series of documents relating to the Prime Minister's meetings, telephone conversations and messages to and from foreign leaders can most easily be accessed via the Foundation website at www.margaretthatcher.org, as can a lot of other relevant material.

My thanks are due also to Andrew Riley, archivist in charge of the Thatcher papers at Churchill College, Cambridge and to numerous friends and former colleagues who have helped with various sections of the book. Robert Armstrong and David Goodall gave invaluable help with Chapter VII on the Anglo-Irish Agreement. David Wilson and Tony Galsworthy kindly vetted the chapter on Hong Kong, and Stephen Wall those on the European negotiations.

There are many others who should be thanked, none more so than my own mentors in the Foreign Office, Nicholas Henderson and Tony Parsons, who exerted great influence on Margaret Thatcher and never failed to entertain me with their accounts of their dealings with her, supplementing my own, mainly later experiences of her.

I am indebted to Eddie George, late Governor of the Bank of England, for his impressions of the discussions on the European Exchange Rate Mechanism (Chapter XIV), in which he was a key participant.

Margaret Thatcher was a frequent visitor to the British embassy in Washington in the period in which she was writing her memoirs. Those visits afforded me an opportunity to discuss further with her many of the episodes described in this book.

Her memoirs themselves – *The Path to Power* and *The Downing Street Years* – published by HarperCollins, are also a meticulously researched and very important resource. I hope that this account will encourage others to read or re-read them.

Marie-France Renwick gave invaluable help in sourcing the illustrations, as did Katie Gareh in numerous ways.

I am extremely grateful to Iain Dale, Hollie Teague and the team at Biteback for their help and encouragement in producing this book in time for the anniversary of the Falklands War.

NOTES

1   Margaret Thatcher, *The Downing Street Years*, HarperCollins, 1993, p. 543
2   Nigel Lawson's description in *Memoirs of a Tory Radical*, Biteback, 2010, p. 83
3   Michael Butler, *Europe: More than a Continent*, Heinemann, 1986, p. 116
4   *The Economist*, 2 June 1979
5   Lawson, *Memoirs of a Tory Radical*, pp. 92–3
6   George Shultz, *Turmoil and Triumph*, Charles Scribner, 1993, p. 495
7   John Major, *Autobiography*, HarperCollins, 1999, pp. 85, 110
8   John Nott, *Here Today, Gone Tomorrow*, Politico's, 2002, p. 189
9   Noel Annan, *Our Age*, Random House, 1990, p. 424
10 Thatcher, *The Downing Street Years*, p. 129
11 Nott, *Here Today, Gone Tomorrow*, p. 321
12 Thatcher, *The Downing Street Years*, p. 167
13 Margaret Thatcher, *The Path to Power*, HarperCollins, 1995, pp. 483, 492
14 Hugo Young, *One of Us*, Pan Books, 1989, p. 25
15 Thatcher, *The Path to Power*, p. 69
16 Peter Rawlinson, *A Price Too High*, Weidenfeld & Nicolson, 1989, pp. 246–7
17 Young, *One of Us*, p. 47
18 Thatcher, *The Path to Power*, p. 134
19 John Campbell, *Margaret Thatcher, Volume I, The Grocer's Daughter*, Jonathan Cape, 2000, p. 341
20 *The Guardian*, 14 January 1974, quoted in Campbell, p. 256
21 Barbara Castle, *The Castle Diaries 1974–1976*, Weidenfeld & Nicholson, 1980, p. 309
22 Douglas Hurd, *Memoirs*, Little, Brown, 2004, p. 242; Woodrow Wyatt, *Journals*, Macmillan, 1998, Volume I, p. 22
23 *Wall Street Journal*, 20 August 1995
24 Thatcher, *The Path to Power*, p. 372
25 Hansard, 8 June, 29 June and 27 July 1976; Dominic Sandbrook, *Seasons in the Sun: The Battle for Britain, 1974–1979*, Allen Lane, 2012, p. 653

26 Thatcher, *The Downing Street Years*, p. 73
27 Peter Carrington, *Reflect on Things Past: The Memoirs of Lord Carrington*, HarperCollins, 1988, p. 277
28 Hurd, *Memoirs*, p. 324
29 No. 10 record of conversation between Margaret Thatcher and Carrington, 14 August 1980 PREM 19/110 f205; www.margaretthatcher.org document 116994
30 No. 10 record of meeting between Margaret Thatcher and General Walls, 6 December 1980 PREM 19/116 pt2f.162; www.margaretthatcher.org documents 116125 and 116126
31 Admiral Leach, *Endure No Makeshifts*, Leo Cooper, 1993, pp. 210, 219–23, 227
32 Leach, *Endure No Makeshifts*, pp. 219–23, 227
33 Falkland Islands Review (The Franks Report), Cmnd 8787, London HMSO, 1983 pp. 33–34; D. R. Thorpe, *Supermac, Life of Harold Macmillan*, Chatto and Windus, 2010, p. 603
34 Franks Report pp. 33–4; Callaghan in the House of Commons, 9 February 1982
35 Thatcher, *The Downing Street Years*, p. 177
36 CAB 148, 25 March 1982, National Archives
37 Reagan to Thatcher, 1 April 1982; James Rentschler, *Falklands diary*, p. 2, www.margaretthatcher.org
38 CAB 148, 2 April 1982
39 Thatcher, *The Downing Street Years*, pp. 181–2
40 CAB 148, 6 April 1982
41 Caspar Weinberger, *Fighting for Peace*, Michael Joseph, 1990, p. 146
42 Rentschler, *Falklands diary*, p. 2
43 Ibid., pp. 3–4; No. 10 record PREM 19/616 f165; US embassy telephone call to State Dept, 8 April 1982, PDF496K; Haig to Reagan, 9 April 1982, Reagan Library NSC records, Falklands War, Box 91365
44 Alexander Haig Jr, *Caveat*, Weidenfeld & Nicholson, 1984, pp. 179–80
45 Rentschler, *Falklands diary*, p. 10; No. 10 record, 12 April 1982, PREM 19/617 f227 and f189
46 CAB 148, 12 April 1982
47 OD (SA), 13 April 1982
48 Robin Renwick, *Fighting with Allies*, Random House, 1996, p. 332
49 Haig telephone calls to Thatcher, 14 April 1982, PREM 19/617 f76 and f70
50 Reagan to Thatcher, 15 April 1982, PREM 19/618 f8
51 CAB 148, 22 April 1982
52 OD (SA), 24 April 1982 and PREM 19/621f252; Thatcher, *The Downing Street Years*, p. 208
53 CAB 148, 28 April 1982
54 Reagan message to Thatcher, 29 April 1982; Douglas Brinkley ed. *The Reagan Diaries*, HarperCollins, 2007, p. 80; Richard Aldous, *Reagan and Thatcher: The Difficult Relationship*, Heinemann, 2012, pp. 88–9
55 NSC minutes, 29 April 1982, Reagan Library, NSC meeting file, Box 91284; Aldous, *Reagan and Thatcher*, p. 90
56 Aldous, *Reagan and Thatcher*, p. 88

57 Reagan press conference, www.margaretthatcher.org

58 Thatcher, *The Downing Street Years*, p. 226

59 OD (SA) ad hoc meeting, 2 May 1982 and Wade-Gery to Omand, PREM 19/623 f14

60 Reagan to Thatcher, 5 May 1982, PREM 19/624 f118; Thatcher to Reagan, 5 May 1982, PREM 19/624 f47; CAB 148 and Armstrong note, 5 May 1982; UKE Washington telegram 1597 050400Z

61 Thatcher, *The Downing Street Years*, p. 218

62 Pérez de Cuéllar in *Margaret Thatcher: A Tribute in Words and Pictures*, ed. by Iain Dale, Weidenfeld & Nicolson, 2005, p. 86; Thatcher, *The Downing Street Years*, p. 218

63 Reagan/Thatcher telephone call, 13 May 1982; Nicholas Henderson, *Mandarin*, Weidenfield & Nicolson, 1994, p. 463

64 Henderson, *Mandarin*, pp. 461–3

65 John Campbell, *Margaret Thatcher, Volume 2, The Iron Lady*, Jonathan Cape, 2003, p. 139. Julian Thompson in Dale, *Margaret Thatcher: A Tribute in Words and Pictures*, p. 103

66 Sir Anthony Parsons to the author

67 Thatcher to Mitterrand, 18 May 1982, www.margaretthatcher.org

68 OD (SA) and CAB 148, 18 May 1982

69 Thatcher, *The Downing Street Years*, p. 229

70 OD (SA), 4 May 1982 (check)

71 OD (SA), 24 May 1982

72 Reagan telephone call to Thatcher, 31 May 1982, Reagan Library NSC file (UK) Box 20; No. 10 record PREM 19/633 f161; Rentschler, p. 34; Thatcher, pp. 230–231; Ronald Reagan, *An American Life*, Hutchinson, 1990, p. 360

73 Draft message to Galtieri, www.margaretthatcher.org

74 Henderson, *Mandarin*, pp. 646–7

75 Thatcher, *The Downing Street Years*, p. 232

76 Reagan speech, 8 June 1982, Ronald Reagan Presidential Library

77 Henderson, *Mandarin*, p. 480

78 OD (SA), 12 July 1982

79 Shultz, *Turmoil and Triumph*, p. 153

80 Christopher Meyer, *DC Confidential*, Weidenfeld & Nicolson, 2005, p. 225

81 Haig, *Caveat*, pp. 297–8

82 Mike Deaver to the author

83 Rex Hunt, *My Falklands Days*, David and Charles, 1992, pp. 370–75; Carol Thatcher, *Below the Parapet, Biography of Denis Thatcher*, HarperCollins, 1996, p. 201

84 Percy Cradock, *Experiences of China*, John Murray, 1994, p. 118

85 Ibid., pp. 175–8

86 Ibid.

87 Ibid., pp. 185–6

88 Ibid., pp. 189–91

89 Geoffrey Howe, *Conflict of Loyalty*, Pan Books, 1995, pp. 371–2, 376–8

90 Thatcher, *The Downing Street Years*, p. 492

91 Chris Patten, *East and West*, Macmillan, 1998, pp. 61–2

92   Cradock, *In Pursuit of British Interests*, John Murray, 1997, p. 20
93   Ian Gilmour, *Dancing with Dogma: Britain under Thatcherism*, Simon and Schuster, 1992, p. 238
94   Thatcher, *The Downing Street Years*, p. 309
95   Ibid., p. 385
96   Garret FitzGerald, *All in a Life*, Autobiography, Macmillan, 1991, pp. 262–3, 284–7
97   David Goodall, *An Agreement to Remember*, The Dublin Review of Books, December 2009 and Robert Armstrong to the author
98   Goodall, *An Agreement to Remember*
99   Armstrong to the author; Fitzgerald, *All in a Life*, pp. 475–8
100 Thatcher, *Below the Parapet*, p. 221
101 Simon Jenkins, *Thatcher and Sons*, Allen Lane, 2006, p. 101; Thatcher, *Below the Parapet*, p. 219
102 Goodall, *An Agreement to Remember*
103 Hurd, *Memoirs*, pp. 302–5
104 Goodall, *An Agreement to Remember*
105 Fitzgerald, *All in a Life*, pp. 515–23; Howe, *Conflict of Loyalty*, p. 416
106 Thatcher, *The Downing Street Years*, pp. 401–3; Howe, *Conflict of Loyalty*, p. 307; Edward Pearce in Iain Dale, *Margaret Thatcher: A Tribute in Words and Pictures*, p. 114
107 Hurd, *Memoirs*, pp. 308–9
108 Henderson, *Mandarin*, pp. 315–20
109 Young, *One of Us*, p. 231
110 Thatcher, *The Downing Street Years*, p. 157
111 Renwick, *Fighting with Allies*, p. 191
112 Douglas Brinkley (ed.), *The Reagan Diaries*, HarperCollins, 2007, p. 88
113 Henderson, *Mandarin*, pp. 385–8
114 Lou Cannon, *President Reagan: The Role of a Lifetime*, Simon and Schuster, 1991, p. 299
115 Henderson, *Mandarin*, p. 406
116 Thatcher, *The Downing Street Years*, p. 247
117 Henderson, *Mandarin*, p. 479
118 Reagan speech, 8 June 1982
119 Reagan, *An American Life*, p. 354
120 Thatcher, *The Downing Street Years*, pp. 463–4
121 Ibid., pp. 324–5
122 Shultz, *Turmoil and Triumph*, p. 340
123 Bernard Ingham, *Kill the Messenger*, HarperCollins, 1994, p. 257
124 George Shultz to the author and *Turmoil and Triumph*, p. 509
125 Robert McFarlane, *Special Trust*, Cadell and Davies, 1994, p. 307
126 Reagan, *An American Life*, p. 635
127 Colin Powell, *A Soldier's Way*, Hutchinson, 1995, pp. 309–10
128 Walters, p. 145
129 Thatcher, *The Downing Street Years*, p. 447
130 Renwick, *Fighting with Allies*, p. 360
131 Thatcher, *The Downing Street Years*, p. 448
132 Campbell, *Margaret Thatcher, Volume 2, The Iron Lady*, p. 338

133 Colin Powell and Richard Perle to the author
134 Thatcher, *The Downing Street Years*, pp. 471–3
135 Reagan, *An American Life*, p. 517
136 Powell, *A Soldier's Way*, p. 375
137 Aldous, *Reagan and Thatcher*, p. 265
138 Margaret Thatcher, *The National Review*, 20 December 1988
139 Roderic Braithwaite, *Across the Moscow River*, Yale University Press, 2002, pp. 51–2
140 Mikhail Gorbachev, *Memoirs*, Doubleday, pp. 160–1; Thatcher, *The Downing Street Years*, pp. 459–63
141 Charles Powell in Dale, *Margaret Thatcher: A Tribute in Words and Pictures*, p. 233; Campbell, *Margaret Thatcher, Volume 2, The Iron Lady*, p. 298; Anatoly Chernyaev, *My Six Years with Gorbachev*, Pennsylvania State University Press, 2000, pp. 99–103
142 Gorbachev, *Memoirs*, p. 547; Chernyaev, *My Six Years with Gorbachev*, pp. 102–4
143 George H. W. Bush and Brent Scowcroft, *A World Transformed*, Vintage, 1998, p. 4
144 Thatcher, *The Downing Street Years*, p. 802
145 Shultz, *Turmoil and Triumph*, p. 568
146 Bush and Scowcroft, *A World Transformed*, p. 143; Thatcher, *The Downing Street Years*, p. 804
147 Braithwaite, *Across the Moscow River*, p. 143
148 Gorbachev, *Memoirs*, pp. 546–7
149 Thatcher, *The Downing Street Years*, p. 529
150 See also Ingham, *Kill the Messenger*, p. 276
151 Thatcher, *The Downing Street Years*, pp. 517
152 Nelson Mandela, *Long Walk to Freedom*, Abacus, 1994, pp. 669, 700
153 Thatcher, *The Downing Street Years*, pp. 533–4
154 Stephen Wall, *A Stranger in Europe*, Oxford University Press, 2008, pp. 74–6, 79
155 Lawson, *Memoirs of a Tory Radical*, pp. 484–99; Howe, *Conflict of Loyalty*, pp. 448–5; Thatcher, *The Downing Street Years*, pp. 691–8
156 Jenkins, *Thatcher and Sons*, p. 138
157 Lawson, *Memoirs of a Tory Radical*, pp. 585–9; Thatcher, *The Downing Street Years*, pp. 708–13; Howe, *Conflict of Loyalty*, pp. 574–80; Wall, *A Stranger in Europe*, p. 82
158 Major, *Autobiography*, pp. 157–64; Thatcher, *The Downing Street Years*, pp. 719–23
159 Thatcher, *The Downing Street Years*, pp. 782–3
160 Bush and Scowcroft, *A World Transformed*, pp. 69–70
161 Charles Powell to the author
162 Bush and Scowcroft, *A World Transformed*, pp. 80–84
163 Major, *Autobiography*, p. 122
164 Bush and Scowcroft, *A World Transformed*, p. 190; Helmut Kohl, *Erinnerungen 1982–90*, Droemer Knaur, 2005
165 Margaret Thatcher Foundation, Chequers seminar on Germany, 25 March 1990

166 Bush and Scowcroft, *A World Transformed*, p. 301

167 Ibid., pp. 218, 222; Thatcher, *The Downing Street Years*, p. 810

168 Percy Cradock, *In Pursuit of British Interests*, p. 14; Bush and Scowcroft, *A World Transformed*, pp. 252, 265; Carol Thatcher, *Below the Parapet*, p. 258

169 Bush and Scowcroft, *A World Transformed*, p. 84; Major, *Autobiography*, p. 234; Thatcher, *The Downing Street Years*, p. 747

170 Thatcher, *The Downing Street Years*, p. 832

171 Kenneth Baker, *The Years of Turbulence*, Faber, 1993, p. 274

172 Bush and Scowcroft, *A World Transformed*, p. 317

173 Powell, *A Soldier's Way*, p. 465

174 Bush and Scowcroft, *A World Transformed*, pp. 351–2

175 Ibid., pp. 384–5

176 James Baker, *The Politics of Diplomacy*, GP Putnam, 1995, p. 279

177 Baker, *The Politics of Diplomacy*, pp. 313–4

178 Peter de la Billière, *Storm Command*, HarperCollins, 1992, pp.123–5

179 Bush and Scowcroft, *A World Transformed*, p. 410

180 Thatcher, *The Downing Street Years*, p. 822

181 Lawson, *Memoirs of a Tory Radical*, p. 641

182 Ibid., pp. 342–3

183 Howe, *Conflict of Loyalty*, pp. 665–7

184 Thatcher, *The Downing Street Years*, p. 840

185 Hurd, *Memoirs*, p. 402

186 Thatcher, *The Downing Street Years*, p. 846

187 Cecil Parkinson, *Right at the Centre*, Weidenfeld & Nicolson, 1992, p. 245; Thatcher, *The Downing Street Years*, p. 852

188 Hansard, 22 November 1990

189 Major, *Autobiography*, p. 169

190 Although generally attributed to Edmund Burke and certainly reflective of his thinking, this is nowhere to be found in his writings

191 Margaret Thatcher, *Collected Speeches*, HarperCollins, 1977, p. 541

192 Hansard, 26 June 1991

193 Hansard, 20 November 1991

194 David Hannay, *Britain's Quest for a Role*, IB Tauris, 2012, pp. 124, 139

195 Margaret Thatcher, *Statecraft*, HarperCollins, 2002, p. 275

196 Thatcher, *The Path to Power*, p. 620

197 Jenkins, *Thatcher and Sons*, p. 161

198 Wall, *A Stranger in Europe*, p. 76

199 Robert Zoellick, *The Times*, 1 July 2012

200 Angela Merkel, The *Financial Times*, 28 December 2012

201 Kissinger in Dale, *Margaret Thatcher: A Tribute in Words and Pictures*, p. 74

202 Thatcher, *The Path to Power*, p. 603

203 Thatcher, *The Downing Street Years*, pp. 640–41

204 Lawson, *Memoirs of a Tory Radical*, pp. 531–6

205 Ibid.,p. 623; Howe, *Conflict of Loyalty*, p. 691; Hurd, *Memoirs*, p. 399

206 Alastair Campbell, *Diaries*, Hutchinson, 2012, Vol. III, p. 384, Vol. IV, p. 30

207 Andrew Marr, *History of Modern Britain*, Macmillan, 2007, p. 274; Francis Pym, *The Politics of Consent*, Hamish Hamilton, 1984, p. 1

208 Jenkins, *Thatcher and Sons*, pp. 1–10

INDEX